Python Microservices Development

Second Edition

Build efficient and lightweight microservices using the Python tooling ecosystem

Simon Fraser

Tarek Ziadé

BIRMINGHAM — MUMBAI

Python Microservices Development

Second Edition

Producer: Shailesh Jain

Acquisition Editor – Peer Reviews: Saby D'Silva

Project Editor: Rianna Rodrigues

Content Development Editor: Alex Patterson

Copy Editor: Safis Editing

Technical Editor: Karan Sonawane

Proofreader: Safis Editing

Indexer: Rekha Nair

Presentation Designer: Pranit Padwal

First published: July 2017

Second edition: September 2021

Production reference: 2291221

Published by Packt Publishing Ltd.
Livery Place
35 Livery Street
Birmingham
B3 2PB, UK.

ISBN 978-1-80107-630-2

www.packt.com

Contributors

About the authors

Simon Fraser is a Site Reliability Engineer for Cisco Meraki. He has over twenty years of experience in computing, both developing and running systems. He has worked as a Systems Administrator for an internet service provider; an infrastructure and high-performance computing engineer at the Welcome Sanger Institute, and as a Firefox Release Engineer at Mozilla. He studied Cybernetics and Computer Science at the University of Reading and has also taught academic courses in programming for scientists.

I would like to thank Emma Apted and Helen Cook for their frequent support and encouragement, ranging from proofreading to miming a book opening when I'm clearly not working. My father George Fraser passed on his immeasurable skill at finishing a project just before the deadline, and my mother Elizabeth Fraser showed me how to explain concepts and inform people through years of teaching. This book would also not be possible without Tarek Ziadé's work on the 1st edition and the solid base on which to build, as well as the work of Development Editor Alex Patterson, Reviewer William Kahn-Greene, and Project Editor Rianna Rodrigues.

We might stand on the shoulders of giants, but we also build on a huge structure made by every one of us, so I would also like to thank everyone I've worked with over the years in all my different teams. Yes, even you.

Tarek Ziadé is a Software Engineer, located in Burgundy, France. He works at Elastic, building tools for developers. Before Elastic, he worked at Mozilla for 10 years, and he founded a French Python user group, called *AFPy*. Tarek has also written several articles about Python for various magazines, and a few books in French and English.

I would like to thank Freya, Suki, Milo, and Amina for being so supportive of all my book projects.

About the reviewer

Will Kahn-Greene has been building things in Python and other languages since the late 90s. He manages the crash ingestion pipeline at Mozilla and maintains several Python libraries. When he's waiting for CI to run tests, he builds things with wood, tends his tomato plants, and cooks for four.

Table of Contents

Preface

Python Microservices Development introduces the design and creation of a microservice-based application using the popular Python programming language, and the Quart web framework. In this book, you will learn about microservice architecture and how it differs from the traditional monolithic approach, what the benefits are, as well as potential trouble that needs overcoming.

Who this book is for

This book is for people familiar with the fundamentals of the Python programming language who want to start writing web services, or who have inherited a web service they want to modernize. It is expected that the reader will be familiar with simple Python structures such as functions and loops, as well as some more advanced features such as decorators. Some familiarity with using web applications would be helpful, although the fundamentals of application design are covered.

What this book covers

Chapter 1, *Understanding Microservices*, introduces the concepts behind microservices, the differences between monolithic applications and microservices, common benefits and pitfalls, as well as testing and scaling.

Chapter 2, *Discovering Quart*, covers the Quart web framework and the ways in which it can respond to requests, create templated documents, act as middleware, handle errors, and read configuration.

Chapter 3, Coding, Testing, and Documentation: the Virtuous Cycle, teaches you about the different types of testing that are possible, what benefits each type has, and how to set up automatic testing, as well as generating documentation in CI pipelines.

Chapter 4, Designing Jeeves, looks at Jeeves, which is the sample application we use in this book to explain the various concepts behind microservices. We introduce what we need Jeeves to do and describe a monolithic approach to application design, covering the web API interface, database use, and worker pools.

Chapter 5, Splitting the Monolith, builds on the monolithic Jeeves described in previous chapter. This chapter offers guidance on how to identify components that may be good microservices, measuring the effects of changes on the software architecture, and how to cleanly migrate features to new microservices.

Chapter 6, Interacting with Other Services, explains how to make web requests to other services, how to configure and decide where to send those queries, and how to cache results, as well as make the data transfer more efficient.

Chapter 7, Securing Your Services, looks at how authentication, tokens, encryption, and security vulnerabilities are all essential topics to consider for any service, and here we build an authentication microservice for Jeeves, as well as discuss various things to consider when making an application secure against attack.

Chapter 8, Making a Dashboard, discusses how many applications will have a human view. In this chapter we add a dashboard to Jeeves so that it can be controlled using a ReactJS application, as well as discussing where best to add the front-end into the microservice architecture.

Chapter 9, Packaging and Running Python, shows how, once created, an application needs to be packaged so that it can be deployed and run. In this chapter, we will learn about creating and publishing Python packages, as well as managing dependencies.

Chapter 10, Deploying on AWS, looks at how cloud services provide a flexible platform to run a web service. This chapter covers creating containers for our application and deploying it in Amazon Web Services.

Chapter 11, What's Next?, summarizes the main things we have learned so far, and the topics that would make good further reading, as well as technologies that will prove useful for different types of application.

To get the most out of this book

Readers will find the book easier to follow with some Python programming experience, or experience in a very similar programming language. The basics of Python are not covered, and for the fundamentals we recommend a book such as *Learn Python Programming*, also from Packt Publishing.

Running the code samples from this book requires a computer with Python 3.8 or greater installed on it. Python is available for free for all popular operating systems, such as Windows, macOS and Linux, among others.

The author recommends not only running the code samples, but also experimenting with them to try different things out.

Download the example code files

The code bundle for the book is hosted on GitHub at https://github.com/PacktPublishing/Python-Microservices-Development-2nd-Edition. We also have other code bundles from our rich catalog of books and videos available at https://github.com/PacktPublishing/. Check them out!

Download the color images

We also provide a PDF file that has color images of the screenshots/diagrams used in this book. You can download it here: https://static.packt-cdn.com/downloads/9781801076302_ColorImages.pdf.

Conventions used

There are a number of text conventions used throughout this book.

CodeInText: Indicates code words in text, database table names, folder names, filenames, file extensions, pathnames, dummy URLs, user input, and Twitter handles. For example; " The __name__ variable, whose value will be __main__ when you run that single Python module, is the name of the application package."

A block of code is set as follows:

```
@app.route('/api', methods=['POST', 'DELETE', 'GET'])
def my_microservice():
    return {'Hello': 'World!'}
```

Any command-line input or output is written as follows:

```
pip install quart
```

Bold: Indicates a new term, an important word, or words that you see on the screen, for example, in menus or dialog boxes. For example: "There are many great synchronous frameworks to build microservices with Python, like **Bottle**, **Pyramid** with **Cornice**, or **Flask**."

 Warnings or important notes appear like this.

 Tips and tricks appear like this.

Get in touch

Feedback from our readers is always welcome.

General feedback: Email feedback@packtpub.com, and mention the book's title in the subject of your message. If you have questions about any aspect of this book, please email us at questions@packtpub.com.

Errata: Although we have taken every care to ensure the accuracy of our content, mistakes do happen. If you have found a mistake in this book we would be grateful if you would report this to us. Please visit http://www.packtpub.com/submit-errata, selecting your book, clicking on the Errata Submission Form link, and entering the details.

Piracy: If you come across any illegal copies of our works in any form on the Internet, we would be grateful if you would provide us with the location address or website name. Please contact us at copyright@packtpub.com with a link to the material.

If you are interested in becoming an author: If there is a topic that you have expertise in and you are interested in either writing or contributing to a book, please visit http://authors.packtpub.com.

Share your thoughts

Once you've read *Python Microservices Development, Second Edition*, we'd love to hear your thoughts! Scan the QR code below to go straight to the Amazon review page for this book and share your feedback.

https://packt.link/r/1801076308

Your review is important to us and the tech community and will help us make sure we're delivering excellent quality content.

1

Understanding Microservices

We are always trying to improve how we create software. Computer programming is less than 100 years old, and we have evolved rapidly through technology, design, and philosophy to improve the tools and applications we produce.

Microservices have revolutionized software products by improving the readability and scalability of services, and have allowed organizations to speed up their release cycles and be more responsive to the needs of their customers. Everybody wants to ship new products and new features to their customers as fast as possible. They want to be *agile* by iterating often, and they want to ship, ship, and ship again.

With thousands of customers using your service simultaneously, it is considered good practice to push an experimental feature to production and remove it again if needed, instead of waiting for months to publish it and many other features at the same time.

Companies such, as Netflix, are promoting their continuous delivery techniques where small changes are made very often in production and tested on a subset of the user base. They've developed tools such as **Spinnaker** (http://www.spinnaker.io/) to automate as many steps as possible to update production and ship their features in the cloud as independent microservices.

But if you read Hacker News or Reddit, it can be quite hard to untangle what's useful for you and what's just buzzword-compliant journalistic-style information. As *Edsger Dijkstra*, noted computer science researcher and discoverer of the famous shortest-path routing algorithm, put it:

"Write a paper promising salvation, make it a structured something or a virtual something, or abstract, distributed or higher-order or applicative and you can almost be certain of having started a new cult."

–Edsger W. Dijkstra

This book will take you through the creation of a traditional monolithic service and provide guidance on how to identify components that will be more effective as microservices. We will cover ways to integrate with other services, pass messages and schedule tasks, and securely deploy our service in Amazon Web Services.

This chapter is going to help you understand what microservices are, and will then focus on the various ways in which you can implement them using Python. It is composed of the following sections:

- The origins of service-oriented architecture
- The monolithic approach to building an application
- The microservices approach to building applications
- Benefits of microservices
- Potential pitfalls in microservices
- Implementing microservices with Python

Hopefully, once you've reached the end of the chapter, you will be able to dive into the rest of the book and build microservices with a good understanding of what they are and what they're not—and how you can use Python.

The origins of service-oriented architecture

There is no official standard for microservices, so it is helpful to look at a bit of the history in this area of software design. When discussing microservices, **Service-Oriented Architecture (SOA)** is often used as a starting point. SOA is a way of thinking about software architecture that encourages reusable software components that provide well-defined interfaces. This allows those components to be reused and applied to new situations.

Each unit in the preceding definition is a self-contained service that implements one facet of a business and provides its feature through some interface.

While SOA clearly states that services should be standalone processes, it does not enforce what protocols should be used for those processes to interact with each other and is quite vague about how you deploy and organize your application.

If you read the **SOA Manifesto** (`http://www.soa-manifesto.org`), first published on the web circa 2009, the authors don't even mention whether the services interact via a network, although contemporary understanding of the principles mostly involves networked services.

SOA services could communicate via **Inter-Process Communication** (**IPC**) using sockets on the same machine, through shared memory, through indirect message queues, or even with **Remote Procedure Calls** (**RPC**). The options are extensive, and SOA is a useful set of principles for a wide variety of situations.

However, it is common to say that microservices are one specialization of SOA, because they allow us to focus on the needs of the organization, its safety, and the scaling and separation of its software.

If we want to give a complete definition of microservices, the best way to understand it is in the context of different software architectures. We will start with a monolith, and then discuss how microservices are different.

The monolithic approach

With a monolith, everything about the service is in one place – the API, database, and all associated tools are managed as part of one code base. Let's take a very simple example of a traditional monolithic application: a hotel booking website.

Besides the static HTML content, the website has a booking feature that will let its users book hotels in any city in the world. Users can search for hotels, then book them with their credit cards.

When a user performs a search on the hotel website, the application goes through the following steps:

1. It runs a couple of SQL queries against its hotel database.
2. An HTTP request is made to a partner's service to add more hotels to the list.
3. Results are sent to the JavaScript embedded in the web page, to render the information for the viewer.

From there, once the user has found the perfect hotel and selected the booking option, the application performs these steps:

1.   The customer gets created in the database, if needed, and has to authenticate
2.   Payment is carried out by interacting with the bank's web service
3.   The app saves the payment details in the database for legal reasons
4.   A receipt is generated using a PDF generator
5.   A recap email is sent to the user using the email service
6.   A reservation email is forwarded to the third-party hotel using the email service
7.   A database entry is added to keep track of the reservation

This process is a simplified model, of course, but describes enough for us to learn from.

The application interacts with a database that contains the hotel's information, the reservation details, the billing, the user information, and so on. It also interacts with external services for sending emails, making payments, and getting more hotels from partners.

In the early days of the web, a new service would commonly use a **LAMP (Linux-Apache-MySQL-Perl/PHP/Python)** architecture. With this approach, every incoming request generates a cascade of SQL queries on the database, and a few network calls to external services, then the server generates the HTML response using a template engine.

The following diagram illustrates this centralized architecture:

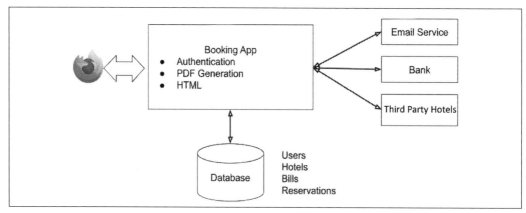

Figure 1.1: A sample monolithic service architecture

This application is a typical monolith, and it has a lot of benefits. The biggest one is that the whole application is in a single code base, and when the project coding starts, it makes everything simpler. Building a good test coverage is easy, and you can organize your code in a clean and structured way inside the code base. Storing all the data in a single database also simplifies the development of the application. You can tweak the data model, and how the code will query it.

The deployment is also straightforward; we can build a package, install it, and run it somewhere. To scale up, we can run several instances of the booking app, and run several databases with some replication mechanism in place.

If your application stays small, this model works well and is easy to maintain for a single team. But projects usually grow, and they get bigger than what was first intended. And having the whole application in a single code base brings some nasty issues along the way. For instance, if you need to make a sweeping change that is large in scope, such as changing your banking service or your database layer, the risks impact the whole application. These changes can have a huge impact on the project and need to be tested well before being deployed, and such testing often can't be exhaustive. Changes like this will happen in a project's life.

Small changes can also generate collateral damage because different parts of the system have different uptime and stability requirements. Putting the billing and reservation processes at risk because the function that creates a PDF crashes the server is a bit of a problem.

Uncontrolled growth is another issue. The application is bound to get new features, and with developers leaving and joining the project, the code might start to get messy, the tests a bit slower, and the deployment more fragile. This growth usually ends up with a spaghetti code base that's hard to maintain, with a hairy database that needs complicated migration plans every time some developer refactors the data model.

The other form of growth that makes the project interesting is capacity management. If just one element in the application needs to scale very differently than the rest, then scaling the application becomes much trickier; for example, if the hotel room availability starts being used to generate website advertising, as well as serving people visiting the website.

Large software projects usually take a couple of years to mature, and then they slowly start to turn into an incomprehensible mess that's hard to maintain. And it does not happen because developers are bad. It happens because as the complexity grows, fewer people fully understand the implications of every small change they make.

So, they try to work in isolation with a fragment of the code base, and the mess only becomes visible when you view the entire structure of the project. We've all been there.

It's not fun, and developers who work on such a project dream of building the application from scratch with the newest framework. And by doing so, they usually face the same issues again – the same story is repeated.

To summarize, with a monolithic architecture there are benefits:

- Starting a project as a monolith is easy, and probably the best approach.
- A centralized database simplifies the design and organization of the data.
- Deploying one application is simple.

However:

- Any change in the code can impact unrelated features. When something breaks, the whole application may break.
- Solutions to scale your application are limited: you can deploy several instances, but if one particular feature inside the app takes all the resources, it impacts everything.
- As the code base grows, it's hard to keep it clean and under control.

There are, of course, some ways to avoid some of the issues described here.

The obvious solution is to split the application into separate pieces, even if the resulting code is still going to run in a single process. Developers do this by building their apps with external libraries and frameworks. Those tools can be in-house or from the **Open-Source Software** (**OSS**) community.

If you build a web app in Python using a framework like **Quart** or **Flask**, you are able to focus on the business logic, and it becomes very appealing to externalize some of your code into framework extensions and small Python packages. And splitting your code into small packages is often a good idea to control your application growth.

"Small is beautiful."

— The UNIX philosophy

For instance, the PDF generator described in the hotel booking app could be a separate Python package that uses **ReportLab** and some templates to do the work. It's highly likely that this package could be reused in some other applications, and maybe even published to the **Python Package Index** (**PyPI**) for the community.

But you're still building a single application and some problems persist, like the inability to scale parts differently, or any indirect issue introduced by a buggy dependency.

You'll even face new challenges because you're now using dependencies. One problem that you'll face is *dependency hell*. If two parts of your application use the same library, you could get into the situation where one part of your application requires a new version for a feature that has been added, but another component can't use the newer one because something else has changed, and you are now in *dependency hell*. There's a good chance you will eventually have some ugly workaround for this problem in a large project, such as having a copy of the dependency that you now need to maintain separately to keep the fix up to date.

Of course, all the problems described in this section do not appear on day one when the project starts, but rather pile up over time.

Let's now look at how the same application would look if we were to use microservices to build it.

The microservice approach

If we were to build the same application using microservices, we would organize the code into several separate components that run in separate processes. We have already discussed the PDF report generator, and we can examine the rest of the application and see where we could split it into different microservices, as shown in the following diagram:

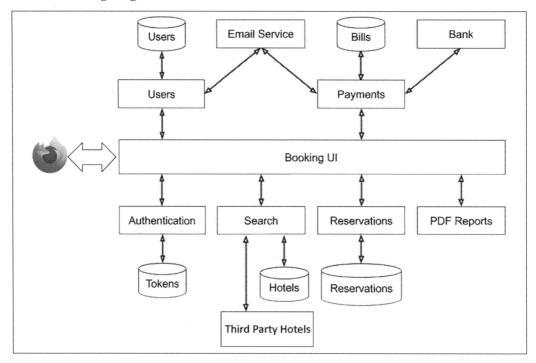

Figure 1.2: A sample microservice architecture

Don't be afraid of the number of components displayed in this diagram. The internal interactions of the monolithic application are just being made visible by separate pieces. We've shifted some of the complexity and ended up with these seven standalone components:

1. **Booking UI**: A frontend service that generates the web user interface, and interacts with all the other microservices.

2. **PDF reports**: A very simple service that will create PDFs for receipts or any other document given a template and some data. Also known as the PDF reporting service.

3. **Search**: A service that can be queried to get a list of hotels when given a location. This service has its own database.

4. **Payments**: A service that interacts with the third-party bank service, and manages a billing database. It also sends emails on successful payment.

5. **Reservations**: Manages reservations and changes to bookings.

6. **Users**: Stores the user information, and interacts with users via emails.

7. **Authentication**: An OAuth 2-based service that returns authentication tokens, which each microservice can use to authenticate when calling others.

Those microservices, along with a few external services, like the email service, would provide a feature set similar to the monolithic application. In this design, each component communicates using the HTTP protocol, and features are made available through RESTful web services.

There's no centralized database, as each microservice deals internally with its own data structures, and the data that gets in and out uses a language-agnostic format like JSON. It could use XML or YAML as long as it can be produced and consumed by any language, and travel through HTTP requests and responses.

The Booking UI service is a bit particular in that regard, since it generates the **User Interface (UI)**. Depending on the frontend framework used to build the UI, the Booking UI output could be a mix of HTML and JSON, or even plain JSON if the interface uses a static JavaScript-based client-side tool to generate the interface directly in the browser.

But besides this particular UI case, a web application designed with microservices is a composition of several microservices, which may interact with each other through HTTP to provide the whole system.

In that context, microservices are logical units that focus on a very particular task. Here's a full definition attempt:

 A microservice is a lightweight application that provides a narrow list of features with a well-defined contract. It's a component with a single responsibility that can be developed and deployed independently.

This definition does not mention HTTP or JSON, because you could consider, for example, a small UDP-based service that exchanges binary data as a microservice, or a service that communicates using gRPC. (gRPC is a recursive acronym that stands for gRPC Remote Procedure Call, an open-source remote procedure call system.)

But in our case, and throughout the book, all our microservices are just simple web applications that use the HTTP protocol and consume and produce JSON when it's not a UI.

Microservice benefits

While the microservices architecture looks more complicated than its monolithic counterpart, it offers multiple advantages. It offers the following:

- Separation of concerns
- Smaller projects to deal with
- More scaling and deployment options

We will discuss them in more detail in the following sections.

Separation of concerns

First of all, each microservice can be developed independently by a separate team. For instance, building a reservation service can be a full project on its own. The team in charge can code it in the programming language and database of their choice, as long as it has a well-documented HTTP API.

That also means the evolution of the app is more under control than with monoliths. For example, if the payment system changes its underlying interactions with the bank, the impact is localized inside that service, and the rest of the application stays stable and is probably unaffected.

This is known as loose coupling, and improves the overall project velocity as we apply, at the service level, a philosophy similar to the *single responsibility* principle. By contrast, a tightly coupled payment service would need inside knowledge of how the system represents its data or performs its task.

Robert Martin, the author of many widely respected books about software engineering, defined the single responsibility principle to explain that a class should have only one reason to change; in other words, each class should provide a single, well-defined feature. Applied to microservices, it means that we want to make sure that each microservice focuses on a single role.

Smaller projects

The second benefit is breaking the complexity of the project. When you add a feature to an application such as PDF reporting, even if you do it cleanly, you make the code base bigger, more complicated, and sometimes slower. Building that feature in a separate application avoids this problem and makes it easier to write it with whatever tools you want. You can refactor it often, shorten your release cycles, and stay on top of things. The growth of the application remains under your control.

Dealing with a smaller project also reduces risks when improving the application: if a team wants to try out the latest programming language or framework, they can iterate quickly on a prototype that implements the same microservice API, try it out, and decide whether or not to stick with it.

One real-life example is the Firefox Sync storage microservice. There were experiments to switch from storing data in MySQL, to an implementation that stores users' data in standalone SQLite databases. The risks of an experimental prototype were mitigated by isolating the storage feature in a microservice with a well-defined HTTP API. This minimized the unexpected interactions with other components and allowed a small subset of the user base to try out the new version of the service.

Reducing the size of each component also makes it easier to think about for developers, especially new ones joining the team or ones who are stressed about handling an outage with the service. Instead of having to work through an entire system, a developer can focus on a smaller area and not worry about the rest of the application's features.

Scaling and deployment

Finally, having your application split into components makes it easier to scale depending on your constraints. Let's say your business grows and there are many more customers who book hotels each day, and the PDF generation starts to use more resources and slows down. To tackle this problem, you can deploy that specific microservice in some servers that have bigger CPUs or more memory.

Another typical example is a high memory usage microservice, such as ones that interact with in-memory databases such as **Redis** or **Memcached**. You could tweak your deployments, consequently, by using servers with less CPU and a lot more RAM.

We can, thus, summarize the benefits of microservices as follows:

- A team can develop each microservice independently, and use whatever technology stack makes sense. They can define a custom release cycle. All they need to define is a language-agnostic HTTP API.

- Developers split the application complexity into logical components. Each microservice focuses on doing one thing well.

- Since microservices are standalone applications, there's finer control over deployments, which makes scaling easier.

The microservices architecture is good at solving a lot of the problems that may arise once your application starts to grow. However, we need to be aware of some of the new issues that are brought along.

Pitfalls of microservices

As discussed earlier, building an application with microservices has many benefits, but it's not a silver bullet by any means.

You need to be aware of these main problems you might have to deal with when coding microservices:

- Illogical splitting
- More network interactions
- Data storing and sharing
- Compatibility issues
- Testing

These issues will be covered in detail in the following sections.

Illogical splitting

The first issue of a microservice architecture is how it gets designed. There's no way a team can come up with the perfect microservice architecture on their first shot. Some microservices like the PDF generator are an obvious use case. But as soon as you deal with the business logic, there's a good chance that your code will move around before you get a good grasp of how to split things into the right set of microservices.

The design needs to mature with some try-and-fail cycles. And adding and removing microservices can be more painful than refactoring a monolithic application. You can mitigate this problem by avoiding splitting your app into microservices if the split is not evident.

If there's any doubt that the split makes sense, keeping the code in the same app is the safe bet. It's always easier to split apart some of the code into a new microservice later than to merge two microservices back in the same code base because the decision turned out to be wrong.

For instance, if you always have to deploy two microservices together, or if one change in a microservice impacts the data model of the other one, the odds are that you did not split the application correctly and that those two services should be reunited.

More network interactions

The second problem is the number of network interactions added to build the same application. In the monolithic version, even if the code gets messy, everything happens in the same process, and you can send back the result without having to call too many backend services to build the actual response.

That requires extra attention to how each backend service is called and raises a lot of questions, like the following:

- What happens when the Booking UI cannot reach the PDF reporting service because of a network split or a laggy service?
- Does the Booking UI call the other services synchronously or asynchronously?
- How will that impact the response time?

We will need to have a solid strategy to be able to answer all those questions, and we will address those in *Chapter 6, Interacting with Other Services*.

Data storing and sharing

Another problem is data storing and sharing. An effective microservice needs to be independent of other microservices, and ideally, should not share a database. What does this mean for our hotel booking app?

Again, that raises a lot of questions, such as the following:

- Do we use the same users' IDs across all databases, or do we have independent IDs in each service and keep it as a hidden implementation detail?
- Once a user is added to the system, do we replicate some of her information in other services' databases via strategies like data pumping, or is that overkill?
- How do we deal with data removal?

These are hard questions to answer, and there are many different ways to solve those problems, as we'll learn throughout the book.

> Avoiding data duplication as much as possible while keeping microservices in isolation is one of the biggest challenges in designing microservices-based applications.

Compatibility issues

Another problem happens when a feature change impacts several microservices. If a change affects, in a backward-incompatible way, the data that travels between services, you're in for some trouble.

Can you deploy your new service, and will it work with older versions of other services? Or do you need to change and deploy several services at once? Does it mean you've just stumbled on some services that should probably be merged back together?

Good versioning and API design hygiene helps to mitigate those issues, as we will discover in the second part of the book, when we'll build our application.

Testing

Lastly, when you want to do some end-to-end tests and deploy your whole app, you have to deal with many components. You need to have a robust and agile deployment process to be efficient. You need to be able to play with your whole application when you develop it. You can't fully test things out with just one piece of the puzzle, although having a clean and well-defined interface does help.

Many of the recent developments in cloud orchestration tools, such as Kubernetes, Terraform, and CloudFormation make life much easier when deploying an application that consists of several components. They can be used to create test and staging environments as well as production, customer-facing deployments. The popularity of these tools has helped in the success and adoption of microservices.

> Microservices-style architecture boosts deployment tools' innovation, and deployment tools lower the bar for the approval of microservices-style architecture.

The pitfalls of using microservices can be summarized as follows:

- Premature splitting of an application into microservices can lead to architectural problems.
- Network interactions between microservices add potential points of failure and additional overhead.
- Testing and deploying microservices can be complex.
- And the biggest challenge—data sharing between microservices is hard.

You should not worry too much about all the pitfalls described in this section for now. They may seem overwhelming, and the traditional monolithic application may look like a safer bet, but in the long term, splitting your project into microservices will make many of your tasks, as a developer or as an **operations person** (**ops**), easier. It can also make running a service cheaper. To add more capacity to a monolithic application, you need a larger server, or the ability to add more large servers. If the architecture is distributed and based around microservices, then extra resources can be added in smaller increments, holding far closer to the amount actually needed. And as we will discover in *Chapter 9: Deployment, Running, and Scaling*, it can be easier to set a cloud service provider up to automatically scale based on demand.

Implementing microservices with Python

Python is an amazingly versatile language. As you probably already know, Python is used to build many different kinds of applications – from simple system scripts that perform tasks on a server to large object-oriented applications that run services for millions of users. Python is also used in machine learning and data analysis tools.

Python sits comfortably in the top five languages in the TIOBE index (http://www.tiobe.com/tiobe-index/), and has reached as high as number two. It's probably even bigger in the web development world since languages like C are rarely used as main languages to build web applications.

 This book makes the assumption that you are already familiar with the Python programming language. If you are not an experienced Python developer, you can read the book *Expert Python Programming, Third Edition*, where you will learn advanced programming skills in Python.

However, some developers criticize Python for being slow and unfit for building efficient web services. Python is slow, and this is undeniable, though it is fast enough for most situations. But it still is the language of choice for building microservices, and many major companies happily use it.

This section will give you some background on the different ways you can write microservices using Python, offer some insights on asynchronous versus synchronous programming, and conclude with some details on Python performance.

How web services work

If we imagine a simple program that answers queries on the web, the description is straightforward. A new connection is made, and the protocol is negotiated. A request is made, and some processing is done: perhaps a database is queried. Then a response is structured and sent, and the connection is closed. This is often how we want to think about our application's logic, because it keeps things simple for the developer as well as anyone else responsible for the program once it's running.

The web is a big, complicated place, though. Various parts of the internet will try to do malicious things to a vulnerable web service they find. Others just behave badly because they have not been set up well. Even when things are working well, there are different HTTP protocol versions, encryption, load balancing, access control, and a whole set of other things to think about.

Rather than reinvent all of this technology, there are **interfaces** and **frameworks** that let us use the tools that other people have built, and spend more of our time working on our own applications. They let us use web servers such as **Apache** and **nginx** and let them handle the difficult parts of being on the web, such as certificate management, load balancing, and handling multiple website identities. Our application then has a smaller, more manageable configuration to control its behavior.

The WSGI standard

What strikes most web developers who start with Python is how easy it is to get a web application up and running.

Inspired by the older **Common Gateway Interface (CGI)**, the Python web community has created a standard called the **Web Server Gateway Interface (WSGI)**. It simplifies how you can write a Python application in order to serve HTTP requests. When your code uses this standard, your project can be executed by standard web servers like Apache or nginx, using WSGI extensions like `uwsgi` or `mod_wsgi`.

Your application just has to deal with incoming requests and send back JSON responses, and Python includes all that goodness in its standard library.

You can create a fully functional microservice that returns the server's local time with a vanilla Python module of fewer than 10 lines:

```
import json
import time

def application(environ, start_response):
    headers = [('Content-type', 'application/json')]
    start_response('200 OK', headers)
    return [bytes(json.dumps({'time': time.time()}), 'utf8')]
```

Since its introduction, the WSGI protocol has become an essential standard, and the Python web community has widely adopted it. Developers have written middleware, which are functions you can hook before or after the WSGI application function itself, to do something within the environment.

Some web frameworks, such as **Bottle** (`http://bottlepy.org`), were created specifically around that standard, and soon enough, every framework out there could be used through WSGI in one way or another.

The biggest problem with WSGI, though, is its synchronous nature. More recently, the **Asynchronous Server Gateway Interface** (**ASGI**) has emerged as a successor to WSGI, allowing frameworks to operate asynchronously with the same seamless behavior as before. What are synchronous and asynchronous applications? We will cover that now.

Workers, threads, and synchronicity

Thinking back to our simple application that handles requests, our model of the program is synchronous. This means that it accepts a piece of work, does that work, and returns the result, but while it's doing all of that, the program can't do anything else. Any other requests that come in when it's already working on something will have to wait.

There are several approaches to solving this problem, from using worker pools to early context switching environments, and more recently, full asynchronous Python.

A worker pool approach

Accepting a new request is often very fast, and the bulk of the time is taken up by doing the work that has been requested. Reading a request that tells you "Give me a list of all our customers in Paris" takes much less time than putting the list together and sending it back.

When an application has lots of requests arriving, an effective strategy is to ensure that all the heavy lifting is done using other processes or threads. Starting a new thread can be slow, and starting a new process is even slower, and so a common technique is to start these workers early and keep them around, giving them new work to do as it arrives.

This is an old technique and a very effective one, but it does have limitations. As far as each worker is concerned, it receives work, and can't do anything else until it has finished. This means that if you have eight worker processes, you can only handle eight simultaneous requests. Your application could create more workers if it is running low, but there is always a bottleneck.

There is also a practical limit to the number of processes and threads that an application can create, and swapping between them takes a lot of time that a responsive application can't always afford.

Being asynchronous

One important thing to realize is that computers interacting with each other is a slow process. Not from a human perspective, where a new message from a family member can appear on our phones in the blink of an eye, but from the perspective of the computer itself.

There are several charts available that suggest *"Latency Numbers Every Programmer Should Know,"* originally by *Jeff Dean* and *Peter Norvig*. A version of it can be found at https://colin-scott.github.io/personal_website/research/interactive_latency.html.

There are a lot of numbers in these tables, but the important ones for us are the ones about network traffic. We can learn that reading about 1 MB from a computer's memory takes about 3,000 ns, but sending a packet over the network to a computer in the same building, and getting a response, can take about 500,000 ns. Talking to a computer on another continent can take hundreds of milliseconds.

To put this in human terms: it might take you a few seconds to remember that you need to ask someone a question. Sending them the question and hearing back that they've read it, whether or not you get the answer you need, might take two days.

You don't really want to be sitting there doing nothing while waiting for an answer, but that's what a process usually does if it's synchronous. An asynchronous program is aware that some tasks it has been told to perform might take a long time, and so it can get on with some other work while it is waiting, without necessarily having to use other processes or threads.

Twisted, Tornado, Greenlets, and Gevent

For a long time, non-WSGI frameworks like **Twisted** and **Tornado** were the popular answers for concurrency when using Python, allowing developers to specify **callbacks** for many simultaneous requests. In a sequential program, you might call a function and wait for it to return a value to you. A callback is a technique where the calling part of the program doesn't wait but instead tells the function what it should do with the result it generates. Often this is another function that it should call.

Another popular approach involved Greenlets and Gevent. The **Greenlet** project (`https://github.com/python-greenlet/greenlet`) is a package based on the **Stackless** project, a particular CPython implementation, and provides *greenlets*.

Greenlets are *pseudo-threads* that are very cheap to instantiate, unlike real threads, and that can be used to call Python functions. Within those functions, you can *switch*, and give back the control to another function. The switching is done with an event loop and allows you to write an asynchronous application using a thread-like interface paradigm.

However, switching from one greenlet to another has to be done explicitly, and the resulting code can quickly become messy and hard to understand. That's where Gevent can become very useful. The **Gevent** project (`http://www.gevent.org/`) is built on top of Greenlet and offers an implicit and automatic way of switching between greenlets, among many other things.

With the experience from all of these options, Python now has `asyncio` as a core feature of the language since 3.5, and this is what we will be using in our code.

Asynchronous Python

When *Guido van Rossum* started to work on adding async features in Python 3, part of the community pushed for a Gevent-like solution, because it made a lot of sense to write applications in a synchronous, sequential fashion rather than having to add explicit callbacks like in Tornado or Twisted.

But Guido picked the explicit technique and experimented in a project called **Tulip** inspired by Twisted. Eventually, the `asyncio` module was born out of that side project and added into Python.

In hindsight, implementing an explicit event loop mechanism in Python instead of going the Gevent way makes a lot of sense. The way the Python core developers coded asyncio, and how they extended the language with the `async` and `await` keywords to implement coroutines, made asynchronous applications built with vanilla Python 3.5+ code look very elegant and close to synchronous programming.

Python 3 has introduced a full set of features and helpers in the asyncio package to build asynchronous applications; refer to `https://docs.python.org/3/library/asyncio.html`.

aiohttp (`http://aiohttp.readthedocs.io`) is one of the most mature asyncio packages, and building the earlier "time" microservice with it would simply need these few lines:

```python
from aiohttp import web
import time

async def handle(request):
    return web.json_response({'time': time.time()})


if __name__ == '__main__':
    app = web.Application()
    app.router.add_get('/', handle)
    web.run_app(app)
```

In this small example, we're very close to how we would implement a synchronous app. The only hint we're using asynchronous code is the `async` keyword, which marks the `handle` function as being a coroutine.

And this concept is what's going to be used at every level of an async Python app going forward. Here's another example using `aiopg`, a PostgreSQL library for asyncio from the project documentation:

```python
import asyncio
import aiopg
# Start an example postgres instance with:
# docker run -p5432:5432 --name some-postgres \
# -e POSTGRES_PASSWORD=mysecretpassword -d postgres

dsn = "dbname=postgres user=postgres password=mysecretpassword
host=127.0.0.1"

async def go():
    pool = await aiopg.create_pool(dsn)
    async with pool.acquire() as conn:
        async with conn.cursor() as cur:
            await cur.execute("SELECT 1")
            ret = []
```

```
            async for row in cur:
                ret.append(row)
            assert ret == [(1,)]
        await pool.clear()

    loop = asyncio.get_event_loop()
    loop.run_until_complete(go())
```

With a few `async` and `await` prefixes, the function that performs an SQL query and sends back the result looks a lot like a synchronous function. We will explain more about this code in later chapters.

If you need to use a library that is not asynchronous in your code, to use it from your asynchronous code means that you will need to go through some extra and challenging work if you want the different libraries to work well together.

There are many great synchronous frameworks to build microservices with Python, like **Bottle**, **Pyramid** with **Cornice**, or **Flask**. We will be using one that is very similar to Flask, but is also asynchronous: **Quart**.

 Keep in mind that whatever Python web framework you use, you should be able to transpose all the examples in this book. This is because most of the coding involved when building microservices is very close to plain Python, and the framework is mostly to route the requests and offer a few helpers.

Language performance

In the previous sections, we went through the two different ways to write microservices: asynchronous versus synchronous, and whatever technique you use, the speed of Python directly impacts the performance of your microservice.

Of course, everyone knows Python is slower than Java or Go, but execution speed is not always the top priority. A microservice is often a thin layer of code that sits most of its life waiting for some network responses from other services. Its core speed is usually less important than how fast your SQL queries will take to return from your Postgres server, because the latter will represent most of the time spent building the response.

It's also important to remember that how long you spend developing the software can be just as important. If your services are rapidly changing, or a new developer joins and has to understand the code, it is important to have code that is easy to understand, develop, and deploy.

But wanting an application that's as fast as possible is legitimate.

One controversial topic in the Python community around speeding up the language is how the **Global Interpreter Lock (GIL)** can affect performance, because multi-threaded applications cannot use several processes.

The GIL has good reasons to exist. It protects non-thread-safe parts of the CPython interpreter and exists in other languages like Ruby. And all attempts to remove it so far have failed to produce a faster CPython implementation.

For microservices, besides preventing the usage of multiple cores in the same process, the GIL will slightly degrade performance under high load because of the system calls overhead introduced by the mutex.

However, all the scrutiny around the GIL has been beneficial: work has been done in the past to reduce GIL contention in the interpreter, and in some areas, Python's performance has improved a lot. Changes in Python 3.8 to introduce subinterpreters and multiple locks have also helped with some areas.

Bear in mind that even if the core team removes all the GIL performance issues, Python is an interpreted and garbage collected language and suffers performance penalties for those properties.

Python provides the `dis` module if you are interested in seeing how the interpreter decomposes a function. In the following example, the interpreter will decompose a simple function that yields incremented values from a sequence in no less than 22 steps:

```
>>> def myfunc(data):
...     for value in data:
...         yield value + 1
...
>>> import dis
>>> dis.dis(myfunc)
  2           0 LOAD_FAST                0 (data)
              2 GET_ITER
        >>    4 FOR_ITER                14 (to 20)
              6 STORE_FAST               1 (value)

  3           8 LOAD_FAST                1 (value)
             10 LOAD_CONST               1 (1)
             12 BINARY_ADD
             14 YIELD_VALUE
             16 POP_TOP
```

```
        18 JUMP_ABSOLUTE            4
>>      20 LOAD_CONST              0 (None)
        22 RETURN_VALUE
```

A similar function written in a statically compiled language will dramatically reduce the number of operations required to produce the same result. There are ways to speed up Python execution, though.

One is to write a part of your code in compiled code by building extensions in C, Rust, or another compiled language, or using a static extension of the language like **Cython** (http://cython.org/), but that makes your code more complicated.

Another solution is by simply running your application using the **PyPy** interpreter (http://pypy.org/). This can give noticeable performance improvements just by swapping out the Python interpreter.

PyPy implements a **Just-In-Time (JIT)** compiler. This compiler directly replaces, at runtime, pieces of Python with machine code that can be directly used by the CPU. The whole trick for the JIT compiler is to detect in real time, ahead of the execution, when and how to do it.

Even if PyPy is always a few Python versions behind CPython, it has reached a point where you can use it in production, and its performance can be quite amazing. In one of our projects at Mozilla that needs fast execution, the PyPy version was almost as fast as the Go version, and we decided to use Python there instead.

 The Pypy Speed Center website is a great place to look at how PyPy compares to CPython (http://speed.pypy.org/).

However, if your program uses C extensions or has any other compiled dependencies, you will need to recompile them for PyPy, and that extra work must be balanced against the speed improvements, especially if you are depending on another project or other developers to maintain the extensions you are using.

But if you build your microservice with a standard set of libraries, chances are that it will work out of the box with the PyPy interpreter, so that's worth a try. In any case, for most projects, the benefits of Python and its ecosystem largely surpass the performance issues described in this section, because the overhead in a microservice is rarely a problem. And if performance is a problem, the microservice approach allows you to rewrite and scale performance-critical components without affecting the rest of the system.

Summary

In this chapter, we've compared the monolithic and microservice approaches to building web applications, and it became apparent that there's not a binary choice where you have to pick one model on day one and stick with it.

You should see microservices as an improvement of an application that started its life as a monolith. As the project matures, parts of the service logic should migrate into microservices. It is a useful approach, as we've learned in this chapter, but it should be done carefully to avoid falling into some common traps.

Another important lesson is that Python is considered to be one of the best languages to write web applications and, therefore, microservices. For the same reasons, it's a language of choice in other areas, and also because it provides many mature frameworks and packages to do the work.

Python can be a slow language, and that can be a problem in very specific cases. Knowing what makes it slow, and the different solutions to avoid this issue, will usually be enough to work through any trouble.

We've rapidly looked at several frameworks, both synchronous and asynchronous, and for the rest of the book, we'll be using Quart. The next chapter will introduce this fantastic framework.

2
Discovering Quart

Quart was started in 2017 as an evolution of the popular **Flask** framework. Quart shares many of the same design decisions as Flask, and so a lot of the advice for one will work with the other. This book will focus on Quart to allow us to support asynchronous operations and to explore features such as WebSockets and HTTP/2 support.

Quart and Flask are not the only Python frameworks. There is a long history of projects aimed at providing services on the web, such as **Bottle**, **cherrypy**, and **Django**. All of these tools are used around the web, and they all share a similar goal: to offer the Python community simple tools for building web applications quickly.

The smaller frameworks, such as Quart and Bottle, are often called microframeworks; however, the term can be a bit misleading. It does not mean you can only create micro-applications. Using those tools, you can build any application, large or small. The prefix "micro" means that the framework tries to make as few decisions as possible. It lets you freely organize your application code and use whichever libraries you want.

A microframework acts as the glue code that delivers requests to your system and sends back responses. It does not enforce any particular paradigm on your project.

A typical example of this philosophy is when you need to interact with a SQL database. A framework such as Django is batteries-included and provides everything you need to build your web app, including an **Object-Relational Mapper** (**ORM**) to bind objects with database query results.

If you want to use an alternative ORM such as SQLAlchemy in Django to benefit from some of its great features, you'd be choosing a difficult path that would involve rewriting a lot of the Django library you are hoping to make use of, because of the tight integration Django has with the ORM it comes with. For certain applications, that's a good thing, but not necessarily for producing a microservice.

Quart, on the other hand, does not have a built-in library to interact with your data, leaving you free to choose your own. The framework will only attempt to make sure it has enough hooks to be extended by external libraries to provide various kinds of features. In other words, using an ORM in Quart, and making sure you're doing the right thing with SQL sessions and transactions, will mostly consist of adding a package such as SQLAlchemy to your project. If you don't like how a particular library integrates, you're free to use another one or to build your own integration. Quart can also make use of the more common Flask extensions, although there is a performance risk there as they are unlikely to be asynchronous and could block your application's work.

Of course, that's not a silver bullet. Being completely free in your choices also means that it is easier to make poor decisions and build an application that relies on defective libraries, or one that is not well designed. But fear not! This chapter will make sure you know what Quart has to offer, and how to organize your code for building microservices.

This chapter covers the following topics:

- Making sure we have Python
- How Quart handles requests
- Quart's built-in features
- A microservice skeleton

The goal of this chapter is to give you all the information needed to build microservices with Quart. By doing so, it inevitably duplicates some of the information you can find in Quart's official documentation, but focuses on providing interesting details and anything relevant when building microservices. Quart and Flask have good online documentation.

Make sure you take a look at Quart's and Flask's documentation, listed respectively:

- `https://pgjones.gitlab.io/quart/index.html`
- `https://flask.palletsprojects.com/`

Both should serve as a great complement to this chapter. The source code is located at https://gitlab.com/pgjones/quart.

This is worth being aware of, as the source code is always the ultimate truth when you need to understand how the software works.

Making sure we have Python

Before we start digging into its features, we should make sure that we have Python installed and working!

You might see some documentation or posts online that mention *Python version 2*. There was a long transition from Python 2 to Python 3, and had this book been written a few years earlier, we would be discussing the merits of each. However, Python 3 is fully capable of everything the majority of people need to do, and Python 2 stopped being supported by the core Python team in 2020. This book uses the latest Python 3.9 stable release for all its code examples, but they are likely to work on Python 3.7 or later, as that's the minimum version that Quart requires in order to work.

 If your computer does not have at least Python 3.7, you can download a new version from Python's own website, where installation instructions are provided: https://www.python.org/downloads/.

You will find it easier if all the code examples in this book are run in a virtual environment, or virtualenv (https://docs.python.org/3/library/venv.html). A virtual environment is Python's way of keeping each project separate, as it means you can install Quart and any other libraries you need; it will only affect the application you are currently working on. Other applications and projects can have different libraries, or different versions of the same library, without them getting in the way of each other. Using a virtualenv also means that you can easily recreate your project's dependencies somewhere else, which will be very useful when we deploy a microservice in a later chapter.

Some code editors, such as PyCharm or Visual Studio, may manage a virtual environment for you. Every code example in the book runs in a terminal, and so we will use a terminal to create our virtualenv. This also shows how things work in more detail than viewing a program's output on the web, or in log files, and will be helpful when fixing any problems in the future.

In a terminal, such as a macOS Terminal application, or a Windows Subsystem for Linux, change to the directory you would like to work in and run the following command:

```
python -m venv my-venv
```

Depending on how you installed Python, you may need to use python3 to create the virtual environment.

This creates a new virtual environment called my-venv in the current directory. You could give it another path if you like, but it's important to remember where it is. To use the virtual environment, you must activate it:

```
source my-venv/bin/activate
```

For most of the command-line examples in this book, we assume you are running on Linux, as that is what most services online use, so it is good to be familiar with it. This means that most of the commands will also work on macOS or on Windows using the Windows Subsystem for Linux. It's also possible to run Docker containers on all these systems, and we will describe containers later on when we discuss deploying your microservice.

Now, let's install Quart so that we can run our example code:

```
pip install quart
```

To stop using the virtual environment without closing the terminal, you can type deactivate. For now, though, let's keep the virtualenv active and look at how Quart will work.

How Quart handles requests

The framework entry point is the Quart class in the quart.app module. Running a Quart application means running one single instance of this class, which will take care of handling incoming **Asynchronous Server Gateway Interface (ASGI)** and **Web Server Gateway Interface (WSGI)** requests, dispatch them to the right code, and then return a response. Remember that in *Chapter 1, Understanding Microservices*, we discussed ASGI and WSGI, and how they define the interface between a web server and a Python application.

The Quart class offers a route method, which can decorate your functions. When you decorate a function this way, it becomes a view and is registered in the routing system.

When a request arrives, it will be to a specific endpoint—usually a web address (such as `https://duckduckgo.com/?q=quart`) or part of an address, such as `/api`. The routing system is how Quart connects an endpoint to the view—the bit of code that will run to process the request.

Here's a very basic example of a fully functional Quart application:

```
# quart_basic.py
from quart import Quart

app = Quart(__name__)

@app.route("/api")
def my_microservice():
    return {"Hello": "World!"}

if __name__ == "__main__":
    app.run()
```

All the code samples are available on GitHub at `https://github.com/PacktPublishing/Python-Microservices-Development-2nd-Edition/tree/main/CodeSamples`.

We see that our function returns a dictionary, and Quart knows that this should be encoded as a JSON object to be transferred. However, only querying the `/api` endpoint returns the value. Every other endpoint would return a 404 Error, indicating that it can't find the resource you requested because we haven't told it about any!

The __name__ variable, whose value will be __main__ when you run that single Python module, is the name of the application package. It's used by Quart to create a new logger with that name to format all the log messages, and to find where the file is located on the disk. Quart will use the directory as the root for helpers, such as the configuration that is associated with your app, and to determine default locations for the `static` and `templates` directories, which we will discuss later.

If you run that module in a terminal, the Quart app will run its own development web server, and start listening to incoming connections on port 5000. Here, we assume that you are still in the virtual environment created earlier and that the code above is in a file called quart_basic.py:

```
$ python quart_basic.py
 * Serving Quart app 'quart_basic'
 * Environment: production
 * Please use an ASGI server (e.g. Hypercorn) directly in production
 * Debug mode: False
```

```
 * Running on http://localhost:5000 (CTRL + C to quit)
 [2020-12-10 14:05:18,948] Running on http://localhost:5000 (CTRL + C to
 quit)
```

Visiting `http://localhost:5000/api` in your browser or with the `curl` command will return a valid JSON response with the right headers:

```
$ curl -v http://localhost:5000/api
*    Trying localhost...
...
< HTTP/1.1 200
< content-type: application/json
< content-length: 18
< date: Wed, 02 Dec 2020 20:29:19 GMT
< server: hypercorn-h11
<
* Connection #0 to host localhost left intact
{"Hello":"World!"}* Closing connection 0
```

The `curl` command is going to be used a lot in this book. If you are under Linux or macOS, it should be pre-installed; refer to `https://curl.haxx.se/`.

If you are not developing your application on the same computer as the one that you are testing it on, you may need to adjust some of the settings, such as which IP addresses it should use to listen for connections. When we discuss deploying a microservice, we will cover some of the better ways of changing its configuration, but for now, the `app.run` line can be changed to use a different `host` and `port`:

```
app.run(host="0.0.0.0", port=8000)
```

While many web frameworks explicitly pass a `request` object to your code, Quart provides a global `request` variable, which points to the current `request` object it built for the incoming HTTP request.

This design decision makes the code for the simpler views very concise. As in our example, if you don't have to look at the request content to reply, there is no need to have it around. As long as your view returns what the client should get and Quart can serialize it, everything happens as you would hope. For other views, they can just import that variable and use it.

The `request` variable is global, but it is unique to each incoming request and is thread-safe. Let's add some `print` method calls here and there so that we can see what's happening under the hood. We will also explicitly make a `Response` object using `jsonify`, instead of letting Quart do that for us, so that we can examine it:

```python
# quart_details.py
from quart import Quart, request, jsonify

app = Quart(__name__)

@app.route("/api", provide_automatic_options=False)
async def my_microservice():
    print(dir(request))
    response = jsonify({"Hello": "World!"})
    print(response)
    print(await response.get_data())
    return response

if __name__ == "__main__":
    print(app.url_map)
    app.run()
```

Running that new version in conjunction with the curl command in another terminal, you get a lot of details, including the following:

```
$ python quart_details.py
QuartMap([<QuartRule '/api' (HEAD, GET, OPTIONS) -> my_microservice>,
 <QuartRule '/static/<filename>' (HEAD, GET, OPTIONS) -> static>])
Running on http://localhost:5000 (CTRL + C to quit)

[… '_load_field_storage', '_load_form_data', '_load_json_data',
'_send_push_promise', 'accept_charsets', 'accept_encodings',
'accept_languages', 'accept_mimetypes', 'access_control_request_
headers', 'access_control_request_method', 'access_route', 'args',
'authorization', 'base_url', 'blueprint', 'body', 'body_class', 'body_
timeout', 'cache_control', 'charset', 'content_encoding', 'content_
length', 'content_md5', 'content_type', 'cookies', 'data', 'date',
'dict_storage_class', 'encoding_errors', 'endpoint', 'files', 'form',
'full_path', 'get_data', 'get_json', 'headers', 'host', 'host_url',
'http_version', 'if_match', 'if_modified_since', 'if_none_match',
'if_range', 'if_unmodified_since', 'is_json', 'is_secure', 'json',
'list_storage_class', 'max_forwards', 'method', 'mimetype', 'mimetype_
params', 'on_json_loading_failed', 'origin', 'parameter_storage_class',
'path', 'pragma', 'query_string', 'range', 'referrer', 'remote_addr',
'root_path', 'routing_exception', 'scheme', 'scope', 'send_push_
promise', 'url', 'url_charset', 'url_root', 'url_rule', 'values',
'view_args']
Response(200)
b'{"Hello":"World!"}'
```

Let's explore what's happening here:

- **Routing:** When the service starts, Quart creates the QuartMap object, and we can see here what it knows about endpoints and the associated views.

- **Request:** Quart creates a Request object and my_microservice is showing us that it is a GET request to /api.

- **dir()** shows us which methods and variables are in a class, such as get_data() to retrieve any data that was sent with the request.

- **Response:** A Response object to be sent back to the client; in this case, curl. It has an HTTP response code of 200, indicating that everything is fine, and its data is the 'Hello world' dictionary we told it to send.

Routing

Routing happens in app.url_map, which is an instance of the QuartMap class that uses a library called Werkzeug. That class uses regular expressions to determine whether a function decorated by @app.route matches the incoming request. The routing only looks at the path you provided in the route call to see whether it matches the client's request.

By default, the mapper will only accept GET, OPTIONS, and HEAD methods on a declared route. Sending an HTTP request to a valid endpoint with an unsupported method will return a 405 Method Not Allowed response together with a list of supported methods in the allow header:

```
$ curl -v -XDELETE  http://localhost:5000/api
**   Trying 127.0.0.1...
* TCP_NODELAY set
* Connected to localhost (127.0.0.1) port 5000 (#0)
> DELETE /api HTTP/1.1
> Host: localhost:5000
> User-Agent: curl/7.64.1
> Accept: */*
>
< HTTP/1.1 405
< content-type: text/html
< allow: GET, OPTIONS, HEAD
< content-length: 137
< date: Wed, 02 Dec 2020 21:14:36 GMT
< server: hypercorn-h11
<
```

```
<!doctype html>
<title>405 Method Not Allowed</title>
<h1>Method Not Allowed</h1>
Specified method is invalid for this resource
* Connection #0 to host 127.0.0.1 left intact
    * Closing connection 0
```

If you want to support specific methods allowing you to POST to an endpoint or DELETE some data, you can pass them to the route decorator with the methods argument, as follows:

```
@app.route('/api', methods=['POST', 'DELETE', 'GET'])
def my_microservice():
    return {'Hello': 'World!'}
```

Note that the OPTIONS and HEAD methods are implicitly added in all rules since it is automatically managed by the request handler. You can deactivate this behavior by giving the provide_automatic_options=False argument to the route function. This can be useful when you want to add custom headers to the response when OPTIONS is called, such as when dealing with **Cross-Origin Resource Sharing** (**CORS**), in which you need to add several Access-Control-Allow-* headers.

For more information regarding HTTP request methods, a good resource is the Mozilla Developer Network: https://developer.mozilla.org/en-US/docs/Web/HTTP/Methods.

Variables and converters

A common requirement for an API is the ability to specify exactly which data we want to request. For example, if you have a system where each person has a unique number to identify them, you might want to create a function that handles all requests sent to the /person/N endpoint, so that /person/3 only deals with ID number 3, and /person/412 only affects the person with ID 412.

You can do this with variables in the route, using the <VARIABLE_NAME> syntax. This notation is pretty standard (Bottle also uses it), and allows you to describe endpoints with dynamic values. If we create a route such as /person/<person_id>, then, when Quart calls your function, it converts the value it finds in the URL to a function argument with the same name:

```
@app.route('/person/<person_id>')
def person(person_id):
    return {'Hello': person_id}
```

```
$ curl localhost:5000/person/3
{"Hello": "3"}
```

If you have several routes that match the same URL, the mapper uses a particular set of rules to determine which one it calls. Quart and Flask both use Werkzeug to organize their routing; this is the implementation description taken from Werkzeug's routing module:

1. Rules without any arguments come first for performance. This is because we expect them to match faster and some common rules usually don't have any arguments (index pages, and so on).

2. The more complex rules come first, so the second argument is the negative length of the number of weights.

3. Lastly, we order by the actual weights.

Werkzeug's rules have, therefore, weights that are used to sort them, and this is not used or made visible in Quart. So, it boils down to picking views with more variables first, and then the others, in order of appearance, when Python imports the different modules. The rule of thumb is to make sure that every declared route in your app is unique, otherwise tracking which one gets picked will give you a headache.

This also means that our new route will not respond to queries sent to /person, or /person/3/help, or any other variation—only to /person/ followed by some set of characters. Characters include letters and punctuation, though, and we have already decided that /api/apiperson_id is a number! This is where converters are useful.

We can tell the route that a variable has a specific type. Since /api/apiperson_id is an integer, we can use <int:person_id>, as in the previous example, so that our code only responds when we give a number, and not when we give a name. You can also see that instead of the string "3", person_id is a number, with no quotes:

```
@app.route('/person/<int:person_id>')
def person(person_id):
    return {'Hello': person_id}
```

```
$ curl localhost:5000/person/3
{
  "Hello": 3
}
$ curl localhost:5000/person/simon
<!doctype html>
<title>404 Not Found</title>
<h1>Not Found</h1>
Nothing matches the given URI
```

If we had two routes, one for /person/<int:person_id> and one for /person/<person_id> (with different function names!), then the more specific one, which needs an integer, would get all the requests that had a number in the right place, and the other function would get the remaining requests.

Built-in converters are string (the default is a Unicode string), int, float, path, any, and uuid.

The path converter is like the default converter, but includes forward slashes, so that a request to a URL, /api/some/path/like/this, would match the route /api/<path:my_path>, and the function would get an argument called my_path containing some/path/like/this. If you are familiar with regular expressions, it's similar to matching [^/].*?.

int and float are for integers and floating-point—decimal—numbers. The any converter allows you to combine several values. It can be a bit confusing to use at first, but it might be useful if you need to route several specific strings to the same place. A route of /<any(about, help, contact):page_name> will match requests to /about, /help, or /contact, and which one was chosen will be in the page_name variable passed to the function.

The uuid converter matches the UUID strings, such as those that you get from Python's uuid module, providing unique identifiers. Examples of all these converters in action are also in the code samples for this chapter on GitHub.

It's quite easy to create your custom converter. For example, if you want to match user IDs with usernames, you could create a converter that looks up a database and converts the integer into a username. To do this, you need to create a class derived from the BaseConverter class, which implements two methods: the to_python() method to convert the value to a Python object for the view, and the to_url() method to go the other way (used by url_for(), which is described in the next section):

```python
# quart_converter.py
from quart import Quart, request
from werkzeug.routing import BaseConverter, ValidationError


_USERS = {"1": "Alice", "2": "Bob"}
_IDS = {val: user_id for user_id, val in _USERS.items()}

class RegisteredUser(BaseConverter):
    def to_python(self, value):
        if value in _USERS:
            return _USERS[value]
```

```
        raise ValidationError()

    def to_url(self, value):
        return _IDS[value]


app = Quart(__name__)
app.url_map.converters["registered"] = RegisteredUser

@app.route("/api/person/<registered:name>")
def person(name):
    return {"Hello": name}


if __name__ == "__main__":
    app.run()
```

The `ValidationError` method is raised in case the conversion fails, and the mapper will consider that the `route` simply does not match that request. Let's try a few calls to see how that works in practice:

```
$ curl localhost:5000/api/person/1
{
  "Hello hey": "Alice"
}

$ curl localhost:5000/api/person/2
{
  "Hello hey": "Bob"
}

$ curl localhost:5000/api/person/3

<!doctype html>
<title>404 Not Found</title>
<h1>Not Found</h1>
Nothing matches the given URI
```

 Be aware that the above is just an example of demonstrating the power of converters—an API that handles personal information in this way could give a lot of information away to malicious people. It can also be painful to change all the routes when the code evolves, so it is best to only use this sort of technique when necessary.

The best practice for routing is to keep it as static and straightforward as possible. This is especially true as moving all the endpoints requires changing all of the software that connects to them! It is often a good idea to include a version in the URL for an endpoint so that it is immediately clear that the behavior will be different between, for example, /v1/person and /v2/person.

The url_for function

The last interesting feature of Quart's routing system is the url_for() function. Given any view, it will return its actual URL. Here's an example of using Python interactively:

```
>>> from quart_converter import app
>>> from quart import url_for
>>> import asyncio
>>> async def run_url_for():
...     async with app.test_request_context("/", method="GET"):
...         print(url_for('person', name='Alice'))
...
>>> loop = asyncio.get_event_loop()
>>> loop.run_until_complete(run_url_for())
/api/person/1
```

The previous example uses the **Read-Eval-Print Loop** (**REPL**), which you can get by running the Python executable directly. There is also some extra code there to set up an asynchronous program because here, Quart is not doing that for us.

The url_for feature is quite useful in templates when you want to display the URLs of some views—depending on the execution context. Instead of hardcoding some links, you can just point the function name to url_for to get it.

Request

When a request comes in, Quart calls the view and uses a Request Context to make sure that each request has an isolated environment, specific to that request. We saw an example of that in the code above, where we were testing things using the helper method, test_request_context(). In other words, when you access the global request object in your view, you are guaranteed that it is unique to the handling of your specific request.

As we saw earlier when calling `dir(request)`, the `Request` object contains a lot of methods when it comes to getting information about what is happening, such as the address of the computer making the request, what sort of request it is, and other information such as authorization headers. Feel free to experiment with some of these request methods using the example code as a starting point.

In the following example, an HTTP Basic Authentication request that is sent by the client is always converted to a base64 form when sent to the server. Quart will detect the Basic prefix and will parse it into `username` and `password` fields in the `request.authorization` attribute:

```python
# quart_auth.py
from quart import Quart, request

app = Quart(__name__)

@app.route("/")
def auth():
    print("Quart's Authorization information")
    print(request.authorization)
    return ""

if __name__ == "__main__":
    app.run()
```

```
$ python quart_auth.py
* Running on http://localhost:5000/ (Press CTRL+C to quit)
Quart's Authorization information
{'username': 'alice', 'password': 'password'}
[2020-12-03 18:34:50,387] 127.0.0.1:55615 GET / 1.1 200 0 3066

$ curl http://localhost:5000/ --user alice:password
```

This behavior makes it easy to implement a pluggable authentication system on top of the `request` object. Other common request elements, such as cookies and files, are all accessible via other attributes, as we will discover throughout this book.

Response

In many of the previous examples, we have simply returned a Python dictionary and left Quart to produce a response for us that the client will understand. Sometimes, we have called `jsonify()` to ensure that the result is a JSON object.

There are other ways to make a response for our web application, along with some other values that are automatically converted to the proper object for us. We could return any of the following, and Quart would do the right thing:

- `Response()`: Creates a `Response` object manually.
- `str`: A string will be encoded as a text/html object in the response. This is especially useful for HTML pages.
- `dict`: A dictionary will be encoded as application/json using `jsonify()`.
- A generator or asynchronous generator object can be returned so that data can be streamed to the client.
- A `(response, status)` tuple: The response will be converted to a `response` object if it matches one of the preceding data types, and the status will be the HTTP response code used.
- A `(response, status, headers)` tuple: The response will be converted, and the `response` object will use a dictionary provided as headers that should be added to the response.

In most cases, a microservice will be returning data that some other software will interpret and choose how to display, and so we will be returning Python dictionaries or using `jsonify()` if we want to return a list or other object that can be serialized as JSON.

Here's an example with YAML, another popular way of representing data: the `yamlify()` function will return a `(response, status, headers)` tuple, which will be converted by Quart into a proper `Response` object:

```python
# yamlify.py
from quart import Quart
import yaml  # requires PyYAML

app = Quart(__name__)

def yamlify(data, status=200, headers=None):
    _headers = {"Content-Type": "application/x-yaml"}
    if headers is not None:
        _headers.update(headers)
    return yaml.safe_dump(data), status, _headers

@app.route("/api")
def my_microservice():
    return yamlify(["Hello", "YAML", "World!"])

if __name__ == "__main__":
    app.run()
```

The way Quart handles requests can be summarized as follows:

1. When the application starts, any function decorated with @app.route() is registered as a view and stored in app.url_map.
2. A call is dispatched to the right view depending on its endpoint and method.
3. A Request object is created in a local, isolated execution context.
4. A Response object wraps the content to send back.

These four steps are roughly all you need to know to start building apps using Quart. The next section will summarize the most important built-in features that Quart offers, alongside this request-response mechanism.

Quart's built-in features

The previous section gave us a good understanding of how Quart processes a request, and that's good enough to get you started. There are more helpers that will prove useful. We'll discover the following main ones in this section:

- The session object: Cookie-based data
- **Globals**: Storing data in the request context
- **Signals**: Sending and intercepting events
- **Extensions and middleware**: Adding features
- **Templates**: Building text-based content
- **Configuring**: Grouping your running options in a config file
- **Blueprints**: Organizing your code in namespaces
- **Error handling and debugging**: Dealing with errors in your app

The session object

Like the request object, Quart creates a session object, which is unique to the request context. It's a dict-like object, which Quart serializes into a cookie on the user side. The data contained in the session mapping is dumped into a JSON mapping, then compressed using zlib to make it smaller, and finally encoded in base64.

When the session gets serialized, the **itsdangerous** (https://pythonhosted.org/itsdangerous/) library signs the content using a secret_key value defined in the application. The signing uses **HMAC** (https://en.wikipedia.org/wiki/Hash-based_message_authentication_code) and SHA1.

This signature, which is added to the data as a suffix, ensures that the client cannot tamper with the data that is stored in a cookie unless they know the secret key to sign the session value. Note that the data itself is not encrypted. Quart will let you customize the signing algorithm to use, but HMAC + SHA1 is good enough when you need to store data in cookies.

However, when you're building microservices that are not producing HTML, you rarely rely on cookies as they are specific to web browsers. However, the idea of keeping a volatile key-value storage for each user can be extremely useful for speeding up some of the server-side work. For instance, if you need to perform some database look-ups to get some information pertaining to a user every time they connect, caching this information in a `session`-like object on the server side and retrieving the values based on their authentication details makes a lot of sense.

Globals

As discussed earlier in this chapter, Quart provides a mechanism for storing global variables that are unique to a particular `request` context. That is used for `request` and `session`, but is also available to store any custom object.

The `quart.g` variable contains all globals, and you can set whatever attributes you want on it. In Quart, the `@app.before_request` decorator can be used to point to a function that the app will call every time a request is made, just before it dispatches the `request` to a view.

It's a typical pattern in Quart to use `before_request` to set values in the globals. That way, all the functions that are called within the request context can interact with the special global variable called g and get the data. In the following example, we copy the `username` provided when the client performs an HTTP Basic Authentication in the user attribute:

```python
# globals.py
from quart import Quart, g, request

app = Quart(__name__)


@app.before_request
def authenticate():
    if request.authorization:
        g.user = request.authorization["username"]
    else:
        g.user = "Anonymous"
```

```
@app.route("/api")
def my_microservice():
    return {"Hello": g.user}


if __name__ == "__main__":
    app.run()
```

When a client requests the /api view, the authenticate function will set g.user depending on the headers provided:

```
$ curl http://localhost:5000/api
{
  "Hello": "Anonymous"
}
$ curl http://localhost:5000/api --user alice:password
{
  "Hello": "alice"
}
```

Any data you may think of that's specific to a request context, and that would be usefully shared throughout your code, can be added to quart.g.

Signals

Sometimes in an application, we want to send a message from one place to another, when components are not directly connected. One way in which we can send such messages is to use signals. Quart integrates with Blinker (https://pythonhosted. org/blinker/), which is a signal library that lets you subscribe a function to an event.

Events are instances of the AsyncNamedSignal class, which is based on the blinker.base.NamedSignal class. It is created with a unique label, and Quart instantiates 10 of them in version 0.13. Quart triggers signals at critical moments during the processing of a request. Since Quart and Flask use the same system, we can refer to the following full list: http://flask.pocoo.org/docs/latest/api/#core-signals-list.

Registering to a particular event is done by calling the signal's connect method. Signals are triggered when some code calls the signal's send method. The send method accepts extra arguments to pass data to all the registered functions.

In the following example, we register the finished function to the `request_finished` signal. That function will receive the `response` object:

```
# signals.py
from quart import Quart, g, request_finished
from quart.signals import signals_available

app = Quart(__name__)

def finished(sender, response, **extra):
    print("About to send a Response")
    print(response)

request_finished.connect(finished)

@app.route("/api")
async def my_microservice():
    return {"Hello": "World"}

if __name__ == "__main__":
    app.run()
```

The `signal` feature is provided by `Blinker`, which is installed by default as a dependency when you install `Quart`.

Some signals implemented in Quart are not useful in microservices, such as the ones occurring when the framework renders a template. However, there are some interesting signals that Quart triggers throughout the `request` life, which can be used to log what's going on. For instance, the `got_request_exception` signal is triggered when an exception occurs before the framework does something with it. That's how **Sentry**'s (`https://sentry.io`) Python client hooks itself in to log exceptions.

It can also be interesting to implement custom signals in your apps when you want to trigger some of your features with events and decouple the code. For example, if your microservice produces PDF reports, and you want to have the reports cryptographically signed, you could trigger a `report_ready` signal, and have a signer register to that event.

One important aspect of the signals implementation is that the registered functions are not called in any particular order, and so if there are dependencies between the functions that get called, this may cause trouble. If you need to do more complex or time-consuming work, then consider using a queue such as **RabbitMQ** (https://www.rabbitmq.com/) or one provided by a cloud platform such as Amazon Simple Queue Service or Google PubSub to send a message to another service. These message queues offer far more options than a basic signal and allow two components to communicate easily without even necessarily being on the same computer. We will cover an example of message queues in *Chapter 6, Interacting with Other Services*.

Extensions and middleware

Quart extensions are simply Python projects that, once installed, provide a package or a module named quart_something. They can be useful for avoiding having to reinvent anything when wanting to do things such as authentication or sending an email.

Because Quart can support some of the extensions available to Flask, you can often find something to help in Flask's list of extensions: Search for Framework::Flask in the Python package index at https://pypi.org/. To use Flask extensions, you must first import a patch module to ensure that it will work. For example, to import Flask's login extension, use the following commands:

```
import quart.flask_patch
import flask_login
```

The most up-to-date list of Flask extensions that are known to work with Quart will be at the address below. This is a good place to start looking when searching for extra features that your microservice needs: http://pgjones.gitlab.io/quart/how_to_guides/flask_extensions.html.

The other mechanism for extending Quart is to use ASGI or WSGI middleware. These extend the application by wrapping themselves around an endpoint and changing the data that goes in and comes out again.

In the example that follows, the middleware fakes an X-Forwarded-For header, so the Quart application thinks it's behind a proxy such as nginx. This is useful in a testing environment when you want to make sure your application behaves properly when it tries to get the remote IP address, since the remote_addr attribute will get the IP of the proxy, and not the real client. In this example, we have to create a new Headers object, as the existing one is immutable:

```python
# middleware.py
from quart import Quart, request
from werkzeug.datastructures import Headers

class XFFMiddleware:
    def __init__(self, app, real_ip="10.1.1.1"):
        self.app = app
        self.real_ip = real_ip

    async def __call__(self, scope, receive, send):
        if "headers" in scope and "HTTP_X_FORWARDED_FOR" not in
scope["headers"]:
            new_headers = scope["headers"].raw_items() + [
                (
                    b"X-Forwarded-For",
                    f"{self.real_ip}, 10.3.4.5, 127.0.0.1".encode(),
                )
            ]
            scope["headers"] = Headers(new_headers)
        return await self.app(scope, receive, send)


app = Quart(__name__)
app.asgi_app = XFFMiddleware(app.asgi_app)


@app.route("/api")
def my_microservice():
    if "X-Forwarded-For" in request.headers:
        ips = [ip.strip() for ip in request.headers["X-Forwarded-For"].
split(",")]
        ip = ips[0]
    else:
        ip = request.remote_addr
    return {"Hello": ip}


if __name__ == "__main__":
    app.run()
```

Notice that we use `app.asgi_app` here to wrap the ASGI application. `app.asgi_app` is where the application is stored to let people wrap it in this way. The `send` and `receive` parameters are channels through which we can communicate. It's worth remembering that if the middleware returns a response to the client, then the rest of the `Quart` app will never see the request!

In most situations, we won't have to write our own middleware, and it will be enough to include an extension to add a feature that someone else has produced.

Templates

Sending back JSON or YAML documents is easy enough, as we have seen in the examples so far. It's also true that most microservices produce machine-readable data and if a human needs to read it, the frontend must format it properly, using, for example, JavaScript on a web page. In some cases, though, we might need to create documents with some layout, whether it's an HTML page, a PDF report, or an email.

For anything that's text-based, Quart integrates a template engine called **Jinja** (`https://jinja.palletsprojects.com/`). You will often find examples showing Jinja being used to create HTML documents, but it works with any text-based document. Configuration management tools such as Ansible use Jinja to create configuration files from a template so that a computer's settings can be kept up to date automatically.

Most of the time, Quart will use Jinja to produce HTML documents, email messages, or some other piece of communication meant for a human—such as an SMS message or a bot that talks to people on tools such as Slack or Discord. Quart provides helpers such as `render_template`, which generate responses by picking a Jinja template, and provides the output given some data.

For example, if your microservice sends emails instead of relying on the standard library's email package to produce the email content, which can be cumbersome, you could use Jinja. The following example email template should be saved as `email_template.j2` in order for the later code examples to work:

```
Date: {{date}}
From: {{from}}
Subject: {{subject}}
To: {{to}}
Content-Type: text/plain

Hello {{name}},
```

```
We have received your payment!

Below is the list of items we will deliver for lunch:

{% for item in items %}- {{item['name']}} ({{item['price']}} Euros)
{% endfor %}

Thank you for your business!

--
My Fictional Burger Place
```

Jinja uses double brackets for marking variables that will be replaced by a value. Variables can be anything that is passed to Jinja at execution time. You can also use Python's if and for blocks directly in your templates with the {% for x in y % }... {% endfor %} and {% if x %}...{% endif %} notations.

The following is a Python script that uses the email template to produce an entirely valid RFC 822 message, which you can send via SMTP:

```python
# email_render.py
from datetime import datetime
from jinja2 import Template
from email.utils import format_datetime

def render_email(**data):
    with open("email_template.j2") as f:
        template = Template(f.read())
    return template.render(**data)


data = {
    "date": format_datetime(datetime.now()),
    "to": "bob@example.com",
    "from": "shopping@example-shop.com",
    "subject": "Your Burger order",
    "name": "Bob",
    "items": [
        {"name": "Cheeseburger", "price": 4.5},
        {"name": "Fries", "price": 2.0},
```

```
        {"name": "Root Beer", "price": 3.0},
    ],
}

print(render_email(**data))
```

The render_email function uses the Template class to generate the email using the data provided.

Jinja is a powerful tool and comes with many features that would take too much space to describe here. If you need to do some templating work in your microservices, it is a good choice, also being present in Quart. Check out the following for full documentation on Jinja's features: https://jinja.palletsprojects.com/.

Configuration

When building applications, you will need to expose options to run them, such as the information needed to connect to a database, the contact email address to use, or any other variable that is specific to a deployment.

Quart uses a mechanism similar to Django in its configuration approach. The Quart object comes with an object called config, which contains some built-in variables, and which can be updated when you start your Quart app via your configuration objects. For example, you can define a Config class in a Python-format file as follows:

```
# prod_settings.py
class Config:
    DEBUG = False
    SQLURI = "postgres://username:xxx@localhost/db"
```

It can then be loaded from your app object using app.config.from_object:

```
>>> from quart import Quart
>>> import pprint
>>> pp = pprint.PrettyPrinter(indent=4)
>>> app = Quart(__name__)
>>> app.config.from_object('prod_settings.Config')
>>> pp.pprint(app.config)
{   'APPLICATION_ROOT': None,
    'BODY_TIMEOUT': 60,
    'DEBUG': False,
```

```
    'ENV': 'production',
    'JSONIFY_MIMETYPE': 'application/json',
    'JSONIFY_PRETTYPRINT_REGULAR': False,
    'JSON_AS_ASCII': True,
    'JSON_SORT_KEYS': True,
    'MAX_CONTENT_LENGTH': 16777216,
    'PERMANENT_SESSION_LIFETIME': datetime.timedelta(days=31),
    'PREFER_SECURE_URLS': False,
    'PROPAGATE_EXCEPTIONS': None,
    'RESPONSE_TIMEOUT': 60,
    'SECRET_KEY': None,
    'SEND_FILE_MAX_AGE_DEFAULT': datetime.timedelta(seconds=43200),
    'SERVER_NAME': None,
    'SESSION_COOKIE_DOMAIN': None,
    'SESSION_COOKIE_HTTPONLY': True,
    'SESSION_COOKIE_NAME': 'session',
    'SESSION_COOKIE_PATH': None,
    'SESSION_COOKIE_SAMESITE': None,
    'SESSION_COOKIE_SECURE': False,
    'SESSION_REFRESH_EACH_REQUEST': True,
    'SQLURI': 'postgres://username:xxx@localhost/db',
    'TEMPLATES_AUTO_RELOAD': None,
    'TESTING': False,
    'TRAP_HTTP_EXCEPTIONS': False}
```

However, there are two significant drawbacks when using Python modules as configuration files. Firstly, since these configuration modules are Python files, it can be tempting to add code to them as well as simple values. By doing so, you will have to treat those modules like the rest of the application code; this can be a complicated way to ensure that it always produces the right value, especially if the configuration is produced with a template! Usually, when an application is deployed, the configuration is managed separately from the code.

Secondly, if another team is in charge of managing the configuration file of your application, they will need to edit the Python code to do so. While this is usually fine, it makes it increase the chance that some problems will be introduced, as it assumes that the other people are familiar with Python and how your application is structured. It is often good practice to make sure that someone who just needs to change the configuration doesn't also need to know how the code works.

Since Quart exposes its configuration via `app.config`, it is quite simple to load additional options from a JSON, YAML, or other popular text-based configuration formats. All of the following examples are equivalent:

```
>>> from quart import Quart
>>> import yaml
>>> from pathlib import Path
>>> app = Quart(__name__)
>>> print(Path("prod_settings.json").read_text())
{
    "DEBUG": false,
    "SQLURI":"postgres://username:xxx@localhost/db"
}
>>> app.config.from_json("prod_settings.json")
>>> app.config["SQLURI"]
'postgres://username:xxx@localhost/db'

>>> print(Path("prod_settings.yml").read_text())
---
DEBUG: False
SQLURI: "postgres://username:xxx@localhost/db"

>>> app.config.from_file("prod_settings.yml", yaml.safe_load)
```

You can give `from_file` a function to use to understand the data, such as `yaml.safe_load`, `toml.load`, and `json.load`. If you prefer the INI format with [`sections`] along with `name = value`, then many extensions exist to help, and the standard library's `ConfigParser` is also straightforward.

Blueprints

When you write microservices that have more than a single endpoint, you will end up with a number of different decorated functions—remember those are functions with a decorator above, such as `@app.route`. The first logical step to organize your code is to have one module per endpoint, and when you create your app instance, make sure they get imported so that Quart registers the views.

For example, if your microservice manages a company's employees database, you could have one endpoint to interact with all employees, and one with teams. You could organize your application into these three modules:

- app.py: To contain the Quart app object, and to run the app
- employees.py: To provide all the views related to employees
- teams.py: To provide all the views related to teams

From there, employees and teams can be seen as a subset of the app, and might have a few specific utilities and configurations. This is a standard way of structuring any Python application.

Blueprints take this logic a step further by providing a way to group your views into namespaces, making the structure used in separate files and giving it some special framework assistance. You can create a Blueprint object that looks like a Quart app object, and then use it to arrange some views. The initialization process can then register blueprints with app.register_blueprint to make sure that all the views defined in the blueprint are part of the app. A possible implementation of the employee's blueprint could be as follows:

```python
# blueprints.py
from quart import Blueprint

teams = Blueprint("teams", __name__)

_DEVS = ["Alice", "Bob"]
_OPS = ["Charles"]
_TEAMS = {1: _DEVS, 2: _OPS}


@teams.route("/teams")
def get_all():
    return _TEAMS

@teams.route("/teams/<int:team_id>")
def get_team(team_id):
    return _TEAMS[team_id]
```

The main module (app.py) can then import this file, and register its blueprint with app.register_blueprint(teams). This mechanism is also interesting when you want to reuse a generic set of views in another application or several times in the same application—it's easy to imagine a situation where, for example, both the inventory management area and a sales area might want to have the same ability to look at current stock levels.

Error handling

When something goes wrong in your application, it is important to be able to control what responses the clients will receive. In HTML web apps, you usually get specific HTML pages when you encounter a 404 (Resource not found) or 5xx (Server error), and that's how Quart works out of the box. But when building microservices, you need to have more control of what should be sent back to the client—that's where custom error handlers are useful.

The other important feature is the ability to debug your code when an unexpected error occurs; Quart comes with a built-in debugger, which can be activated when your app runs in debug mode.

Custom error handler

When your code does not handle an exception, Quart returns an HTTP 500 response without providing any specific information, like the traceback. Producing a generic error is a safe default behavior to avoid leaking any private information to users in the body of the error. The default 500 response is a simple HTML page along with the right status code:

```
$ curl http://localhost:5000/api
<!doctype html>
<title>500 Internal Server Error</title>
<h1>Internal Server Error</h1>
Server got itself in trouble
```

When implementing microservices using JSON, it is good practice to make sure that every response sent to clients, including any exception, is JSON-formatted. Consumers of your microservice will expect every response to be machine-parseable. It's far better to tell a client that you had an error and have it set up to process that message and show it to a human than to give a client something it doesn't understand and have it raise its own errors.

Quart lets you customize the app error handling via a couple of functions. The first one is the @app.errorhandler decorator, which works like @app.route. But instead of providing an endpoint, the decorator links a function to a specific error code.

In the following example, we use it to connect a function that will return a JSON-formatted error when Quart returns a 500 server response (any code exception):

```python
# error_handler.py
from quart import Quart
```

```
app = Quart(__name__)

@app.errorhandler(500)
def error_handling(error):
    return {"Error": str(error)}, 500

@app.route("/api")
def my_microservice():
    raise TypeError("Some Exception")

if __name__ == "__main__":
    app.run()
```

Quart will call this error view no matter what exception the code raises. However, in case your application issues an HTTP 404 or any other 4xx or 5xx response, you will be back to the default HTML responses that Quart sends. To make sure your app sends JSON for every 4xx and 5xx response, we need to register that function to each error code.

One place where you can find the list of errors is in the abort.mapping dict. In the following code snippet, we register the error_handling function to every error using app.register_error_handler, which is similar to the @app.errorhandler decorator:

```
# catch_all_errors.py
from quart import Quart, jsonify, abort
from werkzeug.exceptions import HTTPException, default_exceptions

def jsonify_errors(app):
    def error_handling(error):
        if isinstance(error, HTTPException):
            result = {
                "code": error.code,
                "description": error.description,
                "message": str(error),
            }
        else:
            description = abort.mapping[ error.code].description
            result = {"code":  error.code, "description": description,
"message": str(error)}

        resp = jsonify(result)
        resp.status_code = result["code"]
        return resp
```

```
        for code in default_exceptions.keys():
            app.register_error_handler(code, error_handling)

        return app

    app = Quart(__name__)
    app = jsonify_errors(app)

    @app.route("/api")
    def my_microservice():
        raise TypeError("Some Exception")

    if __name__ == "__main__":
        app.run()
```

The jsonify_errors function modifies a Quart app instance and sets up the custom JSON error handler for every 4xx and 5xx error that might occur.

A microservice skeleton

So far in this chapter, we have looked at how Quart works, and at most of the built-in features it provides—all of which we will be using throughout this book. One topic we have not yet covered is how to organize the code in your projects, and how to instantiate your Quart app. Every example so far has used a single Python module and the app.run() call to run the service.

Having everything in a module is possible, but will create a lot of headaches unless your code is just a few lines. Since we will want to release and deploy the code, it's better to have it inside a Python package so that we can use standard packaging tools such as pip and setuptools.

It is also a good idea to organize views into blueprints, and have one module per blueprint. This lets us keep better track of what each bit of code does, and re-use code whenever possible.

Lastly, the run() call can be removed from the code since Quart provides a generic run command that looks for an application using information from the QUART_APP environment variable. Using that runner offers extra options, such as the ability to configure the host and port that will be used to run the app without going into the settings each time.

The microservice project on GitHub was created for this book and is a generic Quart project that you can use to start a microservice. It implements a simple layout, which works well for building microservices. You can install and run, and then modify it. The project can be found at `https://github.com/PythonMicroservices/microservice-skeleton`.

The `microservice` project skeleton contains the following structure:

- `setup.py`: Distutils' setup file, which is used to install and release the project.
- `Makefile`: A Makefile that contains a few useful targets to make, build, and run the project.
- `settings.yml`: The application default settings in a YAML file.
- `requirements.txt`: The project dependencies following the `pip` format produced by `pip freeze`.
- `myservices/`: The actual package
    - `__init__.py`
    - `app.py`: The app module, which contains the app itself
    - `views/`: A directory containing the views organized in blueprints
        - `__init__.py`
        - `home.py`: The home blueprint, which serves the root endpoint
    - `tests/`: The directory containing all the tests
        - `__init__.py`
        - `test_home.py`: Tests for the home blueprint views

In the following code, the `app.py` file instantiates a `Quart` app using a helper function called `create_app` to register the blueprints and update the settings:

```python
import os
from myservice.views import blueprints
from quart import Quart

_HERE = os.path.dirname(__file__)
_SETTINGS = os.path.join(_HERE, "settings.ini")


def create_app(name=__name__, blueprints=None, settings=None):
    app = Quart(name)

    # load configuration
    settings = os.environ.get("QUART_SETTINGS", settings)
```

```
        if settings is not None:
            app.config.from_pyfile(settings)

        # register blueprints
        if blueprints is not None:
            for bp in blueprints:
                app.register_blueprint(bp)

        return app

    app = create_app(blueprints=blueprints, settings=_SETTINGS)
```

The home.py view uses a blueprint to create a simple route that doesn't return anything:

```
from quart import Blueprint

home = Blueprint("home", __name__)

@home.route("/")
def index():
    """Home view.

    This view will return an empty JSON mapping.
    """
    return {}
```

This example application can run via Quart's built-in command line, using the package name:

```
$ QUART_APP=myservice quart run
 * Serving Quart app 'myservice.app'
 * Environment: production
 * Please use an ASGI server (e.g. Hypercorn) directly in production
 * Debug mode: False
 * Running on http://localhost:5000 (CTRL + C to quit)
[2020-12-06 20:17:28,203] Running on http://127.0.0.1:5000 (CTRL + C to quit)
```

From there, building JSON views for your microservice consists of adding modules to microservices/views, and their corresponding tests.

Summary

This chapter gave us a detailed overview of the Quart framework and how it can be used to build microservices. The main things to remember are:

- Quart wraps a simple request-response mechanism around the ASGI protocol, which lets you write your applications in almost vanilla Python.

- Quart is easy to extend and can use Flask extensions if required.

- Quart comes with some useful built-in features: blueprints, globals, signals, a template engine, and error handlers.

- The microservice project is a Quart skeleton, which will be used to write microservices throughout this book.

The next chapter will focus on development methodology: how to continuously code, test, and document your microservices.

3
Coding, Testing, and Documentation: the Virtuous Cycle

We write software because we want it to do something useful. But how do we know that the code does what we want it to? The obvious answer is that we test it. Sometimes we run a piece of code we've just written and look at what it does, to see if it is doing the right thing. There's often a lot of code, though, and there are a lot of things we want to ensure are working—and continue to work as we add new features.

Thankfully, most languages come with a way to automate testing your code, and Python is no exception. When we create tests along with the code we are writing, it will increase the likelihood of spotting an error. Bugs in our code cost time, and can cost a company money. Bugs are also impossible to eliminate completely—the best we can do is take reasonable steps to prevent as many as we can.

Writing tests helps to provide a clearer idea of what software is meant to do. Take, for example, a function that is meant to return the five highest numbers in a list:

```python
def filter(some_numbers):
    some_numbers.sort()
    return some_numbers[-5:]
```

It's a very simple function, so it probably does what we want. Or does it? The `.sort()` method works in place instead of returning a new value, so we've changed the order of the variable that we passed in as an argument; this can have unintended consequences in other areas of the program. The function also doesn't check to see that it's returning numbers, so what should be done if there are other objects in the list? If there are not enough numbers to return five of them, is that acceptable, or should the function raise an error?

By writing tests, we get a clear idea not just about what we want the function to do, but also how it should behave in different situations: We keep working towards the objective, but instead of thinking about "How to win" we think about "How to avoid losing."

Test-Driven Development (TDD) is an approach where you write tests alongside the code you are creating and use the tests to guide what the code should do — and to demonstrate that it works as you expect. It will not always improve the quality of your project, but it will catch a lot of errors before they can cause damage, helping to make your team more agile. Developers who need to fix a bug or refactor a part of the application can do so with fewer concerns that they have broken something, and more easily show their team that the work is suitable.

Behavior-Driven Development (BDD) is another approach that can work well in combination with TDD. Using this method, tests describe the desired behavior of the software from a higher-level point of view and are often presented in more human-friendly language. A developer can write code to describe what happens when a test uses phrases such as "the user searches for" and "results are shown for," allowing the people writing the tests to focus on what should happen; for example:

```
Scenario: Basic DuckDuckGo Search
    When the user searches for "panda"
    Then results are shown for "panda"
```

Some good examples of BDD tests are available at: https://github.com/AndyLPK247/behavior-driven-python

Writing tests is time-consuming at first, but in the long term, it is often the best approach to ensure a project is stable as it grows in size and scope. Of course, it's always possible to write bad tests and end up with poor results or create a test suite that is horrible to maintain and takes too long to run. The best tools and processes in the world won't prevent a careless developer from producing bad software.

Figure 3.1: The best tools on offer still won't prevent complacent developers from producing bad software… Credit to: https://xkcd.com/303/

A good set of tests should demonstrate that the software does what we intend it to do and that it should fail in a predictable and fixable way. That means that if you give it invalid data, or a dependency it relies on has broken, the behavior of the code is predictable.

Writing tests is also a good way to get some perspective on your code. Does the API you've designed make sense? Do things fit well together? And when the team gains more people or reorganizes, tests are a good source of information about the state of the code, detailing what its intentions are. The specific needs the software fulfils often change over time as well, meaning that significant refactoring—not just rewriting but changing the architecture—is often needed.

Documentation is a crucial part of a project, although it's often the first area to fall behind. After a while, it becomes rare to see a project's documentation fully up to date with the state of the code, unless some dedicated people work on it. It can be an immense source of frustration for developers to find out that the code examples in the documentation are broken after some refactoring. But there are ways to mitigate these issues; for instance, code extracts in the documentation could be part of the test suite to make sure they work.

In any case, no matter how much energy you expend on tests and documentation, there is one golden rule: testing, documenting, and coding your projects should be done continuously. In other words, updating the tests and documentation is part of the process to update the code. We can make this process easier, as we shall see.

After providing a few general tips on how to test code in Python, this chapter focuses on what testing and documentation tools can be used in the context of building microservices with Quart, and how to set up continuous integration with some popular online services.

The chapter is organized into five parts:

- The different types of tests
- Using pytest and tox
- Developer documentation
- Version control
- Continuous integration

Different kinds of tests

There are many kinds of tests, and it can be confusing sometimes to know what is being spoken about. For instance, when people refer to functional tests, they may be referring to different kinds of tests depending on the project's nature. In microservice land, we can classify tests into these five distinct goals:

- **Unit tests**: These make sure a class or a function works as expected in isolation.
- **Functional tests**: Verify that the microservice does what it says from the consumer's point of view, and behaves correctly, even upon receiving bad requests.
- **Integration tests**: Verify how a microservice integrates with all its network dependencies.
- **Load tests**: Measure the microservice performances.
- **End-to-end tests**: Verify that the whole system works—from initial request to final action—through all its components.

We will dive deeper into the details in the following sections.

Unit tests

Unit tests are the simplest and most self-contained tests to add to a project. The "unit" being tested is a small component of the code; for example, a single unit test might examine a single function, several unit tests might run a battery of tests against that function, and a whole suite of tests might run against the module that the function is in.

Python's standard library comes with everything needed to write unit tests. In most projects, there are functions and classes that can be tested in isolation, and projects based on Quart are no different.

Testing in isolation in Python usually means that you instantiate a class or call a function with specific arguments and verify that you get the expected result. If you have a function that gets given a large data structure and searches for a particular value within it, then that can be easily tested on its own as it is given everything it needs. However, when the class or function calls another piece of code that is not built in Python or its standard library, it is not in isolation anymore.

In some cases, it will be useful to mock those calls to achieve isolation. Mocking means replacing a piece of code with a fake version which will return the value you need for the test, but fake the behavior that the real code performs. An example might be a function which queries a database and formats the data before returning it. In our unit test suite, we probably don't want to run a real database, but we can mock the database query so that it returns a predictable value, and make sure that our function does the right thing with what it gives us.

Mocking comes with its own risks, because it's easy to implement a different behavior in your mocks and end up with some code that works with your tests but not the real thing. That problem often occurs when you update your project's dependencies, or an external service changes what it sends, and your mocks are not updated to reflect the new behaviors.

So, limiting the usage of mocks to the three following use cases is good practice:

- **I/O operations**: When the code performs calls to third-party services or a resource (socket, files, and so on), and you can't run them from within your tests.

- **CPU-intensive operations**: When the call computes something that would make the test suite too slow.

- **Specific behaviors to reproduce**: When you want to write a test to try out your code under specific behaviors (for example, a network error or changing the date or time by mocking the date time and time modules).

Clean code techniques can help make our unit tests much more straightforward by trying to reduce the number of functions that have side effects and gathering all your I/O operations to the highest level possible. Consider the following scenario, where we are reading some data about superheroes from the Mozilla Developer Network's documentation about JSON (`https://developer.mozilla.org/en-US/docs/Learn/JavaScript/Objects/JSON`):

```python
import requests

def query_url(url):
    response = requests.get(url)
    response.raise_for_status()
    return response.json()

def get_hero_names(filter=None):
    url = "https://mdn.github.io/learning-area/javascript/oojs/json/superheroes.json"
    json_body = query_url(url)
    for member in json_body.get("members", []):
        if filter(member):
            yield member["name"]


def format_heroes_over(age=0):
    hero_names = get_hero_names(filter=lambda hero: hero.get("age", 0)
> age)
    formatted_text = ""
    for hero in hero_names:
        formatted_text += f"{hero} is over {age}\n"
    return formatted_text


if __name__ == "__main__":
    print(format_heroes_over(age=30))
```

In order to test the function that constructs the string, or the one that filters the names, we need to create a fake connection to the web. This means several of our functions are relying on mocked connections. Instead, we could write:

```python
# requests_example2.py
import requests

def query_url(url):

    response = requests.get(url)
    response.raise_for_status()
    return response.json()

def get_hero_names(hero_data, hero_filter=None):
    for member in hero_data.get("members", []):
        if hero_filter is None or hero_filter(member):
            yield member

def render_hero_message(heroes, age):
    formatted_text = ""
    for hero in heroes:
        formatted_text += f"{hero['name']} is over {age}\n"
    return formatted_text


def render_heroes_over(age=0):
    url = "https://mdn.github.io/learning-area/javascript/oojs/json/
superheroes.json"
    json_body = query_url(url)
    relevant_heroes = get_hero_names(
        json_body, hero_filter=lambda hero: hero.get("age", 0) > age
    )
    return render_hero_message(relevant_heroes, age)


if __name__ == "__main__":
    print(render_heroes_over(age=30))
```

By rearranging our code this way, the network connection query is "higher up" — we encounter it first. We can write tests to examine and filter the results without ever creating a mocked connection, and it means we can use them in isolation in our code — perhaps we get the same data from a cache instead of the web, or receive it from a client who already has it. Our code is more flexible now, and simpler to test.

Of course, this is a somewhat contrived example, but the principle means that we are arranging our code so that there are functions with well-defined inputs and outputs, and that makes it easier to test. It's an important lesson from the world of functional programming languages, such as Lisp and Haskell, where functions are closer to mathematical functions.

What might the tests look like? Here is a class using unittest that will perform some basic checks, including setting up any prerequisites that our tests have in a method called setUp, and cleaning up after ourselves if we add a method called tearDown. If this was a real service, we might also want to consider other situations, such as what get_hero_names does with no filter, or a filter that returns no results or throws an error. The following example uses request_mock, which is a handy library to mock request-based network calls (see http://requests-mock.readthedocs.io):

```python
import unittest
from unittest import mock

import requests_mock

import requests_example2   # Our previous example code

class TestHeroCode(unittest.TestCase):
    def setUp(self):
        self.fake_heroes = {
            "members": [
                {"name": "Age 20 Hero", "age": 20},
                {"name": "Age 30 Hero", "age": 30},
                {"name": "Age 40 Hero", "age": 40},
            ]
        }

    def test_get_hero_names_age_filter(self):
        result = list(
            requests_example2.get_hero_names(
                self.fake_heroes, filter=lambda x: x.get("age", 0) > 30
            )
        )
        self.assertEqual(result, [{"name": "Age 40 Hero", "age": 40}])

    @requests_mock.mock()
    def test_display_heroes_over(self, mocker):
        mocker.get(requests_mock.ANY, json=self.fake_heroes)
```

```
        rendered_text = requests_example2.render_heroes_over(age=30)
        self.assertEqual(rendered_text, "Age 40 Hero is over 30\n")

if __name__ == "__main__":
    unittest.main()
```

You should keep an eye on all your mocks as the project grows, and make sure they are not the only kind of tests that cover a particular feature. For instance, if the Bugzilla project comes up with a new structure for its REST API, and the server your project uses is updated, your tests will happily pass with your broken code until the mocks reflect the new behavior.

How many tests and how good the test coverage is will depend on what your application is for. Unless your microservice is critical to your business, there is no need to have tests for all the failures you can come up with on day one. In a microservice project unit tests are not a priority, and aiming at 100% test coverage (where every line of your code is called somewhere in your tests) in your unit tests will add a lot of maintenance work for little benefit.

It is better to focus on building a robust set of functional tests.

Functional tests

Functional tests for a microservice project are all the tests that interact with the published API by sending HTTP requests, and asserting that the HTTP responses are the expected ones. These differ from unit tests because they focus more on the behavior of a microservice, or a smaller part of a larger service.

This definition is broad enough to include any test that can call the application, from fuzzing tests (where gibberish is sent to your app and you see what happens) to penetration tests (you try to break the app security), and so on. The key part of a functional test is to investigate whether the software's behavior meets its requirements. As developers, the two most important kinds of functional tests we should focus on are the following:

- Tests that verify that the application does what it was built for
- Tests that ensure an abnormal behavior that was fixed is not happening anymore

The way those scenarios are organized in the test class is up to the developers, but the general pattern is to create an instance of the application in the test class and then interact with it.

In that context, the network layer is not used, and the application is called directly by the tests; the same request-response cycle happens, so it is realistic enough. However, we would still mock out any network calls happening within the application.

Quart includes a `QuartClient` class to build requests, which can be created directly from the app object using its `test_client()` method. The following is an example of a test against the quart_basic app we showed in *Chapter 2, Discovering Quart*, which sends back a JSON body on /api/:

```python
import unittest
import json


from quart_basic import app as tested_app


class TestApp(unittest.IsolatedAsyncioTestCase):
    async def test_help(self):
        # creating a QuartClient instance to interact with the app
        app = tested_app.test_client()

        # calling /api/ endpoint
        hello = await app.get("/api")

        # asserting the body
        body = json.loads(str(await hello.get_data(), "utf8"))
        self.assertEqual(body["Hello"], "World!")


if __name__ == "__main__":
    unittest.main()
```

The `QuartClient` class has one method per HTTP method and sends back `Response` objects that can be used to assert the results. In the preceding example, we used `.get()`, and since it is asynchronous code, we had to await the call and the request to get_data(), as well as tell the unittest module that we were running asynchronous tests.

There is a testing flag in the `Quart` class which you can use to propagate exceptions to the test, but some prefer not to use it by default to get back from the app what a real client would get—for instance, to make sure the body of 5xx or 4xx errors is converted to JSON for API consistency.

In the following example, the /api/ call produces an exception, and we have error handlers for internal server errors and missing pages:

```python
# quart_error.py
from quart import Quart

app = Quart(__name__)

text_404 = (
    "The requested URL was not found on the server.  "
    "If you entered the URL manually please check your "
    "spelling and try again."
)

@app.errorhandler(500)
def error_handling_500(error):
    return {"Error": str(error)}, 500

@app.errorhandler(404)
def error_handling_404(error):
    return {"Error": str(error), "description": text_404}, 404

@app.route("/api")
def my_microservice():
    raise TypeError("This is a testing exception.")

if __name__ == "__main__":
    app.run()
```

With our tests, we are making sure the client gets a proper 500 with a structured JSON body in test_raise(). The test_proper_404() test method does the same tests on a non-existent path, and uses the asynchronous versions of the TestCase class along with its setup and teardown methods:

```python
# test_quart_error.py
import unittest
import json
from quart_error import app as tested_app, text_404

class TestApp(unittest.IsolatedAsyncioTestCase):
    async def asyncSetUp(self):
        # Create a client to interact with the app
```

```python
        self.app = tested_app.test_client()

    async def test_raise(self):
        # This won't raise a Python exception but return a 500
        hello = await self.app.get("/api")
        self.assertEqual(hello.status_code, 500)

    async def test_proper_404(self):
        # Call a non-existing endpoint
        hello = await self.app.get("/dwdwqqwdwqd")

        # It's not there
        self.assertEqual(hello.status_code, 404)

        # but we still get a nice JSON body
        body = json.loads(str(await hello.get_data(), "utf8"))
        self.assertEqual(hello.status_code, 404)
        self.assertEqual(body["Error"], "404 Not Found: The requested
URL was not found on the server. If you entered the URL manually please
check your spelling and try again.")
        self.assertEqual(body["description"], text_404)

if __name__ == "__main__":
    unittest.main()
```

An alternative to the `QuartClient` method is **WebTest** (`https://docs.pylonsproject.org/projects/webtest/`), which offers a few more features out of the box. This will be covered later in this chapter. Also see the following for further details: (`http://webtest.pythonpaste.org`)

Integration tests

Unit tests and functional tests focus on testing your service code without calling other network resources, and so no other microservices in your application, or third-party services such as databases, need to be available. For the sake of speed, isolation, and simplicity, network calls are mocked.

Integration tests are functional tests without any mocking and should be able to run on a real deployment of your application. For example, if your service interacts with Redis and RabbitMQ, they will be called by your service as normal when the integration tests are run. The benefit is that it avoids falling into the problems that were described earlier when mocking network interactions.

You will be sure that your application works in a production execution context only if you try it in a fully integrated, realistic scenario.

The caveat is that running tests against an actual deployment makes it harder to set up test data, or to clean up whatever data was produced from within the service during the test. Patching the application behavior to reproduce a service's response is also a difficult task.

Good configuration management software can help significantly with integration tests, as having an Ansible playbook or Puppet configuration can mean deploying all these components is as simple as running a command. We will discuss this more in *Chapter 10*, *Deploying on AWS*, when we discuss deployment.

Integration tests can also be run on a development or staging deployment of your service. With many developers pushing changes, this may cause contention on this limited resource, but it can be simpler—and less costly—to run all the integration tests while simulating the real environment that closely.

You can use whatever tool you want to write your integration test. A bash script with curl might sometimes be enough on some microservices, while others might require careful orchestration.

It's better for integration tests to be written in Python, and be part of your project's collection of tests. To do this, a Python script that uses requests to call your microservice can do the trick. If you provide a client library for your microservice, this can be a good place to do its integration tests as well.

What differentiates integration tests from functional tests is mostly the fact that real services are being called. We discover the consequences of real interactions with databases, message queues, and other dependencies that the service possesses. What if we could write functional tests that can either be run on a local Quart application or against an actual deployment? This is possible with WebTest, as we will find out later in this chapter.

Load tests

The goal of a load test is to understand how your service performs under stress. Learning where it starts to fail under high load will tell you how to best plan for future eventualities, as well as distribute the workload your application currently has. The first version of your service may well be fast enough for the situation it finds itself in, but understanding its limitations will help you determine how you want to deploy it, and if its design is future-proof in the case of an increased load.

The information from load tests will, alongside numbers collected from the production service, allow you to balance your service's throughput with the number of queries it can reasonably respond to simultaneously, the amount of work that needs doing for a response, how long queries wait for a response, and how much the service will cost—this is known as capacity management.

A good load test can also point you to changes that can be made to remove a bottleneck, such as changing the way writes are made to a database so that they no longer require an exclusive lock.

> *The real problem is that programmers have spent far too much time worrying about efficiency in the wrong places and at the wrong times; premature optimization is the root of all evil (or at least most of it) in programming.*
>
> *–Donald Knuth, The Art of Computer Programming*

It's a common mistake to spend a lot of time on making each microservice as fast as possible, before we even know what the critical path is and what it is best to improve. Taking measurements before making changes allows us to see exactly what the benefits are of each change, and helps us prioritize our time and effort.

Writing load tests can help you answer the following questions:

1. How many users can one instance of my service serve when I deploy it on this machine?
2. What is the average response time when there are 10, 100, or 1,000 concurrent requests? Can I handle that much concurrency?
3. When my service is under stress, is it running out of RAM or is it mainly CPU-bound? Is it waiting on another service?
4. Can I add other instances of the same service and scale horizontally?
5. If my microservice calls other services, can I use pools of connectors, or do I have to serialize all the interactions through a single connection?
6. Can my service run for multiple days at a time without degradation?
7. Is my service working properly after a usage peak?

Depending on the kind of load you want to achieve, there are many tools available, from simple command-line tools to heavier distributed load systems. For performing a simple load test that does not require any specific scenario, Salvo is an **Apache Bench (AB)** equivalent written in Python, which can be used to apply load to your endpoints: `https://github.com/tarekziade/salvo`.

In the following example, Salvo simulates 10 concurrent connections, each making 100 sequential requests against a `Quart` web server on the `/api/` endpoint:

```
$ salvo http://127.0.0.1:5000/api  --concurrency 10 --requests 100
-------- Server info --------

Server Software: hypercorn-h11

-------- Running 100 queries - concurrency 10 --------

[==============================================================>.]
99%

-------- Results --------

Successful calls                    1000
Total time                          13.3234 s
Average                             0.0133 s
Fastest                             0.0038 s
Slowest                             0.0225 s
Amplitude                           0.0187 s
Standard deviation                  0.002573
Requests Per Second                 75.06
Requests Per Minute                 4503.35

-------- Status codes --------
Code 200                            1000 times.

Want to build a more powerful load test ? Try Molotov !
Bye!
```

These numbers don't mean much, as they will vary a lot depending on the deployment, and from where you run them. For instance, if your Flask application is served behind nginx with several workers, then the load will be distributed, some of the overhead will be handled by nginx, and for a complete picture we should test the entire service.

But this small test alone can often catch problems early on, in particular when your code is opening socket connections itself. If something is wrong in the microservice design, these tools make it easier to detect by highlighting unexpected responses, or causing the application to break in ways the developer was not expecting.

Salvo is based on **Molotov** (https://molotov.readthedocs.io/en/stable/) which requires a bit more work to set up, but has more features, such as allowing interactive scenarios with sets of queries and expected responses. In the following example, each function is a possible scenario that gets picked by Molotov to run against the server:

```python
# molotov_example.py
# Run:
# molotov molotov_example.py --processes 10 --workers 200 --duration 60
import json
from molotov import scenario


@scenario(weight=40)
async def scenario_one(session):
    async with session.get("http://localhost:5000/api") as resp:
        res = await resp.json()
        assert res["Hello"] == "World!"
        assert resp.status == 200


@scenario(weight=60)
async def scenario_two(session):
    async with session.get("http://localhost:5000/api") as resp:
        assert resp.status == 200
```

Both tools will give you some metrics, but they are not very accurate because of the network and client CPU variance on the box they are launched from. A load test will stress the resources of the machine running the test, and that will impact the metrics.

When performing a load test, server-side metrics allow greater visibility into your application. At the Quart level, you can use the Flask extension **Flask Profiler** (https://github.com/muatik/flask-profiler), which collects the amount of time each request takes and offers a dashboard that will let you browse the collected times, as shown in *Figure 3.2*.

Figure 3.2: Flask Profiler enables the time taken for requests to be tracked, showing them in a graphical format

For a production service, it is best to use tools such as **Prometheus** (`https://prometheus.io/`), **InfluxDB** (`https://www.influxdata.com/`), or use one of your cloud hosting provider's built-in tools, such as AWS CloudWatch.

End-to-end tests

An end-to-end test will check that the whole system works as expected from the end-user point of view. The test needs to behave like a real client, and call the system through the same **User Interface (UI)**.

Depending on the type of application you are creating, a simple HTTP client might not be enough to simulate a real user. For instance, if the visible part of the system through which users are interacting is a web application with HTML pages that gets rendered on a client side, you will need to use a tool like **Selenium** (`https://www.selenium.dev/`). It will automate your browser in order to make sure that the client requests every CSS and JavaScript file and then renders every page accordingly.

JavaScript frameworks now do a lot of work on the client side to produce pages. Some of them have completely removed the server-side rendering of templates, and simply fetch data from the server to generate the HTML page by manipulating the **Document Object Model (DOM)** through the browser APIs. Calls to the server, in that case, consist of getting all the static JavaScript files needed for rendering a given URL, plus the data.

Writing end-to-end tests is outside the scope of this book, but you can refer to *Selenium Testing Tools Cookbook* to learn more about this.

The following points summarize what we've learned in this section:

- Functional tests are the most important tests to write for a web service, and it is easy to carry out in Quart by instantiating the app in the tests and interacting with it.
- Unit tests are a good complement, but avoid misusing mocks.
- Integration tests are like functional tests but run against a real deployment.
- Load tests are useful to learn about your microservice bottlenecks and plan for the next steps of development.
- End-to-end tests require using the same UI that the client would normally use.

Knowing when you will need to write integration, load, or end-to-end tests depends on how your project is managed—but both unit and functional tests should be written every time you change something. Ideally, each change you make in your code should include a new test or modify an existing one. Unit tests can be written using standard Python, thanks to the excellent `unittest` package included in the standard library—we will see later how the **pytest** (`http://docs.pytest.org`) library adds extra features on top of it.

For functional tests, we shall look in the next section at pytest.

Using pytest and tox

So far, all the tests we have written use `unittest` classes and `unittest.main()` to run them. As your project grows, you will have more and more test modules around.

To automatically discover and run all the tests in a project, the `unittest` package introduced a Test Discovery feature in Python 3.2, which finds and runs tests, given a few options. This feature has been around for a while in projects like **Nose** (`https://nose.readthedocs.io`) and pytest, and that was what inspired the test discovery feature in the `unittest` package in the standard library.

Which runner to use is a matter of taste, and as long as you stick to writing your tests in `TestCase` classes, your tests will be compatible with all of them.

That said, the pytest project is very popular in the Python community, and since it offers extensions, people have started to write useful tools around it. Its runner is also quite efficient, as it starts to run the tests while they are still discovered in the background, making it a little faster than the others. Its output in the console is also beautiful and bright. To use it in your project, you can simply install the `pytest` package with pip, and use the provided pytest command line. In the following example, the pytest command runs all the modules that start with `test_`:

```
$ pytest test_*
======================= test session starts ========================
platform darwin -- Python 3.8.5, pytest-6.2.1, py-1.10.0, pluggy-0.13.1
rootdir: /Users/simon/github/PythonMicroservices/CodeSamples/Chapter3
plugins: requests-mock-1.8.0
collected 9 items

test_quart_basic.py .                                        [ 11%]
test_quart_error.py ..                                       [ 33%]
test_requests_example2.py ..                                 [ 55%]
test_requests_example2_full.py ....                          [100%]

======================= 9 passed in 0.20s ==========================
```

The `pytest` package comes with a lot of extensions, which are listed at `http://plugincompat.herokuapp.com/`.

The code samples in this book have been formatted with `Black`, which is also available as a pytest extension. Other useful extensions are `pytest-cov` (`https://github.com/pytest-dev/pytest-cov`) and `pytest-flake8` (`https://github.com/tholo/pytest-flake8`).

The first one uses the coverage tool (`https://coverage.readthedocs.io`) to display the test coverage of your project, and the second one runs the `Flake8` (`https://gitlab.com/pycqa/flake8`) linter to make sure that your code is following the `PEP8` style, and avoids a variety of other problems. Here is an invocation example with some deliberate style issues:

```
$ pytest --flake8 --black
======================= test session starts ========================
platform darwin -- Python 3.8.5, pytest-6.2.1, py-1.10.0, pluggy-0.13.1
rootdir: /Users/simon/github/PythonMicroservices/CodeSamples/Chapter3
```

```
plugins: flake8-1.0.7, requests-mock-1.8.0, black-0.3.12, cov-2.10.1
collected 29 items

molotov_example1.py ss                                      [  6%]
quart_basic.py ss                                           [ 13%]
quart_error.py ss                                           [ 20%]
quart_profiled.py ss                                        [ 27%]
requests_example1.py ss                                     [ 34%]
requests_example2.py FF                                     [ 41%]
test_quart_basic.py ss.                                     [ 51%]
test_quart_error.py ss..                                    [ 65%]
test_requests_example2.py ss..                              [ 79%]
test_requests_example2_full.py ss....                       [100%]


======================= FAILURES ========================
_____ Black format check _____
--- /Users/simon/github/PythonMicroservices/CodeSamples/Chapter3/
requests_example2.py    2020-12-29 11:56:56.653870 +0000
+++ /Users/simon/github/PythonMicroservices/CodeSamples/Chapter3/
requests_example2.py    2020-12-29 11:56:58.595337 +0000
@@ -24,11 +24,11 @@

 def render_heroes_over(age=0):
     url = "https://mdn.github.io/learning-area/javascript/oojs/json/
superheroes.json"
     json_body = query_url(url)
     relevant_heroes = get_hero_names(
-            json_body, filter =lambda hero: hero.get("age", 0) > age
+            json_body, filter=lambda hero: hero.get("age", 0) > age
     )
     return render_hero_message(relevant_heroes, age)


 if __name__ == "__main__":

_____ FLAKE8-check _____
/Users/simon/github/PythonMicroservices/CodeSamples/Chapter3/requests_
example2.py:26:80: E501 line too long (85 > 79 characters)
/Users/simon/github/PythonMicroservices/CodeSamples/Chapter3/requests_
example2.py:29:26: E251 unexpected spaces around keyword / parameter
equals

---------------------- Captured log call ----------------------
```

```
WARNING  flake8.options.manager:manager.py:207 option --max-complexity:
please update from optparse string `type=` to argparse callable `type=`
-- this will be an error in the future
WARNING  flake8.checker:checker.py:119 The multiprocessing module is
not available. Ignoring --jobs arguments.
====================== short test summary info ======================
FAILED requests_example2.py::BLACK
FAILED requests_example2.py::FLAKE8
============= 2 failed, 9 passed, 18 skipped in 0.51s =============
```

Another useful tool that can be used in conjunction with pytest is **tox** (http://tox.readthedocs.io). If your projects need to run on several versions of Python or in several different environments, tox can automate the creation of these separate environments to run your tests.

Once you have installed tox (using the `pip install tox` command), it requires a configuration file called `tox.ini` in the root directory of your project. Tox assumes that your project is a Python package and therefore has a `setup.py` file in the root directory alongside the `tox.ini` file, but that's the only requirement. The `tox.ini` file contains the command lines to run the tests along with the Python versions that it should be run against:

```
[tox]
envlist = py38,py39

[testenv]
deps = pytest
    pytest-cov
    pytest-flake8

commands =  pytest --cov=quart_basic --flake8 test_*
```

When tox is executed by calling the `tox` command, it will create a separate environment for each Python version, deploy your package and its dependencies in it, and run the tests in it using the `pytest` command.

You can run a single environment with `tox -e`, which is very handy when you want to run the tests in parallel using automated tools. For instance, `tox -e py38` will just run pytest under Python 3.8.

Even if you support a single Python version, using tox will ensure that your project can be installed in a current Python environment and that you have correctly described all the dependencies. We will use tox in our worked example in later chapters.

Developer documentation

So far, we've looked at the different kinds of tests a microservice can have, and we've mentioned that the documentation should evolve with the code. We are talking here about developer documentation. This includes everything a developer should know about your microservices project, most notably:

- How it is designed.
- How to install it.
- How to run the tests.
- What are the exposed APIs and what data moves in and out?

People go to documentation to get their questions answered. There are Who, What, Where, When, Why, and How questions, such as:

- Who should use this software?
- What does this software do?
- Where can it be deployed?
- When is using it helpful?
- Why does it work this way?
- How do I install and configure it?

Good documentation describes why decisions were made so that people—including yourself—returning to the code can decide whether a decision made in the past is worth following, or whether the situation has moved on and decisions need to be revisited. A developer reading the documentation should come away with a clear idea of the answers to Why questions, and information about the more difficult How questions.

It is rare that each line of code or function needs to be mentioned in a separate document. Instead, the source code should have comments in it that help a developer navigate and understand what they are reading. Functions should have docstring comments that explain their purpose, arguments, and return values, unless they are truly short and obvious. These are easier to keep up to date when the code is changed and avoid the need to tightly couple the documentation and the implementation—a design principle that works here as well as when designing the software itself.

Tools for documentation

The **Sphinx** tool (`http://www.sphinx-doc.org/`), which was developed by *Georg Brandl* to document Python itself, became the standard in the Python community. Sphinx treats documents like source code by separating the content from the layout. The usual way to use Sphinx is to have a `docs` directory in the project that contains the unprocessed content for the documentation, and then to generate the HTML files using Sphinx's command-line utility.

Producing an HTML output with Sphinx makes an excellent static website, which can be published on the web; the tool adds index pages, a small JavaScript-based search engine, and navigation features.

The content of the documentation must be written in **reStructuredText (reST)**, which is the standard markup language in the Python community. A reST file is a simple text file with a non-intrusive syntax to mark section headers, links, text styles, and so on. Sphinx adds a few extensions and summarizes reST usage in this document: `https://www.sphinx-doc.org/en/master/usage/restructuredtext/basics.html`

Markdown (`https://daringfireball.net/projects/markdown/`) is another popular markup language used in the open-source community, and you may have encountered it if you have updated README files on GitHub. Markdown and reST are similar enough that moving between the two should be straightforward. This can be quite useful, as Sphinx has limited support for Markdown.

When you start a project with Sphinx using `sphinx-quickstart`, it generates a source tree with an `index.rst` file, which is the landing page of your documentation. From there, calling `sphinx-build` on it will create your documentation. As an example, if you want to generate HTML documentation, you can add a `docs` environment in your `tox.ini` file, and let the tool build the documentation for you as follows:

```
[tox]
envlist = py39,docs
...

[testenv:docs]
basepython=python
deps =
    -rrequirements.txt
    sphinx
commands=
    sphinx-build -W -b html docs/source docs/build
```

Running `tox -e docs` will generate your documentation.

Showing code examples in Sphinx can be done by pasting your code in a literal block prefixed by using a `::` marker or a code-block directive. In HTML, Sphinx will render it using the **Pygments** (`http://pygments.org/`) syntax highlighter:

```
Quart Application
=============
```

Below is the first example of a **Quart** app in the official documentation:

```
.. code-block:: python

    from quart import Quart
    app = Quart(__name__)

    @app.route("/")
    async def hello():
        return "Hello World!"

    if __name__ == "__main__":
        app.run()
```

That snippet is a fully working app!

Adding code snippets in your documentation is helpful to readers, but does mean that they may get overlooked when the code changes and they no longer work. To avoid this deprecation, one approach is to have every code snippet displayed in your documentation extracted from the code itself. To do this, you can document your modules, classes, and functions with their docstrings, and use the Autodoc Sphinx extension: `https://www.sphinx-doc.org/en/master/usage/extensions/autodoc.html`

This will grab docstrings to inject them in the documentation and is also how Python documents its standard library at: `https://docs.python.org/3/library/index.html`

In the following example, the `autofunction` directive will catch the docstring from the index function that is located in the `myservice/views/home.py` module:

```
APIS
====

**myservice** includes one view that's linked to the root path:
```

```
.. autofunction :: myservice.views.home.index
```

When rendered in HTML, the page will display as shown in *Figure 3.3*.

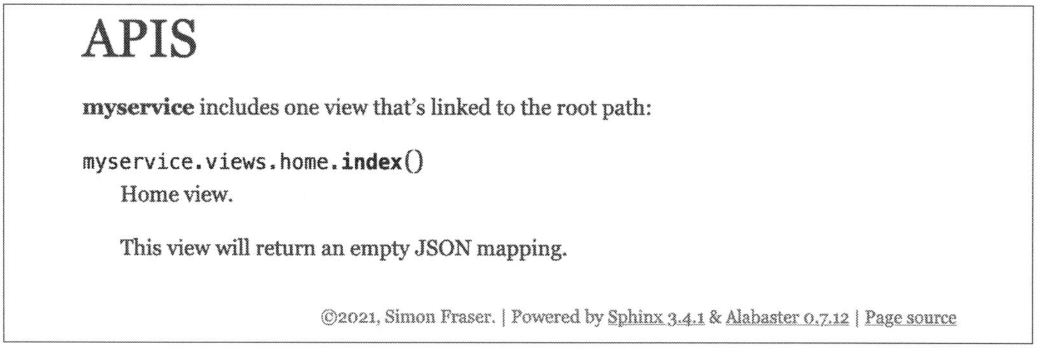

APIS

myservice includes one view that's linked to the root path:

```
myservice.views.home.index()
```
    Home view.

    This view will return an empty JSON mapping.

©2021, Simon Fraser. | Powered by Sphinx 3.4.1 & Alabaster 0.7.12 | Page source

Figure 3.3: The above code, as it is rendered in HTML

The other option is to use a literalinclude directive, which will let you include source code directly. When the file is a Python module, it can be included in the test suite to make sure it works. The following is a full example of project documentation using Sphinx:

```
Myservice
=========

 **myservice** is a simple JSON Quart application.

The application is created with :func:`create_app`:
.. literalinclude:: ../../myservice/app.py

The :file:`settings.ini` file which is passed to :func:`create_app`
contains options for running the Quart app, like the DEBUG flag:
.. literalinclude:: ../../myservice/settings.ini
   :language: ini

Blueprint are imported from :mod:`myservice.views` and one
Blueprint and view example was provided in :file:`myservice/views/home.
py`:

.. literalinclude:: ../../myservice/views/home.py
   :name: home.py
   :emphasize-lines: 13
```

Views can return simple data structures, as we've been using in our example code so far. In that case, they will be converted into a JSON response. When rendered in HTML, the page will display as shown in *Figure 3.4*.

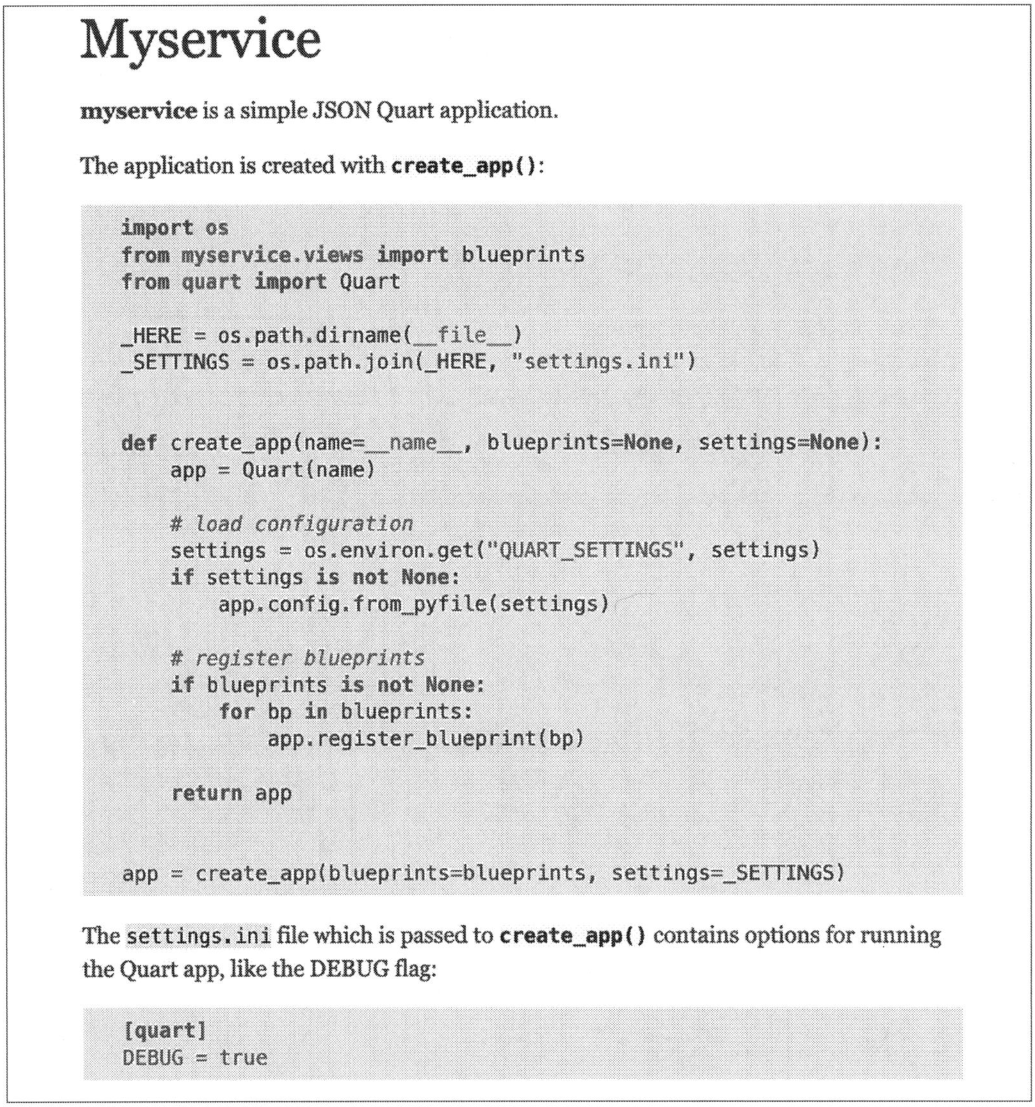

Myservice

myservice is a simple JSON Quart application.

The application is created with **create_app()**:

```python
import os
from myservice.views import blueprints
from quart import Quart

_HERE = os.path.dirname(__file__)
_SETTINGS = os.path.join(_HERE, "settings.ini")


def create_app(name=__name__, blueprints=None, settings=None):
    app = Quart(name)

    # load configuration
    settings = os.environ.get("QUART_SETTINGS", settings)
    if settings is not None:
        app.config.from_pyfile(settings)

    # register blueprints
    if blueprints is not None:
        for bp in blueprints:
            app.register_blueprint(bp)

    return app


app = create_app(blueprints=blueprints, settings=_SETTINGS)
```

The `settings.ini` file which is passed to **create_app()** contains options for running the Quart app, like the DEBUG flag:

```ini
[quart]
DEBUG = true
```

Figure 3.4: Documentation rendered with Sphinx

Of course, using **Autodoc** and **literalinclude** will not fix your processes or design documents—maintaining proper documentation is hard and developers often prioritize changes to the code above changes to the documentation.

It is an easy position to understand, as the code furthers the needs of the organization, but there will be consequences if it is not done. Anything that can be done to automate part of this documentation work is great.

In *Chapter 4*, *Designing Jeeves*, we will see how we can use Sphinx to document the microservice HTTP APIs by using OpenAPI and the Sphinx extension to support it.

The following points summarize this section:

- Sphinx is a powerful tool to document your project.
- Treating your documentation as source code will facilitate its maintenance.
- Tox can be used to rebuild the documentation when something changes.
- If your documentation points to your code, it will be easier to maintain.

Version control

Many of us have worked on projects where we want to keep a copy of something "just in case." This can be homework from school, a project document for work, or, if you're particularly organized, some planning notes for something at home. Often, when we make a lot of changes, we end up with copies of the file with different names that may make sense at the time but quickly get out of control:

```
myplan.txt
myplan.original.txt
myplan.before_feedback.txt
myplan.final.reviewed.final2.suggestions.txt
```

This situation gets even more chaotic when multiple people are working on a project. This is where version control really shines. Using a **Version Control System** (**VCS**) means that each project is kept as a repository of all its files, and every change you commit is kept forever, unless you work really hard to remove it from the repository's history. Accidentally deleted an important paragraph or a useful bit of Python code? It will be in the version control history, so it can easily be recovered. Have more than one person working on something? These tools make it easy to track, compare, and merge changes.

There are many version control systems out there, such as Git, Mercurial, and Subversion. The examples from this book will all work with Git, as we are taking advantage of the features available on GitHub, a popular hosted service for version control—and for our needs, we will be using a free-tier account. If you would like to experiment with the code examples, it is a good idea to sign up for an account at https://github.com/.

Many other services exist that do similar things, with a slightly different set of features or workflows that are possible. For example, **GitLab** (http://gitlab.com) and **Bitbucket** (https://bitbucket.org/) are both excellent services for hosting a Git repository. Other version control software, such as Mercurial and Subversion mentioned above, are also popular choices, and you will see them (and others) in use in organizations around the world.

Hosted services generally offer a wide range of features in addition to the core version control, such as issue tracking, project management, and our next topic: CI/CD systems.

Continuous Integration and Continuous Deployment

Tox can automate many testing steps for your project: running tests on various different Python versions; verifying coverage and code styles; building documentation, and so on. This is still something you would need to run by hand, and would also need to be maintained across several different versions of Python — a task made easier with tools such as **pyenv** (https://github.com/pyenv/pyenv), although still involving some work to keep organized.

A **Continuous Integration** (CI) system solves this issue by listening for changes in your version control system for the right time to run the commands you decide on, and will often take care of the different environments for you. As an example, if you needed to make a change to an open-source project hosted on GitHub, you would be able to clone the repository. You would then have a complete copy of it on your own computer, including all of its history. You then make the change you need, commit it to your own copy's history, and make a **Pull Request** (PR) on GitHub, essentially asking the person who has the original copy of the repository to pull in your changes; allowing random people uncontrolled access is not a good idea!

You know the code you have written is good, but how does this project owner know? They might receive dozens of these requests each week, or each day. If they connect a CI system, they can set things up so that each time someone submits a PR, or a change is merged into their copy, the tests they want to run are done automatically. They can also deploy their software this way by letting the system know what commands to run to automatically build and release a package, update some published documentation, or copy code out to running servers and set up the new version of the software. This is known as **Continuous Deployment** (CD).

We mentioned integration tests earlier, and now we are discussing CI; it's important to remember that CI/CD systems run whatever commands you tell them to. They don't have to be integration tests—there doesn't have to be any integration at all—but they are immensely useful services for testing your code in the way that you want, without having to worry about forgetting or testing many different versions.

GitHub Actions

Many CI systems integrate with popular version control services and so there are many options to run your tests, such as `CircleCI` and `Jenkins`. For more complex requirements, there are also options such as **Taskcluster** (`https://taskcluster.net/`) which is used to build the Firefox web browser and needs to be built on half a dozen platforms and run tens of thousands of tests. However, GitHub comes with its own offering built in, and so to keep things clear, we will be using GitHub `Actions` for the examples in this book.

Most of the services run in a similar way, so it's worth covering how it happens. Once a CI system is connected to your project, it will look for some configuration in your repository. GitHub Actions looks for files in a directory called `github/workflows`, CircleCI looks for a file named `.circleci/config.yml`, and so on. Let's look at an example using GitHub Actions:

```yaml
# .github/workflows/python.yml
---
name: Python package

on: [push]

jobs:
  build:

    runs-on: ubuntu-latest
    strategy:
      matrix:
        python: [3.7, 3.8, 3.9]

    steps:
      - uses: actions/checkout@v2
      - name: Setup Python ${{ matrix.python }}
        uses: actions/setup-python@v2
        with:
```

```
        python-version: ${{ matrix.python }}
    - name: Install Tox and any other packages
      run: pip install tox
    - name: Run Tox
      # Run tox using the version of Python in `PATH`
      run: tox -e py
```

We see that, thanks to on: [push], this will be run every time the repository receives a new change—and this includes a pull request, so we can see whether the tests pass for anyone wanting to give us new code.

The workflow has been told to run three times, using the selection of Python versions listed in the strategy, and for each Python version it will run the steps shown: checking out a copy of the push; setting up Python; installing tox; running tox.

Many different commands or services can be connected in CI/CD pipelines to let us examine code quality, formatting, check for outdated dependencies, building packages, and deploying our service. We will look at documentation control and code test coverage as examples.

Documentation

There are many good options for hosting documentation. GitHub even includes a built-in documentation service called GitHub Pages, although to keep ourselves in line with other Python projects, and to provide examples of using an external service, we will be using **ReadTheDocs (RTD)** (https://docs.readthedocs.io) for our example microservice. Whichever option you choose, a GitHub action or other CI integration can be set up to ensure your documentation is updated whenever a change is made.

Using this approach, your documentation will be in ReStructuredText (.rst) or Markdown (.md) files, which are very easy to create and are a useful format for reading across many different platforms with different accessibility needs. Pages and RTD will create HTML from these documents that are suitable for displaying on the web, and you can apply themes and templates to them to make the resulting web pages appear however you would like.

RTD comes with easy support for different versions of your software so that readers can change views between the documentation for, say, versions 1 and 2. This is very useful when you are maintaining different versions, such as just after a new release, or migrating takes some users a long time. The versioning feature scans git tags and lets you build and publish your documentation per tag and decide which one is the default.

Coveralls

Once a project has tests, a natural question to ask is, "How much of this code is tested?" The answer to this question can be provided through another popular service called **Coveralls** (`https://coveralls.io/`). This service displays your test code coverage in a nice web UI and can be connected to your repository through its CI configuration.

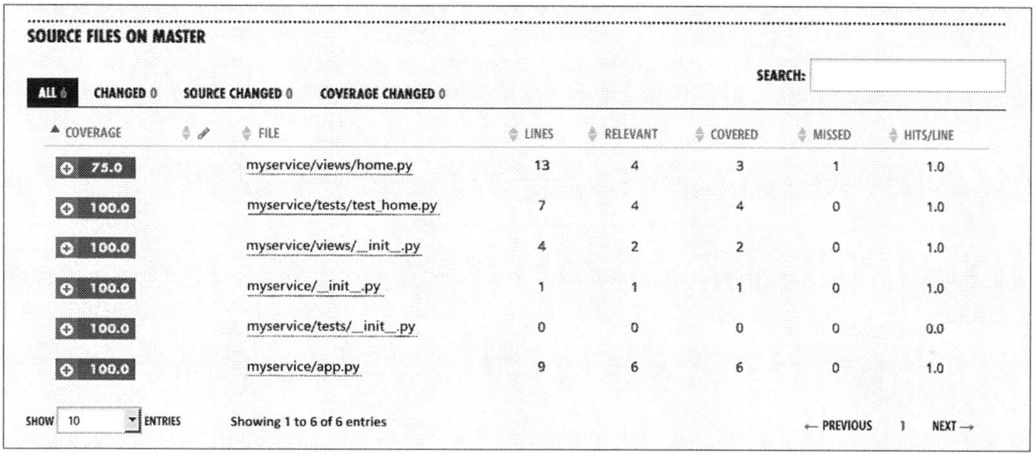

SOURCE FILES ON MASTER

| ALL 6 | CHANGED 0 | SOURCE CHANGED 0 | COVERAGE CHANGED 0 | | SEARCH: | | |

COVERAGE	FILE	LINES	RELEVANT	COVERED	MISSED	HITS/LINE
75.0	myservice/views/home.py	13	4	3	1	1.0
100.0	myservice/tests/test_home.py	7	4	4	0	1.0
100.0	myservice/views/__init__.py	4	2	2	0	1.0
100.0	myservice/__init__.py	1	1	1	0	1.0
100.0	myservice/tests/__init__.py	0	0	0	0	0.0
100.0	myservice/app.py	9	6	6	0	1.0

SHOW 10 ENTRIES   Showing 1 to 6 of 6 entries   ← PREVIOUS   1   NEXT →

Figure 3.5: A Coveralls report about test coverage

Every time you change your project and GitHub Actions triggers a build, it will, in turn, cause Coveralls to display an excellent summary of the coverage and how it evolves over time, similar to that shown in *Figure 3.5*.

Badges

Once you start to add services to your project, it is good practice to use badges in your project's README so the community can see at once the status for each one of them with links to the service. For example, add this README.rst file in your repository:

```
microservice-skeleton

======================


This project is a template for building microservices with Quart.


.. image:: https://coveralls.io/repos/github/PythonMicroservices/
microservice-skeleton/badge.svg?branch=main
```

```
    :target: https://coveralls.io/github/PythonMicroservices/
microservice-skeleton?branch=main


.. image:: https://github.com/PythonMicroservices/microservice-
skeleton/workflows/Python%20Testing/badge.svg
.. image:: https://readthedocs.org/projects/microservice/
badge/?version=latest
    :target: https://microservice.readthedocs.io
```

The preceding file will be displayed as shown in *Figure 3.6* in GitHub on your
project's landing page, demonstrating three different status badges.

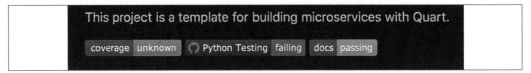

Figure 3.6: GitHub project status badges

Summary

In this chapter, we have covered the different kinds of tests that can be written for
your projects. Functional tests are those that you will write more often, with WebTest
being a great tool to use for such a purpose. To run the tests, pytest combined with
Tox will make your life easier.

We also covered some tips on writing good documentation and ensuring that the
tests are run in an automated way. Last, but not least, if you host your project on
GitHub, you can set up a whole CI system for free, thanks to GitHub Actions. From
there, numerous free services can be hooked to complement the tools available, like
Coveralls. You can also automatically build and publish your documentation on
ReadTheDocs.

If you want to look at how everything fits together, the microservice project
published on GitHub uses GitHub Actions, ReadTheDocs, and coveralls.io to do so:
https://github.com/PythonMicroservices/microservice-skeleton/

Now that we've covered how a Quart project can be continuously developed, tested,
and documented, we can look at how to design a full microservices-based project.
The next chapter will go through the design of such an application.

4

Designing Jeeves

In *Chapter 1, Understanding Microservices*, we said that the natural way to build a microservices-based app is to start with a monolithic version that implements all the features, and then to split it into microservices that make the most sense. When you are designing software, you have enough to worry about with the flow of information through the system, meeting requirements, and working out how it all fits together. Having a design that encounters reality is when you start getting a good idea of what types of components you should have, and as you gain experience, it will become easier to spot potential microservices earlier on.

In this chapter, we will go through this process by building a monolithic application and implementing the required features. We will cover how each component works and why it's there, as well as how information flows through the system.

The chapter is organized into two main sections:

- Presentation of our application and its user stories
- How Jeeves can be built as a monolithic application

Of course, in reality, the splitting process happens over time once the monolithic app design has some time to mature. But for the purpose of this book, we'll assume that the first version of the application has been used for a while and offered us some insights as to how it can be split in the right way, thanks to our time machine.

The Jeeves bot

Jeeves is an example application that was created for this book. Don't look for it in the Apple or Play Store, as it's not released or deployed for real users.

However, the application does work, and you can study its different components on GitHub in the PythonMicroservices organization: `https://github.com/PythonMicroservices/`.

We will be connecting to Slack, a popular communication platform, primarily used to send text messages in channels, similar to the older IRC service. Jeeves will be our personal assistant—a name taken from the stories of *P. G. Wodehouse*—and used for other software bots and at least one search engine. We will be using the name for its familiarity and not because of any connection with other people's work. The Jeeves presented here offers an interactive service to users of a Slack workspace and can be easily adapted to other chat environments. It also offers a web view to configure essential settings.

Once Jeeves is connected to a Slack workspace, a user can send the bot messages and receive replies. Users can also visit the web page and register for any third-party services they might need to connect to thanks to the standard OAuth2 mechanism. See more at `https://oauth.net/2/`.

We will be using **Strava** (`https://www.strava.com`) as an example of a third-party site, although this could easily be GitHub, Google services, Atlassian's JIRA, or some other useful service.

The OAuth2 standard is based on the idea of authorizing a third-party application to call a service with an access token that is unique to the user of the service. The token is generated by the service and usually has a limited scope in what calls can be performed.

Let's dive into the features through their user stories.

User stories

Firstly, what should our application do? A good way to describe our goals is by covering the desired behavior in different scenarios. If you've been involved in Agile development before, this will be familiar in the guise of "user stories." User stories are very simple descriptions of all the interactions a user can have with an application, and is often the first high-level document that is written when a project starts, as some of the stories appear in the justification or proposal for the work to begin.

Attempting to fill lots of detail early on can also make life harder; start with high-level stories and add detail as they are revisited. Sometimes a user story might be discarded if it's not feasible—it depends very much on how the work progresses and on the feasibility of each idea. User stories are also helpful to detect when it's worth splitting a feature into its microservice: a story that stands on its own could be a good candidate.

For Jeeves, we can start with this small set:

- As a Slack workspace user, I can send messages to a bot and get updates about the weather without leaving Slack
- As a Slack workspace user, I expect the bot to remember facts that I have told it about myself, such as my location
- As a Slack workspace user, I can visit the bot's control panel and authenticate third-party services, such as GitHub and Strava
- As an admin of the bot, I can get statistics regarding the bot's usage
- As an admin of the bot, I can disable or change the configuration of various features
- As a user, I can create an account on a third-party site that the bot knows about, and then use the bot to perform tasks there

There are already a few components emerging from this set of user stories. In no particular order, these are as follows:

- The app needs to store the contents of some types of messages it receives. These may be stored against a specific Slack identity.
- A user should be able to navigate to a web interface for third-party site authentication.
- The app will authenticate web users with a password or a URL with a provided token.
- The app should be able to perform periodic scheduled tasks to alert the user if a condition is true, such as for bad weather.

These descriptions are enough to get us started. The next section describes how the application can be designed and coded.

Monolithic design

This section presents extracts from the source code of the monolithic version of Jeeves. If you want to study it in detail, then the whole application can be found at `https://github.com/PacktPublishing/Python-Microservices-Development-2nd-Edition/tree/main/monolith`.

The first thing to consider is the retrieval of data from Slack into our application. There will be a single endpoint for this, as Slack sends all its events to the URL that the application developer configures. Later on, we can also add other endpoints to work with other environments, such as IRC, Microsoft Teams, or Discord.

We will also need a small interface to allow people to adjust the settings outside Slack, as controlling third-party authentication tokens and updating permissions for those tools is much easier using a web page. We will also need a small database to store all this information, along with other settings that we want our microservice to have.

Lastly, we will need some code to actually perform the actions our bot should do on behalf of the person who has sent it messages.

A design pattern that is often referred to when building applications is the **Model-View-Controller** (**MVC**) pattern, which separates the code into three parts:

- **Model**: This manages the data
- **View**: This displays the model for a particular context (web view, PDF view, and so on)
- **Controller**: This manipulates the model to change its state

SQLAlchemy is a library that can aid with the model part, allowing us to specify tables, relationships, and wrappers around reading and writing data in our Python source code. In a microservice, the view and controller distinction can be a bit vague, because what is called a view is a function that receives a request and sends back a response—and that function can both display and manipulate the data, allowing it to act as both a View and as a Controller.

The Django project uses **Model-View-Template** (**MVT**) to describe that pattern, where View is the Python callable, and Template is the template engine, or whatever is in charge of producing a response in a particular format, given some data. Quart uses Jinja2 for all sorts of useful template rendering—most commonly generating HTML and filling in the contents with values that it obtains from variables using the render_template() function. We will use this approach for views that present data to a human; for API views that return JSON, we will use json.dumps() to generate the response. In any case, the first step of designing our application is to define the model.

Model

In a Quart application based on SQLAlchemy, the model is described through classes, which represent the database schema. For Jeeves, the database tables are:

- **User**: This contains information about each user, including their credentials
- **Service**: This is a list of the available services the bot can provide, and whether or not they are active
- **Log**: A log of bot activity

Using the **SQLAlchemy** (https://www.sqlalchemy.org/) library, each table is created as a subclass of the base class provided by the module, allowing us to avoid duplicating effort and leaving the classes in our own code clean and focused on the data that we want to work with. SQLAlchemy has asynchronous interfaces that can be used to keep the performance benefits of our async application while accessing the database. To use these features, we must install both `sqlalchemy` and `aiosqlite`. The full example can be found in the code samples' GitHub repository as the `sqlachemy-async.py` file:

```python
# sqlalchemy-async.py

from sqlalchemy.ext.asyncio import create_async_engine,
AsyncSession
from sqlalchemy.orm import declarative_base, sessionmaker
from sqlalchemy import Column, Integer, String, Boolean, JSON
from sqlalchemy.orm import Session
from sqlalchemy.future import select
from sqlalchemy import update


# Initialize SQLAlchemy with a test database
DATABASE_URL = "sqlite+aiosqlite:///./test.db"
engine = create_async_engine(DATABASE_URL, future=True, echo=True)
async_session = sessionmaker(engine, expire_on_commit=False,
class_=AsyncSession)
Base = declarative_base()

# Data Model
class User(Base):
    __tablename__ = "user"
    id = Column(Integer, primary_key=True, autoincrement=True)
    name = Column(String)
    email = Column(String)
    slack_id = Column(String)
    password = Column(String)
    config = Column(JSON)
    is_active = Column(Boolean, default=True)
```

```
        is_admin = Column(Boolean, default=False)

    def json(self):
        return {"id": self.id, "email": self.email, "config": self.
config}
```

The User table mostly stores some Unicode strings, but it's also worth noting the two Boolean values that guarantee that we do not need to interpret another system's way of storing True and False. There is also a JSON column for storing entire data structures—a feature available in an increasing number of backend databases, including PostgreSQL and SQLite.

When used in a Quart app, SQLAlchemy allows us to write an interface to avoid writing SQL directly; instead, we can call functions that query and filter the data. We can go one step further and create a **data access layer (DAL)** that handles all of the database session management for us. In the following code, we have written an access layer that can be used as a context manager, while providing methods to create and find users. The create_user method is simply using the model we defined previously to create a new Python object—without all the fields, to make the example clearer—and then adding it to the database session, ensuring the data has been written out before returning the value written to the database.

Building on that, we can then use the get_all_users method to return all the records stored using the User model, using select() to retrieve them, and get_user to return just one record, while using the where method to filter the results to only display the ones that match the argument provided:

```
class UserDAL:
    def __init__(self, db_session):
        self.db_session = db_session


    async def create_user(self, name, email, slack_id):
        new_user = User(name=name, email=email, slack_id=slack_id)
        self.db_session.add(new_user)
        await self.db_session.flush()
        return new_user.json()


    async def get_all_users(self):
        query_result = await self.db_session.execute(select(User).
order_by(User.id))
```

```
            return {"users": [user.json() for user in query_result.
 scalars().all()]}


     async def get_user(self, user_id):
         query = select(User).where(User.id == user_id)
         query_result = await self.db_session.execute(query)
         user = query_result.one()
         return user[0].json()
```

With the DAL set up, we can use a feature provided by Python's own `contextlib` to create an asynchronous context manager:

```
@asynccontextmanager
async def user_dal():
    async with async_session() as session:
        async with session.begin():
            yield UserDAL(session)
```

All of this is a lot to set up, but once done, it allows us to access any of the data stored behind the `User` model with only a context manager to control the database session. We will use all this code in our views.

View and template

When a request is received, a view is invoked through the URL mapping, and we can use the context manager we created above to query and update the database. The following `Quart` view will allow us to view all the users in the database when the `/users` endpoint is queried:

```
@app.get("/users")
async def get_all_users():
    async with user_dal() as ud:
        return await ud.get_all_users()
```

When the `user_dal` context is created, we gain access to all the methods within it, and so we can easily call the `get_all_users` method and return the values to the client. Let's put all of the above together into one example application, adding in some of our missing fields:

```
# sqlalchemy-async.py
from contextlib import asynccontextmanager
```

```
from quart import Quart
from sqlalchemy.ext.asyncio import create_async_engine,
AsyncSession
from sqlalchemy.orm import declarative_base, sessionmaker
from sqlalchemy import Column, Integer, String, Boolean, JSON
from sqlalchemy.orm import Session
from sqlalchemy.future import select
from sqlalchemy import update

# Initialize SQLAlchemy with a test database
DATABASE_URL = "sqlite+aiosqlite:///./test.db"
engine = create_async_engine(DATABASE_URL, future=True, echo=True)
async_session = sessionmaker(engine, expire_on_commit=False,
class_=AsyncSession)
Base = declarative_base()




# Data Model
class User(Base):
    __tablename__ = "user"
    id = Column(Integer, primary_key=True, autoincrement=True)
    name = Column(String)
    email = Column(String)
    slack_id = Column(String)
    password = Column(String)
    config = Column(JSON)
    is_active = Column(Boolean, default=True)
    is_admin = Column(Boolean, default=False)



    def json(self):
        return {
            "id": self.id,
            "email": self.email,
            "slack_id": self.slack_id,
            "config": self.config,
            "is_active": self.is_active,
            "is_admin": self.is_admin,
        }

# Data Access Layer
```

```python
    class UserDAL:
        def __init__(self, db_session):
            self.db_session = db_session


        async def create_user(
            self,
            name,
            email,
            slack_id,
            password=None,
            config=None,
            is_active=True,
            is_admin=False,
        ):
            new_user = User(
                name=name,
                email=email,
                slack_id=slack_id,
                password=password,
                config=config,
                is_active=is_active,
                is_admin=is_admin,
            )
            self.db_session.add(new_user)
            await self.db_session.flush()
            return new_user.json()

        async def get_all_users(self):
            query_result = await self.db_session.execute(select(User).
    order_by(User.id))
            return [user.json() for user in query_result.scalars().
    all()]


        async def get_user(self, user_id):
            query = select(User).where(User.id == user_id)
            query_result = await self.db_session.execute(query)
            user = query_result.one()
            return user[0].json()

    app = Quart(__name__)
```

```python
@app.before_serving
async def startup():
    # create db tables
    async with engine.begin() as conn:
        # This resets the database - remove for a real project!
        await conn.run_sync(Base.metadata.drop_all)
        await conn.run_sync(Base.metadata.create_all)
        async with user_dal() as bd:
            await bd.create_user("name", "email", "slack_id")


@asynccontextmanager
async def user_dal():
    async with async_session() as session:
        async with session.begin():
            yield UserDAL(session)


@app.get("/users/<int:user_id>")
async def get_user(user_id):
    async with user_dal() as ud:
        return await ud.get_user(user_id)




@app.get("/users")
async def get_all_users():
    async with user_dal() as ud:
        return await ud.get_all_users()


if __name__ == "__main__":
    app.run()
```

A human-readable view

If we were to want this information presented in an easily readable format, we could use a Jinja2 template and pass the results of the query to fill in the details:

```python
@app.get("/users/page")
async def get_all_users_templated():
    async with user_dal() as ud:
```

```
        users = await ud.get_all_users()
        return await render_template("users.html", users=users)
```

Without any configuration to tell it otherwise, Jinja looks for its templates in a subdirectory of the Python application called `templates/`, which is often enough for small applications.

Our `users.html` template has some HTML in it, but also some directives that are bounded by curly braces. There is a `for` loop that allows us to iterate over the data that is passed to the template, and we can see that instructions sent to Jinja are surrounded by `{%` and `%}`. Another common instruction in a template would be `{% if … %}` to only include a piece of text if the condition is true. Inside the `for` loop, we see some variable expansions inside `{{` and `}}`, signaling to Jinja that it should look for a variable with that name. It's possible to apply filters to variables, which is especially useful when formatting dates. Here is a simple template that loops over all of the users it is given and displays both their email address and Slack ID:

```html
<html>
  <body>
    <h1>User List</h1>
    <ul>
      {% for user in users %}
      <li>
      {{ user.email }} {{ user.slack_id }}
      </li>
      {% endfor %}
    </ul>
  </body>
</html>
```

For editing data through the web, WTForms can be used to generate forms for each model. WTForms is a library that generates HTML forms with Python definitions, takes care of extracting data from incoming requests, and validating them before you update your model. Find out more at `http://wtforms.readthedocs.io`.

The Flask-WTF project wraps WTForms for `Quart` and adds some useful integration, such as securing forms with **Cross-Site Request Forgery (CSRF)** tokens. Find out more at `https://flask-wtf.readthedocs.io/`.

CSRF tokens will ensure that no malicious third-party website can send valid forms to your app when you are logged in. *Chapter 7, Securing Your Services*, will explain in detail how CSRF works and why it is important for your app security.

Designing Jeeves

The following module implements a form for the `User` table, using `FlaskForm` as its basis:

```
import quart.flask_patch
from flask_wtf import FlaskForm
import wtforms as f
from wtforms.validators import DataRequired


class UserForm(FlaskForm):
    email = f.StringField("email", validators=[DataRequired()])
    slack_id = f.StringField("Slack ID")
    password = f.PasswordField("password")

    display = ["email", slack_id, "password"]
```

The `display` attribute is just a helper to assist the template in iterating into a particular ordered list of fields when rendering the form. Everything else is using WTForms basic fields classes to create a form for the user table. The WTForm's Fields documentation provides the full list at `https://wtforms.readthedocs.io/en/2.3.x/fields/`.

Once created, `UserForm` can be used in a view that has two goals. The first one is to display the form on `GET` calls, and the second one is to update the database on `POST` calls when the user submits the form:

```
@app.route("/create_user", methods=["GET", "POST"])
    async def create_user():
        form = UserForm()
        if request.method == "POST" and form.validate():
            async with user_dal() as ud:
                await ud.create_user(form.name.data, form.email.data,
form.slack_id.data)
            return redirect("/users")
        return await render_template("create_user.html", form=form)
```

The `UserForm` class has a method to validate the incoming `POST` data, using the validators we provide. When some data is invalid, the form instance will keep the list of errors in `field.errors` in case the template wants to display them for the user.

The `create_user.html` template iterates through the form field list, and WTForm takes care of rendering the proper HTML tags:

```html
<html>
  <body>
    <form action="" method="POST">
      {{ form.hidden_tag() }}
      <dl>
      {% for field in form.display %}
      <dt>{{ form[field].label }}</dt>
      <dd>{{ form[field]() }}
        {% if form[field].errors %}
          {% for e in form[field].errors %}{{ e }} {% endfor %}
        {% endif %}
        </dd>
      {% endfor %}
      </dl>
      <p>
      <input type=submit value="Publish">
    </form>
  </body>
</html>
```

The form.hidden_tag() method will render all hidden fields, such as the CSRF token. Once this form is working, it's easy to reuse the same pattern for every form needed in the app.

Forms are often adjusted regularly during development and, by necessity, they are tightly coupled to the structure of the database. Because of this, when we look at splitting Jeeves up into microservices, we will consider whether these forms need to be provided by the database microservice to avoid schema dependencies appearing in other services.

Slack workspaces

Slack allows people to connect apps to a workspace. If you are an administrator of the FunCorp Slack instance, you could visit the following link and create a new bot user: https://api.slack.com/apps?new_app=1.

The exact process and web page layout may change—as web services frequently do—but there will be an opportunity to enable Event Subscriptions and provide a URL to which Slack messages should be sent.

A token will be generated, which you should copy and place in your application's settings so that it can authenticate to Slack when sending messages:

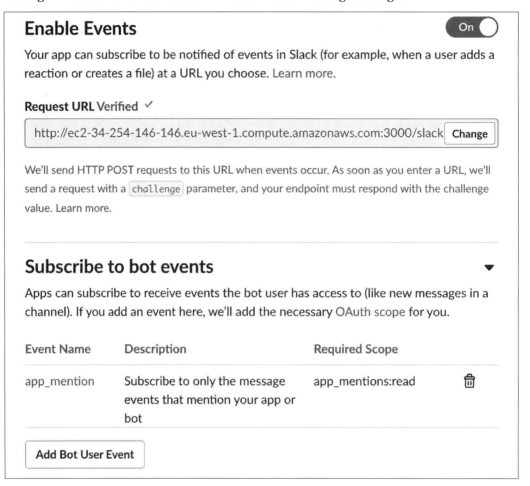

Figure 4.1: Subscribing to Slack bot events

The Request URL that you give to Slack will need to be reachable from Slack's own servers, and so running this on your laptop may not be enough. If you run into trouble, then using a virtual server in a cloud provider is a quick and easy way to get going. We will cover this in more detail in *Chapter 10, Deploying on AWS*, where we discuss deploying our application in the cloud.

Once the bot's endpoint is verified, it will start receiving the messages it has subscribed to. This means that if you have selected app_mention events, then messages that don't mention the bot by name will not be sent, but any others will. Your bot will need some permissions—known as scopes—to read and send messages:

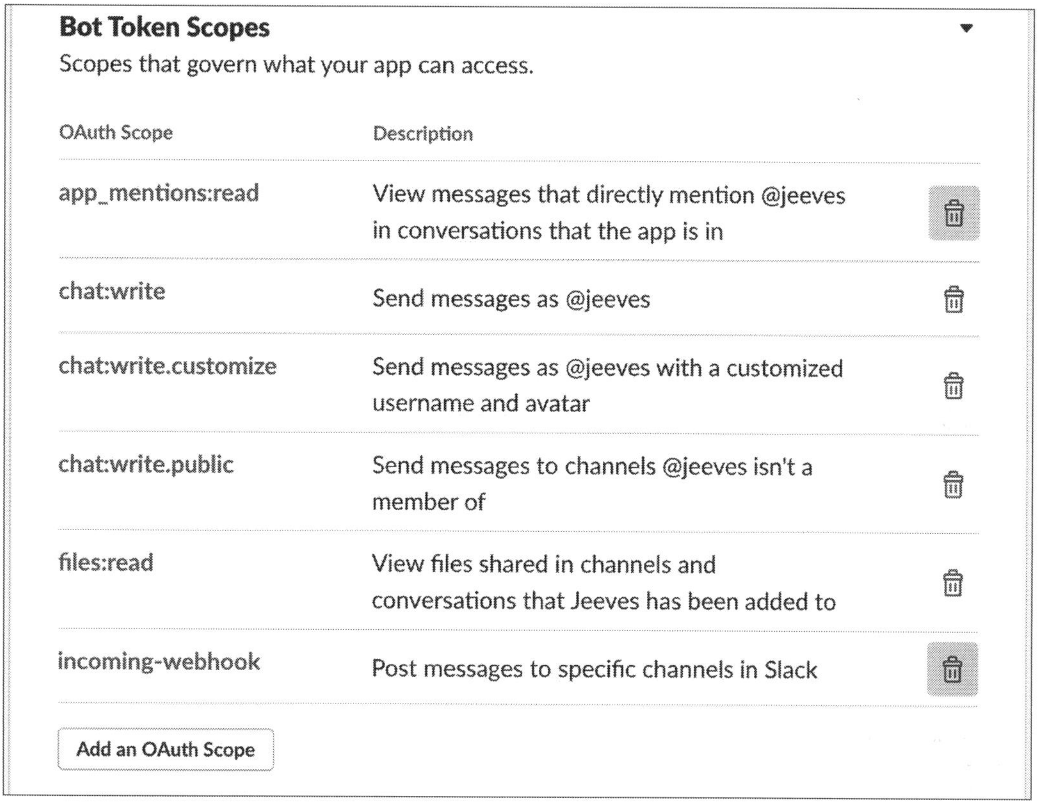

Bot Token Scopes ▼

Scopes that govern what your app can access.

OAuth Scope	Description	
app_mentions:read	View messages that directly mention @jeeves in conversations that the app is in	🗑
chat:write	Send messages as @jeeves	🗑
chat:write.customize	Send messages as @jeeves with a customized username and avatar	🗑
chat:write.public	Send messages to channels @jeeves isn't a member of	🗑
files:read	View files shared in channels and conversations that Jeeves has been added to	🗑
incoming-webhook	Post messages to specific channels in Slack	🗑

Add an OAuth Scope

Figure 4.2: Example Slack bot permissions to receive messages

The JSON data that is sent for an event arrives with all the data categorized. Using the example below, when the person types *@jeeves hello*, the API endpoint will receive a JSON object that identifies the workspace, the timestamp, what sort of event it was, what user typed it, and the component parts of the message itself—such as a mention (@jeeves) and the text, *hello*. Any user ID that is sent will not be recognizable to a human as they are the internal text strings used to represent users and workspaces. This does mean that when we connect a user to our application, we never really learn the username they chose in Slack unless we ask Slack for it.

Here is a trimmed copy of the JSON data our service gets when we ask for the weather in our Slack workspace. It is easy to see that the values for the user and team are not human-friendly, but the JSON is also helpful in that it has already broken up a potentially complicated message into sections for us so that we don't need to worry about safely removing mentions of other users, links, or other special elements that can be in the post:

```
{
    "event": {
        "client_msg_id": "79cd47ec-4586-4677-a50d-4db58bdfcd4b",
        "type": "app_mention",
        "text": "<@U01HYK05BLM>\u00a0weather in London, UK",
        "user": "U136F44A0",
        "ts": "1611254457.003600",
        "team": "T136F4492",
        "blocks": [
            {
                "type": "rich_text",
                "block_id": "pqx",
                "elements": [
                    {
                        "type": "rich_text_section",
                        "elements": [
                            {
                                "type": "user",
                                "user_id": "U01HYK05BLM"
                            },
                            {
                                "type": "text",
                                "text": " weather in London, UK"
                            }
                        ]
                    }
                ]
            }
        ],
        ...
}
```

Taking actions

Our bot should be able to do useful things for the people who send it messages, and we should keep these actions as self-contained as possible. Even without using a microservice-based design, it is far safer to create well-defined boundaries between different components.

How do we know which action to take? After receiving a message from Slack, we need to understand the data we have been given and look for the appropriate keywords. When we find something that matches, we can then check to see what function we should call.

The Quart view we use to handle Slack messages should be as simple as possible, and so we do just enough processing to extract information from the data we are given and pass it on to a message processor. This processor is responsible for examining the text the bot has been sent, and deciding on a course of action. Arranging the code this way also means that if we add support from other chat services, we can use the same message processor, and so consult the same list of actions.

We may require a more complex or dynamic action configuration later, but for now, let's start with a simple mapping in the configuration file. The dictionary keys will be some text to look for at the start of the message, and the value is the name of a function to be called when it matches. Each of those functions will take the same arguments, to make our life simpler:

```python
ACTION_MAP = {
    "help": show_help_text,
    "weather": fetch_weather,
    "config": user_config,
}


def process_message(message, metadata):
    """Decide on an action for a chat message.

    Arguments:
        message (str): The body of the chat message
        metadata (dict): Data about who sent the message,
            the time and channel.
    """
```

```
reply = None

for test, action in ACTION_MAP.items():
    if message.startswith(test):
        reply = action(message.lstrip(test), metadata)
        break

if reply:
    post_to_slack(reply, metadata)
```

By using this approach, adding new actions to our bot does not involve any changes to the process_message function, and so no changes are made to the tests for that function; instead, we just change a dictionary near the top of the file. It will also be easier to move the ACTION_MAP into a database or configuration file later if we discover that this would be useful.

The actions might make good use of the metadata, and so we pass that information along. Looking up the weather, for example, can make use of any stored location that the person has told us about.

OAuth tokens

OAuth2 (https://oauth.net/2/) allows us to make an authenticated request to someone else's site. We could request read-only access to someone's Google calendar, permission to post issues to GitHub, or the ability to read information about our recorded exercises in a fitness application. We can do all of this without ever asking for someone's password to a different site—something no one should ever do!

For our example, we will connect to Slack to allow the people using our bot to log in and update information about themselves. We can also use this to fetch information about them, such as the details of their Slack profile—if they allow us to.

We will present people visiting a web page with a button they can use to log in to the site using Slack, which will send the web browser off to Slack's page to authorize our application. If they agree, then our application is given a code, which we can then use to request an access token. That access token will let us contact Slack and verify that the token is still valid, and let us ask for the information the person has allowed us to view—or change! For this example, we will need HTTPS enabled and a valid site certificate. The easiest way to do this will be to use a proxy and a "Let's Encrypt" certificate. We will cover setting up this proxy and certificate in *Chapter 7, Securing Your Services*. For now, let's look at how we log users in:

```python
# slack_oauth2.py
import os
from quart import Quart, request, render_template
import aiohttp

app = Quart(__name__)

@app.route("/")
async def welcome_page():
    client_id = os.environ["SLACK_CLIENT_ID"]
    return await render_template("welcome.html", client_id=client_
id)

@app.route("/slack/callback")
async def oauth2_slack_callback():
    code = request.args["code"]
    client_id = os.environ["SLACK_CLIENT_ID"]
    client_secret = os.environ["SLACK_CLIENT_SECRET"]
    access_url = f"https://slack.com/api/oauth.v2.access?client_
id={client_id}&client_secret={client_secret}&code={code}"
    async with aiohttp.ClientSession() as session:
        async with session.get(access_url) as resp:
            access_data = await resp.json()
            print(access_data)
    return await render_template("logged_in.html")


if __name__ == "__main__":
    app.run()
```

We have introduced **aiohttp** (https://docs.aiohttp.org/) here, which is a useful asynchronous library for making outgoing web requests. We are also not handling the error responses that our callback view receives, or storing this useful data in a database to use later on. In that view, @login_required and current_user are part of the authentication and authorization processes presented in the next section.

Authentication and authorization

Our monolithic application is almost ready but it also requires a way to handle authentication and authorization. Simply put:

- **Authentication** is proving that you are who you claim to be
- **Authorization** is determining what actions you are permitted to perform

This is a careful—but critically important—distinction to make. In most services, there is an administrator, who must provide authentication—prove who they are— to be granted permission to perform configuration updates. A regular user of the service still must prove who they are, but the things they can do will not include the same access rights as used by administrators.

For Jeeves, we need to connect our Slack users to our web service user interface so that people can authenticate with external services. We are setting up the third-party authentication this way so that we don't need to perform any complicated changes to a standard OAuth process.

Since Slack uses an internal identifier for most users, we won't see—nor do we need to—the friendly name they have chosen to display to other people. Instead, we will know them by a short nine-character string: You can view your own by checking your Slack profile, and it will be visible under the **More** menu. How do we connect that with the web interface? The quickest way would be to get a sign-in link from the bot. If a user sends Jeeves a message asking to log in, Jeeves can reply with a URL. Once visited, that URL will let the user set a password and use all the web features.

For our monolithic solution, we have just seen how we can let people log in using Slack without us ever having to handle a password. Using the quart-auth library makes managing session information for a user straightforward as it provides useful helper functions to create and store session cookies so that we will be remembered between visits.

Looking at the changes, our welcome page no longer presents the login button in its template, but instead now has a new decorator, @login_required, which will only allow the view to be loaded if we have declared that the current visitor has successfully authenticated:

```
@app.route("/")
@login_required
async def welcome_page():
    return await render_template("welcome.html")
```

If a visitor to the site is not authenticated, then their visit will be handled by the errorhandler we set, which here redirects them to the login page. The login page does the same job as our previous welcome page and shows the user the login button to press:

```
@app.route("/slack_login")
async def slack_login():
    client_id = os.environ["SLACK_CLIENT_ID"]
```

```
        return await render_template("login.html", client_id=client_id)


    @app.errorhandler(Unauthorized)
    async def redirect_to_login(_):
        return redirect(url_for("slack_login"))
```

The Slack OAuth2 process continues as it did before, and we receive a message in our callback. If the message indicates that things went well, then we can use the AuthUser calls of quart-auth and the login_user calls to set a session for this user. Let's put the whole thing together in a working example, making use of the secrets library to generate a secure, but temporary, secret key for development:

```
    # logging_in.py
    import os
    from quart import Quart, request, render_template, redirect, url_
for
    from quart_auth import (
        AuthManager,
        login_required,
        logout_user,
        login_user,
        AuthUser,
        Unauthorized,
    )
    import aiohttp
    import secrets


    app = Quart(__name__)
    AuthManager(app)
    app.secret_key = secrets.token_urlsafe(16)



    @app.route("/")
    @login_required
    async def welcome_page():
        return await render_template("welcome.html")



    @app.route("/slack_login")
```

```
    async def slack_login():
        client_id = os.environ["SLACK_CLIENT_ID"]
        return await render_template("login.html", client_id=client_id)


    @app.errorhandler(Unauthorized)
    async def redirect_to_login(_):
        return redirect(url_for("slack_login"))


    @app.route("/slack/callback")
    async def oauth2_slack_callback():
        code = request.args["code"]
        client_id = os.environ["SLACK_CLIENT_ID"]
        client_secret = os.environ["SLACK_CLIENT_SECRET"]
        access_url = f"https://slack.com/api/oauth.v2.access?client_
id={client_id}&client_secret={client_secret}&code={code}"
        async with aiohttp.ClientSession() as session:
            async with session.get(access_url) as resp:
            access_data = await resp.json()
            if access_data["ok"] is True:
                authed_user = access_data["authed_user"]["id"]
                login_user(AuthUser(authed_user))
                return redirect(url_for("welcome_page")
        return redirect(url_for("slack_login"))
```

If you do need to store passwords, the simplest form of protection is to make sure that they are not stored in the clear in a database; instead, store them in a hashed form that cannot be converted back to the original password. That will minimize the risk of leaking passwords if your server is compromised. For the authentication process, it just means that when the user logs in, you need to hash the incoming password to compare it to the stored hash. Always check to see what the latest recommendations are for hashing algorithms, as inventing your own or using one that is obsolete can be very risky.

The transport layer is not usually the weak spot in application security. Thanks to the hard work of security professionals working on **Transport Layer Security (TLS)**, we only need to concern ourselves with what happens inside the service once the request is received.

In the same vein, more granular permission verifications can be done by looking at the current_user variable that quart_auth sets in the application context. For example, you could use this to allow a user to change their data, but prevent them from changing any other users' data.

Background tasks

So far, our application has several features that would be useful to run as scheduled tasks, without user interaction: our weather action could check for weather alerts in a user's area and send a message to them; a calendar action could report on your scheduled meetings at the start of the working day; a monthly report of the actions that have been undertaken could be produced and emailed to the person looking after the bot.

These are background tasks, and they need to run on their own outside the HTTP request/response cycle. Most operating systems have some form of scheduled task feature, such as cron on Unix or Scheduled Tasks in Windows. These features may not be ideal for our application, as it means we are connected to a specific platform when we should ideally be platform-agnostic, and able to run inside containers, or migrate to a serverless platform if our needs change.

A popular way to run repetitive background tasks in Python web apps is to use **Celery**, a distributed task queue that can execute some work in a standalone process: http://docs.celeryproject.org.

To run these pieces of work, an intermediate called a message broker is in charge of passing messages back and forth between the application and Celery. For instance, if the app wants Celery to run something, it will add a message in the broker; Celery will poll it and do the job.

A message broker can be any service that can store messages and provide a way to retrieve them. The Celery project works out of the box with **Advanced Message Queuing Protocol** (**AMQP**) services such as **RabbitMQ** (http://www.rabbitmq.com), **Redis** (http://redis.io), and **Amazon SQS** (https://aws.amazon.com/sqs/). AMQP provides a standard set of techniques for routing and delivering messages in a reliable way. We will be using RabbitMQ in our examples when we investigate the microservices design in more detail in the next chapter, where RabbitMQ will be responsible for making sure that messages reach their destination, and Celery is responsible for acting on those messages.

The component that executes the job is called a worker, and Celery provides a class to start one. To use Celery from a `Quart` application, you can create a `background.py` module that instantiates a Celery object and marks your background tasks with an `@celery.task` decorator.

In the following example, we are using Celery to set up a task that will fetch weather reports for every user who has a location and a Slack username set in our database. While, in practice, we would want people to opt-in to this feature, it allows us to show how a task is constructed.

We will use the database we created earlier in this chapter and assume we have added a location field to it. We should also add a function to let us search for user accounts with a location set:

```python
class UserDAL:
    ...
    async def get_users_with_locations(self):
        query = select(User).where(User.location is not None)
        return await self.db_session.execute(query)
```

Now we can set up a worker to do the task. The only difficulty is needing to wrap the function we call to do the work. To use the asynchronous database engine, it must be an async function, but Celery can only call synchronous functions, so we use a helper found in the `asgiref` library to convert it:

```python
# weather_worker.py
import asyncio


from asgiref.sync import async_to_sync
from celery import Celery
from database import user_dal


celery_app = Celery("tasks", broker="amqp://localhost")


async def fetch_weather(location):
    return "This is where we would call the weather service"


async def post_to_slack(message, options):
```

```
        print(f"This is where we would post {message}")


    async def weather_alerts_async():
        async with user_dal() as ud:
            query_results = await ud.get_users_with_locations()
            for user in query_results:
                user = user[0] # the database returns a tuple
                weather_message = await fetch_weather(user.location)
                username = user.slack_id
                if not username.startswith("@"):
                    username = "@" + username
                await post_to_slack(weather_message, {"channel":
username})


    @celery_app.task
    def do_weather_alerts():
        async_to_sync(weather_alerts_async)()


    @celery_app.on_after_configure.connect
    def setup_periodic_tasks(sender, **kwargs):
        sender.add_periodic_task(10.0, do_weather_alerts, name="fetch
the weather", expires=30)
```

Celery will need RabbitMQ running in order to work—there are tutorials on RabbitMQ's website, but below we assume you have Docker installed and can run containers. If you don't, then don't worry; we will discuss containers in more detail in *Chapter 10*, *Deploying on AWS*. We run the Celery background worker, which will wait for messages to arrive asking it to do work, and in another terminal, we start the scheduler, or beat, which will use the periodic task we set up:

```
    docker run -d -p 5672:5672 rabbitmq
    celery -A background worker  --loglevel=INFO
    celery -A background beat --loglevel=INFO
```

This Celery worker also connects to RabbitMQ using AMQP, so that tasks can be triggered by sending a message through the broker. This will be especially useful if we don't need to send an immediate response to the caller, but instead expect a longer-running process to perform some tasks.

Continuing our setup, we can look at the scheduler. Every 10 seconds is probably a bit too frequent for a report like this. We should instead use the crontab feature from Celery, which lets us specify a schedule while using the more familiar Unix crontab settings:

```
from celery.schedules import crontab

@celery_app.on_after_configure.connect
def setup_periodic_tasks(sender, **kwargs):
    sender.add_periodic_task(
        crontab(hour=7, minute=30, day_of_week='monday'),
        do_weather_alerts, name="fetch the weather", expires=30
    )
```

When the Celery service is invoked by the Quart application by passing messages, it could be considered as a microservice in and of itself. That is also interesting in terms of deployment since both the RabbitMQ server and the Celery app can be deployed on another server. Our asynchronous function can then use the current app context to access the database, run queries, and then use the features of our application to run tasks.

Putting together the monolithic design

This monolithic design is a solid foundation and should be the kind of result you would aim for in your first development iteration. Everything should be created with tests and documentation, as explained in *Chapter 3, Coding, Testing, and Documentation: the Virtuous Cycle*.

It is a short and clean implementation on top of a relational database that can be deployed with a PostgreSQL, MySQL, or a cloud provider's own SQL database. Thanks to the SQLAlchemy abstractions, a local version can run with SQLite 3 and facilitate your day-to-day development and local testing. To build this app, we've used the following extensions and libraries:

- **aiohttp**: This handles all the outgoing HTTP requests
- **SQLAlchemy**: This is used for the model
- **Flask-WTF** and **WTForms**: These are used for all the forms
- **Celery and RabbitMQ**: These are used for background processes and periodic tasks
- **quart-auth**: This is used for managing authentication and authorization

The overall design can be represented in a diagram, as shown in *Figure 4.3*:

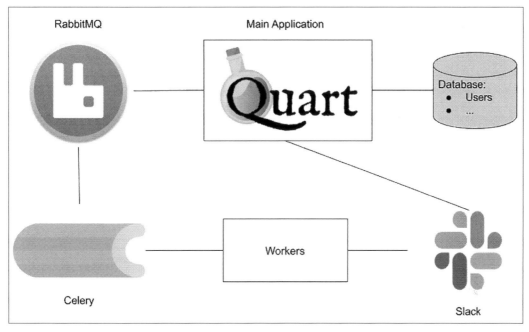

Figure 4.3: The components of our first design

A typical early deployment will put all of these services on the same server. It's certainly simpler that way, and it often feels straightforward to give an application a more powerful computer—this is known as scaling vertically. A single computer, whether it's a virtual machine in a cloud provider or a physical server in your building, has a limited number of resources available, and so there is a practical upper limit to vertical scaling.

Whether your application is running out of memory, network throughput, CPU processing availability, or some other bottleneck, the best solution is to update the architecture so that the service can be run across many different computers. This is scaling horizontally, and is one of the benefits of using microservices. If a microservice needs more I/O throughput to serve all its requests than a single computer can provide, that's not a problem if it can run across dozens or hundreds of computers.

Summary

The Jeeves bot is a typical web app that interacts with a database and a few backend services. The only unusual feature is that it receives most of its workload from one endpoint. Building this application with a monolithic architecture has allowed us to quickly iterate over several choices and get a prototype that works well during development and low-volume usage.

From our discussions about the actions, it should be clear that there are good candidates for migration to a microservice. If we run this bot for dozens or hundreds of Slack workspaces, then we may find that one component is used much more than others, or has reliability issues that are difficult to address in the current architecture. How should the application scale up? What happens when an external service it relies upon is encountering errors? What happens if one of our own components — our database or message broker — goes down?

In the next chapter, we will look at these issues: how to change the architecture of Jeeves so that it is more resilient, and how to make careful, measured changes to the service.

5

Splitting the Monolith

In the previous chapter, we created a monolithic application to serve as an assistant; we did so rapidly, concentrating on adding features rather than long-term architecture. There is nothing wrong with that approach—after all if the application never needs to scale up then the engineering effort is wasted.

But let us assume that our service is very popular, and the number of requests it receives is growing. We now have to make sure it performs well under load, and also ensure that it is easy to maintain for a growing team of developers. How should we proceed from here? In this chapter, we will:

- Examine how to identify the best components to migrate to a new microservice based on code complexity and data we collect about usage
- Show techniques for preparing and performing that migration, as well as checking on its success

Identifying potential microservices

For an application that is familiar to us, we might have a lot of intuition about which components are overloaded or unreliable. After all, either we wrote it, or have rewritten large parts of it, and tested it, along with making decisions about its architecture. It's also natural to have made notes about the database growing larger, or noticing that one particular function takes a long time to run during testing.

Our own intuition may lead us astray, however, and it is a good idea to let our decisions be informed by the data we collect. Developers and operations people will have specific questions that should be answered to make a decision about the future direction of a service. Product management and other business-oriented people will also have questions that need answering, which are often not specific to the technology. Questions a developer may ask include:

- How fast are responses to HTTP requests?
- What are the success and error rates on HTTP requests for different endpoints?
- Which parts of the system are troublesome when making changes?
- How many active connections does a component have to deal with, on average, at peak use?

Some non-technical business questions to consider are:

- Does a slow response mean a user will stop checking with our Slack bot and start using other tools instead?
- In a web-based shop, what is the conversion rate—that is, how many customers viewed items, compared to how many bought something?
- How accurate and up to date is the information we provide through the service?

For our discussion, we will focus on technical questions, but it is always worth remembering why software exists, and how best to answer the questions put forward by the people who need an application—as well as the people who produce it. To make our decisions about splitting our monolithic application, we will keep two questions in mind:

- Which components are the slowest and cause the most delays when they are run?
- Which components are tightly coupled to the rest of the application, and so fragile when changed?

 Two terms often heard are *data-driven* and *data-informed*. To be data-driven involves collecting data about a situation and always basing decisions on that information. Being data-informed also involves collecting data, but using it alongside personal experience and knowledge of the wider situation.

There are many aspects to software and what it does — network connections, reading files, querying databases, and so on. It is tempting to think that collecting everything and looking for patterns in the data will be the best way to monitor the application. There is often too much data to sift through, however, and too many variables to account for. Instead, we should start with a qualitative question.

However, the question should not be, "which parts of the application would work as a microservice?"; instead, we should consider questions such as "which parts of the application are having the most impact on performance?" and "which parts of the application are difficult to change?" The answer might be a microservice — and since this book is about that option, we will investigate it in depth — but there are other performance problems that can arise, and other solutions, such as optimizing a database or caching common query results.

Let us look at some ways that we can identify the parts of an application that need refactoring, and that would make good microservices.

Code complexity and maintenance

As we discussed in *Chapter 1, Understanding Microservices*, as the size of a project increases it becomes more difficult to reason about, especially for people new to the team. Keeping different logical parts of the system separate and having a clean interface between them helps us think more effectively about the interactions between all the different components — making it easier to understand where to make changes — without having to worry about accidentally breaking something in code that seems unrelated.

Many of the decisions made when looking at maintenance will be based on experience: when reading the code, developers get a sense of what areas they understand well, and which areas they do not, as well as how risky it is to change various parts of a project.

We can also take a data-informed approach by using tools that assess the **cyclomatic complexity** of the code. Cyclomatic complexity is a software metric, developed in the 1970s, to assess how many branches and paths of code execution a program has. Understanding the mathematics is outside the scope of this book, so for our purposes we should understand that a higher score indicates more complex code, and code that scores 1.0 has no decisions in it at all.

Radon (`https://pypi.org/project/radon/`) is a Python tool for quickly assessing code complexity; it also groups the complexity scores into bands, similar to academic grades such as A through F. Since our examples so far have been simple, let's run `Radon` against `Quart` itself.

Here, we tell Radon to calculate the cyclomatic complexity and only report on those areas that have a complexity rating of C or worse:

```
$ git clone https://gitlab.com/pgjones/quart
$ cd quart
$ radon  cc .  --average --min c
asgi.py
    M 205:4 ASGIWebsocketConnection.handle_websocket - C
blueprints.py
    M 510:4 Blueprint.register - D
cli.py
    F 278:0 routes_command - C
    M 48:4 ScriptInfo.load_app - C
app.py
    M 1178:4 Quart.run - C
helpers.py
    F 154:0 url_for - C
    F 347:0 send_file - C
testing/utils.py
    F 60:0 make_test_body_with_headers - C

8 blocks (classes, functions, methods) analyzed.
Average complexity: C (15.125)
```

It's easy to think that a high-complexity function is always bad, but that's not necessarily the case. We should strive for simplicity, but not over-simplification to the point where we lose usefulness in the software. We should use scores like these as guides for our decisions.

Now, we will look at other sorts of data we can collect about our code, to help us make informed decisions.

Metrics and Monitoring

It is easy to think of monitoring tools as being useful to alert us when something is broken, but there are other valuable uses. **Operational health** monitoring relies on a wide range of high-resolution metrics that arrive with low latency to allow us to notice and fix problems with the system. To determine if a change in architecture is needed, we might look at the operational health of a service, but we also want to look at the service's quality: **quality assurance** discovers whether or not the service is meeting our standards.

How is this different from operational health? In a complex system, there can be components that are unreliable or slow, but the overall performance of the system is acceptable to the people using it. If we ask software to send an email for us, and it arrives ten seconds later, then most people would consider that quality of service acceptable, even if behind the scenes there are numerous failed nodes, connection timeouts, and retrying operations. Such a service is working but needs maintenance, or it will continue with a higher risk of a large outage or lack of burst capacity.

Gathering data about what our application is doing leaves us more informed about which components need attention, which are slow, and which are responding well. What does it mean to take a measurement? It has historically been tricky to pin down a good definition. Psychologist Stanley Smith Stevens, however, describes it in a useful way:

> *Measurement, in the broadest sense, is defined as the assignment of numerals to objects and events according to rules.*

> *— On the Theory of Scales of Measurement, S. S. Stevens (1946)*

What is a good measurement to make? Giving a firm answer to this is difficult too, although for our purposes, there are three main categories of data we could collect. The first is gauges, which are an absolute measure at a certain point in time. A fuel gauge in a car will tell you how much fuel is remaining, and a tool such as netstat will tell you how many open network connections a server has. Inside a service, a measurement, such as the number of active connections, is a gauge.

Counters are measurements that continue to grow incrementally and cumulatively — you will often see measurements about the amount of network traffic or disk I/O as a counter. Whenever you ask the kernel how many bytes have been transferred out of a network interface, you will get a number that doesn't mean much by itself, as it will be the total amount of traffic since counting started. But ask again one second later, subtract one number from the other, and now you have a value that is bytes per second. Unix tools such as `iostat` and `vmstat` do this for you, which is why the first set of numbers they display is often very high and should be discounted.

It is important to understand what your gauges and counters are collecting, as it changes the ways in which they can be used. Taking an average value — mostly the mean, but sometimes a median — usually gives us a meaningful number. If we record that, in the last second, our laptop's six CPU cores have used 0, 0, 0, 1, 1, and 1 seconds of CPU time, it makes sense to say our average CPU usage is 50%. It is also reasonable to say that we have used a sum of three seconds of CPU time in the last one second. However, if we are measuring the temperature of our laptop and its three sensors tell us the values of 65, 70, and 75°C, the average value is still useful, but it would be meaningless to say the total temperature is 210 degrees!

Ratios are the third category of data we are concerned about. These describe how the other measurements relate to one another. We have already seen a useful ratio when discussing counters, as "the number of bytes transferred" divided by "the time it took" gives us a ratio, as does "the number of bytes transferred" divided by the number of API calls.

Choosing what metrics to collect is often a difficult choice, as there are so many possibilities. It is best to start with specific questions and work toward answering them, rather than trying to collect everything at once. If people report that our application is slow, then we need to discover what parts are slow to respond, and why. Thankfully we can start with two of the easiest things to monitor in a web application:

- Counting how many times each endpoint is visited
- How long each endpoint takes to finish processing a request

Once we have information about these two things, this will hopefully direct us to a specific endpoint that is overloaded, or that takes too long to process requests and falls behind. If it doesn't help, then we need to start investigating similar high-level information about other components of the system, such as the database or network throughput. To investigate this in a cloud-agnostic way, we will turn to a common tool for operational monitoring, called **Prometheus** (https://prometheus.io/). Prometheus operates by scraping endpoints—we configure it with some URLs to query, and it expects some metrics to be returned when it sends a request. To easily integrate metrics into our application, we can use the aioprometheus library. Its documentation can be found at https://aioprometheus.readthedocs.io/en/latest/.

To begin with, we will have to set up the metrics that we want to collect. For now, let's assume that we are interested in how many concurrent requests an endpoint is responding to, and how long each request takes. We can use aioprometheus to set up a Registry object to store these until a Prometheus server asks for the information. The number of active requests is a gauge, since it is a snapshot of the current state at a single point in time. The duration of each request is recorded as a Summary object, as once the data is in Prometheus, we will want to aggregate it, and perhaps look at the distribution of values. We can create both registries and then add them to our application:

```
app.registry = Registry()
app.api_requests_gauge = Gauge(
    "quart_active_requests", "Number of active requests per endpoint"
)
app.request_timer = Summary(
    "request_processing_seconds", "Time spent processing request"
)
```

```
app.registry.register(app.api_requests_gauge)
app.registry.register(app.request_timer)
```

We also need to add an endpoint for Prometheus to reach our application and ask for the metrics that have been collected. aioprometheus also provides a render function to generate this data for us, and so the metrics handler is short:

```
@app.route("/metrics")
async def handle_metrics():
    return render(app.registry, request.headers.getlist("accept"))
```

Once that is done, we can make use of some helper functions provided by aioprometheus to record the duration of a function, and also to automatically increment and decrement a gauge. The contents of the function here are just to provide some content that takes some time—we will sleep for between 1 and 1.5 seconds to generate a set of values for how long the response takes. Let's add it all together into a working example:

```
# quart_metrics.py
import asyncio
from random import randint

from aioprometheus import Gauge, Registry, Summary, inprogress, render, timer
from quart import Quart, request

app = Quart(__name__)
app.registry = Registry()
app.api_requests_gauge = Gauge(
    "quart_active_requests", "Number of active requests per endpoint"
)
app.request_timer = Summary(
    "request_processing_seconds", "Time spent processing request"
)
app.registry.register(app.api_requests_gauge)
app.registry.register(app.request_timer)


@app.route("/")
@timer(app.request_timer, labels={"path": "/"})
@inprogress(app.api_requests_gauge, labels={"path": "/"})
async def index_handler():
```

```python
    await asyncio.sleep(1.0)
    return "index"


@app.route("/endpoint1")
@timer(app.request_timer, labels={"path": "/endpoint1"})
@inprogress(app.api_requests_gauge, labels={"path": "/endpoint1"})
async def endpoint1_handler():
    await asyncio.sleep(randint(1000, 1500) / 1000.0)
    return "endpoint1"


@app.route("/endpoint2")
@timer(app.request_timer, labels={"path": "/endpoint2"})
@inprogress(app.api_requests_gauge, labels={"path": "/endpoint2"})
async def endpoint2_handler():
    await asyncio.sleep(randint(2000, 2500) / 1000.0)
    return "endpoint2"


@app.route("/metrics")
async def handle_metrics():
    return render(app.registry, request.headers.getlist("accept"))


if __name__ == "__main__":
    app.run(host="0.0.0.0")
```

For a production service, the metrics collection service is another component that needs to be deployed and managed; however, for our own experiments while developing, a local copy of Prometheus is enough, and we can run it in a container. If we set up a basic configuration file, we will need to make sure that the targets match the IP address of the computer we are running our application on—it cannot be localhost, as Prometheus is running inside its own container, and so traffic to localhost will never leave that container. Here is our configuration, which we can place in a file called prometheus.yml, which we will then include in the container:

```
# prometheus.yml
---
global:
  scrape_interval: 15s
  external_labels:
    monitor: 'quart-monitor'

scrape_configs:
  - job_name: 'prometheus'
    scrape_interval: 5s
    static_configs:
      - targets: ['192.168.1.100:5000']  # Replace with your app's IP
address
        labels:
          group: 'quart'
```

Now we run Prometheus and visit the web interface, which, if you are running the container on your laptop, will be at `http://localhost:9090/`:

```
docker run \
    -p 9090:9090 \
    -v /path/to/prometheus.yml:/etc/prometheus/prometheus.yml \
    prom/prometheus
```

Figure 5.1 shows the data we collect after running a series of queries against our running application, using the **Boom** (`https://github.com/tarekziade/boom`) tool that we introduced in *Chapter 3, Coding, Testing, and Documentation: the Virtuous Cycle*, when discussing load testing. Because we randomized which endpoints we call in the test, we can see the different rates of use in the graph. The Prometheus query asks for the rate of the number of active requests each minute, using the name of the gauge we set above in `quart_metrics.py`.

More information about querying Prometheus can be found here: `https://prometheus.io/docs/prometheus/latest/getting_started/`.

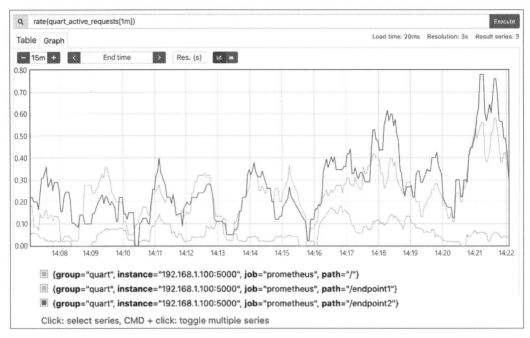

Figure 5.1: An example of Prometheus showing how many active requests each endpoint is serving

Now we have a much clearer picture of how many times each endpoint in our API is queried, and how long those requests take. We could also add extra metrics, such as how much CPU time is used, how much memory is consumed, or how long we are waiting for other network calls to complete. Data like this helps us pinpoint exactly which parts of our application consume the most resources, and which have trouble scaling up.

Logging

Numbers can tell us a lot about what's going on in an application, but not the whole story. We also need to use logging, which is the act of producing some text or data that will be recorded, but is not part of the essential operation of the software. This does not mean that logging isn't important—it is—but the application could run happily without any messages being written out.

Once we have an idea of which parts of a system are operating slowly, the next question is going to be "what, exactly, is it doing?" Reading the code will only give us part of the answer—logging will give us the rest, by recording which decisions were taken, what data was sent, and what errors were encountered.

Recording absolutely everything will increase the I/O requirements of the application, either sending those messages across the network or using up disk resources writing the files locally. We should carefully consider what gets written out, and why. This is especially true when log messages might contain sensitive information, such as personal details about people or passwords. For a service running in production, logs should be sanitized whenever possible, removing anything that might leak personal data.

Python has powerful logging options that can automatically format messages for us, and filter the messages based on their severity. The log message's severity is graded on a scale of debug, info, warning, error, and critical, which allows us to easily change how many messages our application produces with one setting, instead of changing each line that produces a message.

Quart provides an interface that allows the use of Python's built-in logging with ease, within the application. Let's take a look at a basic example where we use `app.logger` to produce log messages whenever `hello_handler` is called:

```python
# quart_logging.py
import logging
from quart import Quart, request

app = Quart(__name__)
app.logger.setLevel(logging.INFO)

@app.route("/hello")
def hello_handler():
    app.logger.info("hello_handler called")
    app.logger.debug(f"The request was {request}")
    return {"Hello": "World!"}

if __name__ == "__main__":
    app.run()
```

When we run our application and the `/hello` endpoint is queried, `Quart` will display one extra message in the terminal where it is running:

```
    [2021-06-26 21:21:41,144] Running on http://127.0.0.1:5000 (CTRL +
C to quit)
    [2021-06-26 21:21:42,743] INFO in quart_logging: hello_handler
called
    [2021-06-26 21:21:42,747] 127.0.0.1:51270 GET /hello 1.1 200 18
4702
```

Why only one message? The second call is using the "debug" severity, and we set the log level to INFO so that only messages of informational importance and above are produced. If we want our debugging messages to appear, we can change app. logger.setLevel(logging.INFO) to app.logger.setLevel(logging.DEBUG).

While there is a specific format to our log messages so far, what gets produced is still a single text string. This can be awkward to process if you have a program that wants to examine the log entries for important errors or find patterns in what is happening.

For log messages that should be readable by a computer, structured logging is the best option. Structured logging is commonly a log message produced in JSON format, so that the date, text description, source of the message, and any other metadata are all separate fields in the JSON. Python's structlog library does a good job of formatting the output correctly, and also makes it easy to add processors to the log message to censor names, passwords, and other similar private information: https://www.structlog.org/en/stable/index.html.

Using it with Quart involves setting up structlog, and replacing the functions used to create log messages:

```python
# quart_structlog.py
import logging
from quart import Quart, request
import structlog
from structlog import wrap_logger
from structlog.processors import JSONRenderer


app = Quart(__name__)

logger = wrap_logger(
app.logger,
    processors=[
        structlog.processors.add_log_level,
        structlog.processors.TimeStamper(),
        JSONRenderer(indent=4, sort_keys=True),
    ],
)
app.logger.setLevel(logging.DEBUG)


@app.route("/hello")
def hello_handler():
    logger.info("hello_handler called")
```

```
    logger.debug(f"The request was {request}")
    return {"Hello": "World!"}


if __name__ == "__main__":
    app.run()
```

Using the code above, we now get structured log entries—still surrounded by human-readable text, but now there are entries that a computer can easily parse:

```
[2021-06-26 21:54:24,208] INFO in _base: {
    "event": "hello_handler called",
    "level": "info",
    "timestamp": 1624740864.2083042
}
[2021-06-26 21:54:24,211] DEBUG in _base: {
    "event": "The request was <Request 'http://localhost:5000/hello'
[GET]>",
    "level": "debug",
    "timestamp": 1624740864.211336
}
```

Further configuration of `structlog` allows you to send the JSON directly to a central logging server, such as **Graylog** (https://www.graylog.org/), which will be useful for collecting logs from multiple different copies of your software running on different computers.

With all this information about code complexity and how well each component in our monolith is working, we should have a good idea as to which areas need the most work, and which would benefit the most from being extracted into their own microservice. Once we have identified those components, we can begin this process.

Splitting a Monolith

Now that we know which components are consuming the most resources and taking the most time, how should we split them up?

It's already possible to move several components in our service to separate servers. RabbitMQ, Celery, and the database all communicate over the network, and so while there are a lot of steps to setting up new servers and configuring them, it is a well-understood process to install those hosts and update our application to use new URLs. This lets our API concentrate on handling network connections and moves the larger tasks to their own workers.

A developer must also consider setting up network security, accounts, access control and other concerns relating to running and securing a service.

The parts of our own application are trickier: we call functions to invoke our own features, and we will need to call a REST API instead. Should this be done using one large deployment and all the changes in one go? Should we run the old and new versions side by side for a while?

A cautious, measured change is always safer. Being cautious does not mean you have to be slow, but it does involve planning. How do we tell if the migration is successful? What happens if we need to reverse the changes? Asking these questions lets us discover difficult situations in the migration before they happen—although things may not always go according to plan. There is an old saying that plans never survive contact with the enemy, but there's an important nuance, attributed to former US President Dwight D. Eisenhower:

> *Plans are worthless, but planning is everything.*

> *– Dwight D. Eisenhower, 1957*

It doesn't matter if the plans you make don't end up being useful. The act of making those plans helps you to better understand a situation and leaves you with the tools to deal with the changing situation in front of you.

An excellent first step with any approach is to return to our service-oriented architecture principles and define a clear interface between the future microservice and the rest of the application. Let's look back at our monolithic application, at the function that works out which action to perform, and the other that gets chosen if the user wants to look up the weather. This code has plenty of issues, but we will address the relevant ones:

```python
# Decide which action to take, and take it.
async def process_message(message, metadata):
    """Decide on an action for a chat message.

    Arguments:
        message (str): The body of the chat message
        metadata (dict): Data about who sent the message,
                         the time and channel.
    """

    reply = None
```

```
    for test, action in ACTION_MAP.items():
        if message.startswith(test):
            reply = await action(message[len(test):] metadata)
            break

    if reply:
        post_to_slack(reply, metadata)

# Process the weather action
async def weather_action(text, metadata):
    if text:
        location = text.strip()
    else:
        with user_dal() as ud:
            user = ud.get_user_by_slack_id(metadata[metadata["sender"]])
            if user.location:
                location = user.location
            else:
                return "I don't know where you are."

    return await fetch_weather(location)
```

We see that our `weather_action` function gets all the information it needs from the `process_message`, but it also needs to understand how to parse the text received as part of the message, and how to interpret the metadata about replying. Ideally only the function that replies needs to understand that metadata. If we wanted to turn the weather feature into a microservice, then we would need to have some way of understanding the messages from different sources, which would require reading the User table to learn where someone is if they haven't told us during the query. We can refactor this to make the function call very clear with regards to what data it needs.

First, it's not easy to test the way in which the location is extracted from the received message. Two new specialist functions should help with that, and ensure that these are more easily tested—the text processing in `extract_location` only relies on its inputs, and `fetch_user_location` is now just a database lookup, which we can mock in testing:

```
async def extract_location(text):
    """Extract location information from free-form text."""
    return re.sub(r'^weather (in )?', '', text)
```

```
async def fetch_user_location(slack_id):
    location = None
    with user_dal() as ud:
            user = ud.get_user_by_slack_id(metadata[metadata["sender"])
        location = user.location
    return location
```

The ability to generate a more complex analysis of the text to find a location within it is now easier too, as it can be done without affecting any other code. What should call these two functions? The answer is a new pre-processor that can accept the freeform text of a message written by a human and try to structure the data within it. We will also adjust our weather action so that it is now very simple and calls a function that performs the web request we need, and passes that text on to the component that sends messages back to Slack:

```
async def process_weather_action(text, metadata):
    potential_location = await extract_location(text)
    if not potential_location:
        potential_location = await fetch_user_
location(metadata["sender"])
    if potential_location:
        await weather_action(potential_location, metadata)
    else:
        await send_response("I don't know where you are", metadata)

async def weather_action(location, metadata):
    reply = await fetch_weather(location)
    await send_response(reply, metadata)
```

Now, when the time comes to move to a microservice, we have a clear model of what the microservice should accept and what data it needs to return. Because the function call can be replaced with one that will perform a web-based query with the same well-structured data, we can incorporate this data into our tests and become more confident that the new microservice will operate as expected. We are also changing the way responses are sent, so that we do not rely on the code that called weather_action, but can instead pass a message on to a dedicated handler. Once we swap to a microservice, the calling code no longer needs to wait for a reply.

Feature Flags

Changing a large codebase often involves multiple large patches, which in professional environments will be reviewed by peers before they are accepted and merged. With large changes, it can be confusing when you must determine exactly which set of patches must exist in order for a new feature to work. Even worse, if something goes wrong and the changes need to be reverted, this can cause problems in a fast-moving environment where others may have already made new changes that make assumptions about what is already there.

A feature flag is a configuration option that exists purely to turn a specific feature on or off. They operate in a similar way to normal configuration options, letting you choose the behavior of the software, but they primarily exist to help with new features, fixes, and migrations. Instead of coordinating multiple large software patches, those changes can arrive in production whenever is most convenient, and they will not be used unless a new configuration option is turned on.

Turning a new feature on is then simply a case of adjusting the configuration file — whether that's through a new release, some configuration management software, or updating a service discovery tool such as **etcd** (https://etcd.io/), which we discuss in *Chapter 10, Deploying on AWS*. There will also be situations — despite all the careful planning — in which you need to turn off a new behavior in a hurry. A feature flag means that this is a simple operation, easily understood by anyone who has to review and understands the change.

A feature flag does not have to be an all-or-nothing switch. Given a choice between either a "call a local function" or "make a web request" path, it could be told to send 99% of the traffic to the first path and 1% to the second to let you examine how successful those queries are. A migration can continue slowly, gradually increasing the proportion of traffic going to the new code. You could also choose to duplicate calls and send real traffic to a test system to see how it copes under the load.

Implementing a feature flag should not be complicated — the code only exists while the migration is happening, after all. A simple on/off flag and a router for a proportion of traffic can be as simple as the following examples. The first example will swap to the new worker completely when the configuration value changes, and the second is configured to send a percentage of the traffic to the new worker to allow a controlled rollout of the new code:

```
@app.route("/migrating_endpoint")
async def migration_example():
    if current_app.config.get("USE_NEW_WORKER"):
```

```
        return await new_worker()
    else:
        return await original_worker()


@app.route("/migrating_gradually")
async def migrating_gradually_example():
    percentage_split = current_app.config.get("NEW_WORKER_PERCENTAGE")
    if percentage_split and random.randint(1,100) <= percentage_split:
        return await new_worker()
    else:
        return await original_worker()
```

Using Prometheus, we can monitor the migration. *Figure 5.2* is an example of a graph showing how the rate of the original_worker and new_worker calls that our application performs change over time with respect to the number of requests they process, as we steadily increase the percentage of calls that should use the new function.

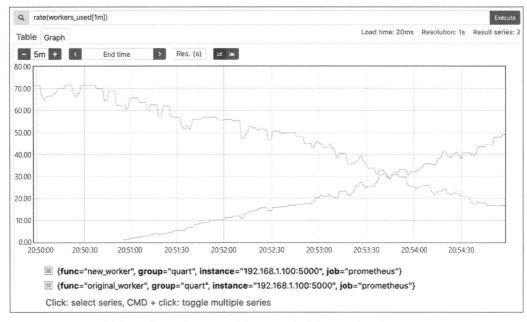

Figure 5.2: Using Prometheus to track how a gradual feature migration is progressing

Once a new feature is stable, the default state for the configuration option can be changed—until now, if the option is missing, the feature is off. By now it should be safe to assume that if the option is missing, it should be turned on. This should catch any piece of the code that is not using the configuration properly! It will let you remove the feature flag, and also let you remove the old version of the feature and any code that checks the flag, finishing a migration.

Refactoring Jeeves

Examining Jeeves to see what aspects could be improved as a microservice, we might discover some external queries are slowing down our responses or using too many resources.

However, we also discover a more fundamental change to the architecture. Responding to an incoming message is purely for the benefit of Slack's infrastructure, as the user does not see that message. Sending messages to Slack is independent of receiving messages, and so those two elements could be separate services. Instead of a monolithic application, we could have a microservice that simply accepts incoming messages, and routes them appropriately to other microservices that perform the actions the user has asked for. Then those services can all contact a microservice that specializes in sending messages to Slack.

Some of these services will need to contact the database, and if we were to keep our current database architecture then each of these new microservices would need the database models. This is a tightly coupled design, meaning that any change in the database schema will need to be duplicated in all these new services, and the deployment managed so that the old and new versions are not running at the same time. To prevent this, we can convert our database into its own microservice, and set it up to answer the questions we know it will get.

No other service needs to know the internal structure of the data, as it must simply know where to ask, and that the answer will always be structured the same way—or be obvious through a version marker in the data that it should read differently.

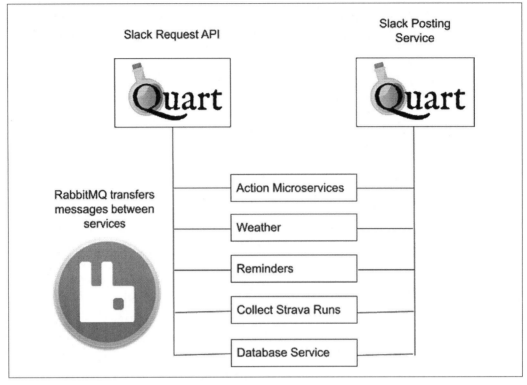

Figure 5.3: Our new microservice architecture; the Celery workers are left out for simplicity

This has an additional benefit: All these microservices can be used by any other tool. We could have a service that receives email, or messages through Signal and Telegram, or reads an IRC channel, and each of those could parse and understand the incoming messages, package up some instructions on how to reply, and send them on to the right service to perform the actions.

With the microservice version of the architecture, we can respond quickly to the needs of the organization and start controlling services, while also processing data in a consistent way, and allowing people flexibility in how they make automated requests and get notified of the results.

Let us look at the workflow in more detail.

Workflow

Everything looks the same from Slack's perspective. When a user types a message, the URL we have configured will be sent some JSON-formatted information. This data is received by our Slack Request API, which is where all the Slack message processing happens, and where we choose the right microservice as a destination. We also build a data structure that can contain information about where to send a reply that will act as an envelope for our message. The action processing services don't need to understand it, but the tools that post a reply to Slack do—and in the future, other ways to reply can be added with their own information in this metadata.

If our Slack Request service then makes a web request to the microservice, we must wait for it to respond, accounting for the time it has to wait for all the calls it makes. This can make our API very slow; its toleration of faults is also poor, as in the event of components breaking the entire chain falls apart and the message is lost.

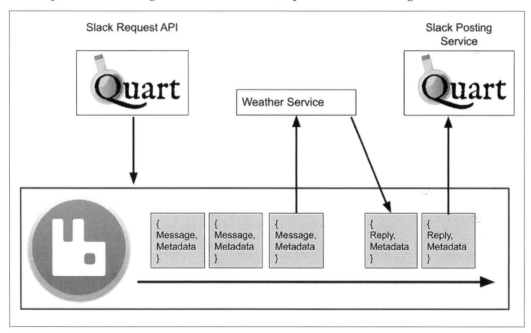

Figure 5.4: How messages traverse the new microservices architecture

Thankfully, we have a message queue! Instead of directly calling each step in sequence, we can pass a message to RabbitMQ and immediately return an appropriate status code to Slack's infrastructure. It will accept the messages and ensure that they are delivered to workers that can perform the actions we need.

If one of our workers has a failure, the messages will queue up and still be there when we come back online—unless we tell them to expire after a certain period of time.

Once a reply has been created, we can then use RabbitMQ again and send a message to the Slack Posting service. We gain the same reliability improvements using the message queue as we do for the incoming messages, only now they are more resilient in the event of any failures.

Summary

In this chapter, we have discussed how to examine a monolithic service and determine which components should be converted to microservices, along with what sort of metrics to collect to allow us to gain a good understanding of a service's operational health and capacity.

This splitting process should be conservative and iterative, otherwise it is quite easy to end up with a system where the overhead for building and maintaining microservices outweighs the benefits of splitting an application up.

However, we have moved from a single application to many that need to interact with each other. Every link in *Figure 5.4* can be a weak point for your application. What happens, for instance, if RabbitMQ goes down, or if there is a network split between the message processor and the Slack Posting service? We also need to consider how quickly our application responds to external requests, so that if a caller does not need to wait around for a response then they do not have to.

The same question goes for every new network link that was added to our architecture. We need to be resilient when something goes wrong. We need to know where we are and what to do when a service that was down is back online.

All these problems are addressed in the next chapter.

6

Interacting with Other Services

In the previous chapter, our monolithic application was split up into several microservices, and consequently, more network interactions between the different parts were included.

More interactions with other components can lead to complications of their own, however, such as a high volume of messages or large data sizes delaying responses, or long-running tasks taking up valuable resources. Since many of our useful tasks involve interacting with third-party services, the techniques to manage these changes are useful both inside our application and for communicating outside of it. Having the ability to loosely couple different parts of the system using some asynchronous messages is useful to prevent blockages and unwanted dependency entanglements.

In any case, the bottom line is that we need to interact with other services through the network, both synchronously and asynchronously. These interactions need to be efficient, and when something goes wrong, we need to have a plan.

The other problem introduced by adding more network connections is **testing**: how do we test a microservice in isolation that also needs to call other microservices to function? In this chapter, we will explore this in detail:

- How one service can call another using synchronous and asynchronous libraries, and how to make these calls more efficient
- How a service can use messages to make asynchronous calls and communicate with other services via events

- We will also see some techniques to test services that have network dependencies

Calling other web resources

As we have seen in the previous chapters, synchronous interactions between microservices can be done via HTTP APIs using JSON payloads. This is by far the pattern most often used, because both HTTP and JSON are common standards. If your web service implements an HTTP API that accepts JSON, any developer using any programming language will be able to use it. Most of these interfaces are also RESTful, meaning that they follow the **Representational State Transfer (REST)** architecture principles of being stateless—with each interaction containing all the information needed instead of relying on previous exchanges—as well as cacheable and having a well-defined interface.

Following a RESTful scheme is not a requirement, however, and some projects implement **Remote Procedure Call (RPC)** APIs, which focus on the action being performed and abstract away the network requests from the code that handles the messages. In REST, the focus is on the resource, and actions are defined by HTTP methods. Some projects are a mix of both and don't strictly follow a given standard. The most important thing is that your service behavior should be consistent and well-documented. This book leans on REST rather than RPC, but is not strict about it, and recognizes that different situations have different solutions.

Sending and receiving JSON payloads is the simplest way for a microservice to interact with others, and only requires microservices to know the entry points and parameters to pass using HTTP requests.

To do this, you just need to use an HTTP client. Python has one as part of the `http. client` module, and in a synchronous Python environment, the `Requests` library is rightfully popular: `https://docs.python-requests.org`.

As we are in an asynchronous environment, we will use `aiohttp`, which has a clean way of creating asynchronous web requests and offers built-in features that make it easier to perform multiple simultaneous asynchronous requests: `https://docs. aiohttp.org/en/stable/`.

HTTP requests in the `aiohttp` library are built around the concept of a session, and the best way to use it is to call `CreateSession`, creating a `Session` object that can be reused every time you interact with any service.

A `Session` object can hold authentication information and some default headers you may want to set for all requests that your application will make. It can also control default error handling behavior, storing cookies, and what timeouts to use. In the following example, the call to `ClientSession` will create an object with the right `Content-Type` headers:

```python
# clientsession.py
import asyncio
import aiohttp

async def make_request(url):
    headers = {
        "Content-Type": "application/json",
    }
    async with aiohttp.ClientSession(headers=headers) as session:
        async with session.get(url) as response:
            print(await response.text())


url = "http://localhost:5000/api"
loop = asyncio.get_event_loop()
loop.run_until_complete(make_request(url))
```

If we should limit how many concurrent requests are being made to an external endpoint, there are two main approaches. `aiohttp` has a concept of connectors, and we can set options to control how many outgoing TCP connections a `session` can operate at once, as well as limiting those numbers for a single destination:

```python
conn = aiohttp.TCPConnector(limit=300, limit_per_host=10)
session = aiohttp.ClientSession(connector=conn)
```

This might be enough for our needs; however, if we make several outgoing connections to complete one request, we could end up in a situation where each piece of work is continuously blocking after each one as we reach the limit. Ideally, we would like a discrete chunk of work to continue until it's done, and for that we can use a semaphore. A semaphore is a simple token that gives code permission to perform a task. If we were to add a semaphore with three slots, then the first three tasks that try to access the semaphore will take a slot each and carry on. Any other task that requests the semaphore will have to wait until one of the slots is free.

Since the most common way to request a semaphore is inside a `with` block, this means that as soon as the context of the `with` block is over, the semaphore is released — inside the semaphore object's __exit__ function:

```python
# clientsession_list.py
import asyncio
import aiohttp
async def make_request(url, session, semaphore):
    async with semaphore, session.get(url) as response:
        print(f"Fetching {url}")
        await asyncio.sleep(1)   # Pretend there is real work happening
        return await response.text()

async def organise_requests(url_list):
    semaphore = asyncio.Semaphore(3)
    tasks = list()

    async with aiohttp.ClientSession() as session:
        for url in url_list:
            tasks.append(make_request(url, session, semaphore))
        await asyncio.gather(*tasks)

urls = [
    "https://www.google.com",
    "https://developer.mozilla.org/en-US/",
    "https://www.packtpub.com/",
    "https://aws.amazon.com/",
]
loop = asyncio.get_event_loop()
loop.run_until_complete(organise_requests(urls))
```

Let us now see how we can generalize this pattern in a Quart app that needs to interact with other services.

This naive implementation is based on the hypothesis that everything will go smoothly, but real life is rarely so easy. We can set up different error handling options in a `ClientSession`, such as retries and timeouts, and we only need to set them up in that one place.

Finding out where to go

When we make a web request to a service, we need to know which **Uniform Resource Locator (URL)** to use. Most of the examples in this book use hardcoded URLs—that is, they are written into the source code. This is nice and easy to read for an example, but can be a problem when maintaining software. What happens when a service gets a new URI, and its hostname or IP address changes? It might move between AWS regions due to a failure or be migrated from Google Cloud Platform to Microsoft Azure. An API update can make the path to a resource change, even if the hostname or IP address has not updated.

We want to pass in data about which URLs to use as configuration to our application. There are several options to manage more configuration options without adding them directly to the code, such as environment variables and service discovery.

Environment variables

Container-based environments are common these days, and we will discuss them in more detail in *Chapter 10, Deploying on AWS*. The most common approach to get configuration options into a container is to pass the container some environment variables. This has the advantage of being straightforward, since the code just needs to examine the environment when processing its configuration:

```python
import os

def create_app(name=__name__, blueprints=None, settings=None):
    app = Quart(name)
    app.config["REMOTE_URL"] = os.environ.get("OTHER_SERVICE_URL",
"https://default.url/here")
```

The downside to this approach is that if the URL changes, then we need to restart the application—and sometimes redeploy it—with the new environment. If you don't expect the configuration to change very often, environment variables are still a good idea due to their simplicity, although we must be careful to not record any secrets that are in environment variables when we log messages.

Service discovery

But what if we did not need to tell our service about all its options when we deploy it? Service discovery is an approach that involves configuring an application with just a few pieces of information: where to ask for configuration and how to identify the right questions to ask.

Services such as etcd (https://etcd.io/) provide a reliable key-value store in which to keep this configuration data. For example, let's use etcd to store the URL of the production and development RabbitMQ instances:

```
$ etcdctl put myservice/production/rabbitmq/url https://my.rabbitmq.
url/
OK
$ etcdctl get myservice/production/rabbitmq/url
myservice/production/rabbitmq/url
https://my.rabbitmq.url/
```

When an application starts up, it can check to see whether it is running in production or in a local development environment and ask etcd for the right value—either myservice/production/rabbitmq/url or myservice/development/rabbitmq/url. With a single option in a deployment, it is possible to change a whole number of configuration options, use different external URLs, bind to different ports, or any other piece of configuration you might think of.

It's also possible to update the values in etcd, and when your application next checks for a new value, it will update and use that instead. Deploying a new version of RabbitMQ can now be done alongside the old version, and the swap will be a value change in etcd—or a change back if it goes wrong.

This approach does add complexity, both as an extra service to run and in terms of updating these values within your application, but it can be a valuable approach in more dynamic environments. We will discuss service discovery more in *Chapter 10, Deploying on AWS*, when we cover deploying an application on containers and in the cloud.

Transferring data

JSON is a human-readable data format. There is a long history of human-readable data transfer on the internet—a good example would be email, as you can quite happily type out the protocol needed to send an email as a human author. This readability is useful for determining exactly what is happening in your code and its connections, especially as JSON maps directly onto Python data structures.

The downside to this readability is the size of the data. Sending HTTP requests and responses with JSON payloads can add some bandwidth overhead in the long run, and serializing and deserializing data from Python objects to JSON structures also adds a bit of CPU overhead.

There are other ways to transfer data that involve caching, compression, binary payloads, or RPC, however.

HTTP cache headers

In the HTTP protocol, there are a few cache mechanisms that can be used to indicate to a client that a page that it's trying to fetch has not changed since its last visit. Caching is something we can do in our microservices on all the read-only API endpoints, such as GETs and HEADs.

The simplest way to implement it is to return, along with a result, an ETag header in the response. An ETag value is a string that can be considered as a version for the resource the client is trying to get. It can be a timestamp, an incremental version, or a hash. It's up to the server to decide what to put in it, but the idea is that it should be unique to the value of the response.

Like web browsers, when the client fetches a response that contains such a header, it can build a local dictionary cache that stores the response bodies and ETags as its values, and the URLs as its keys.

When making a new request, the client can look in its local cache and pass along a stored ETag value in the If-Modified-Since header. If the server sends back a 304 status code, it means that the response has not changed, and the client can use the previously stored one.

This mechanism can greatly reduce the response times from the server, since it can immediately return an empty 304 response when the content has not changed. If it has changed, the client gets the full message in the usual way.

Of course, this means the services that you are calling should implement this caching behavior by adding the proper ETag support. It's not possible to implement a generic solution for this because the cache logic depends on the nature of the data your service is managing. The rule of thumb is to version each resource and change that version every time the data changes. In the following example, the Quart app uses the current server time to create ETag values associated with users' entries. The ETag value is the current time since the epoch, in milliseconds, and is stored in the modified field.

The get_user() method returns a user entry from _USERS and sets the ETag value with response.set_etag. When the view gets some calls, it also looks for the If-None-Match header to compare it to the user's modified field, and returns a 304 response if it matches:

```
# quart_etag.py
from datetime import datetime

from quart import Quart, Response, abort, jsonify, request
```

```
app = Quart(__name__)

def _time2etag():
    return datetime.now().isoformat()

_USERS = {"1": {"name": "Simon", "modified": _time2etag()}}

@app.route("/api/user/<user_id>")
async def get_user(user_id):
    if user_id not in _USERS:
        return abort(404)
    user = _USERS[user_id]

    # returning 304 if If-None-Match matches
    if user["modified"] in request.if_none_match:
        return Response("Not modified", status=304)

    resp = jsonify(user)

    # setting the ETag
    resp.set_etag(user["modified"])
    return resp

if __name__ == "__main__":
    app.run()
```

The change_user() view sets a new modified value when the client modifies a user. In the following client session, we're changing the user, while also making sure that we get a 304 response when providing the new ETag value:

```
$ curl -v http://127.0.0.1:5000/api/user/1
*   Trying 127.0.0.1...
...
< HTTP/1.1 200
< content-type: application/json
< content-length: 56
< etag: "2021-06-29T21:32:25.685907"
< date: Tue, 29 Jun 2021 20:32:30 GMT
< server: hypercorn-h11
<
* Connection #0 to host 127.0.0.1 left intact
```

```
{"modified":"2021-06-29T21:32:25.685907","name":"Simon"}


  $ curl -v -H 'If-None-Match: 2021-06-29T21:32:25.685907'
http://127.0.0.1:5000/api/user/1
...
< HTTP/1.1 304
...
```

This demonstration is a toy implementation that might not work well in production; relying on a server clock to store `ETag` values means you are sure that the clock is never set back in time and that if you have several servers, their clocks are all synchronized with a service, such as ntpdate.

There is also the problem of race conditions if two requests change the same entry within the same millisecond. Depending on your app, it may not be an issue, but then again if it is, then it may be a big one. A cleaner option is to have the modified field handled by your database system directly, and make sure its changes are done in serialized transactions. Sending the `ETag` with a `POST` request is also a good precaution against a race between concurrent updates — the server can use the `ETag` to verify what version of the data the client wants to update from, and if that version doesn't match, it is probably unsafe to update the data, as someone else has changed it first.

Some developers use hash functions for their `ETag` value because it's easy to compute in a distributed architecture, and it doesn't introduce any of the problems timestamps have. But calculating a hash has a CPU cost, and it means you need to pull the whole entry to do it — so it might be as slow as if you were sending back the actual data. That said, with a dedicated table in your database for all your hashes, you can probably come up with a solution that makes your `304` response fast in its return.

As we said earlier, there is no generic solution to implement an efficient HTTP cache logic — but it's worth implementing one if your client is doing a lot of reads on your service. When you have no choice but to send some data back, there are several ways to make it as efficient as possible, as we will see in the next section.

GZIP compression

Compression is an overarching term for reducing the size of data in such a way that the original data can be recovered. There are many different compression algorithms — some of them are general-purpose algorithms that can be used on any sort of data, while some of them are specialized to particular data formats and achieve very good results due to them making assumptions about how the data is structured.

There are trade-offs to make between the size of the compressed data, the speed of compression and decompression, and how widely implemented the compression algorithm is. It might be acceptable to spend a few minutes compressing a large data file if it spends most of its time being stored, as the space savings outweigh the access time taken, but for data that is short-lived or regularly accessed, then the overhead of compression and decompression is more important. For our purposes, we need a compression algorithm that is widely understood by different environments, even if it doesn't always achieve the smallest end result.

GZIP compression is available on almost every single system, and web servers such as Apache or nginx provide native support to compress responses that pass through them—which is far better than implementing your own ad hoc compression at the level of Python. It's important to remember that while this will save network bandwidth, it will use more CPU, and so experimenting with metrics collection activated will let us see the results—and decide whether this option is a good idea.

For example, this nginx configuration will enable GZIP compression for any response produced by the Quart app on port 5000, with an application/json content type:

```
http {
    gzip  on;
    gzip_types application/json;
    gzip_proxied        any;
    gzip_vary .on;

    server {
        listen          80;
        server_name   localhost;

        location / {
            proxy_pass http://localhost:5000;
        }
    }
}
```

From the client side, making an HTTP request to the nginx server at localhost:8080, proxying for the application at localhost:5000 with an Accept-Encoding: gzip header, will trigger the compression:

```
$ curl http://localhost:8080/api -H "Accept-Encoding: gzip"
<some binary output>
```

In Python, requests made using the aiohttp and requests libraries will automatically decompress responses that are GZIP-encoded, so you don't have to worry about doing this when your service is calling another service.

Decompressing the data adds some processing, but Python's GZIP module relies on zlib (http://www.zlib.net/), which is very fast. To accept compressed responses to HTTP queries, we just need to add a header indicating we can deal with a GZIP-encoded response:

```python
import asyncio
import aiohttp

async def make_request():
    url = "http://127.0.0.1:5000/api"
    headers = {
        "Accept-Encoding": "gzip",
    }
    async with aiohttp.ClientSession(headers=headers) as session:
        async with session.get(url) as response:
            print(await response.text())

loop = asyncio.get_event_loop()
loop.run_until_complete(make_request())
```

To compress the data that you are sending to the server, you can use the gzip module and specify a Content-Encoding header:

```python
import asyncio
import gzip
import json

import aiohttp

async def make_request():
    url = "http://127.0.0.1:8080/api_post"
    headers = {
        "Content-Encoding": "gzip",
    }
    data = {"Hello": "World!", "result": "OK"}
    data = bytes(json.dumps(data), "utf8")
    data = gzip.compress(data)
    async with aiohttp.ClientSession(headers=headers) as session:
        async with session.post(url, data=data) as response:
            print(await response.text())

loop = asyncio.get_event_loop()
loop.run_until_complete(make_request())
```

In that case, however, you will get the zipped content in your Quart application, and you will need to decompress it in your Python code, or if you are using an nginx proxy that handles incoming web connections, nginx can decompress the requests for you. We discuss nginx in more detail in *Chapter 10, Deploying on AWS*. To summarize, setting up GZIP compression for all your service responses is a low-effort change with nginx, and your Python client can benefit from it by setting the right header. Sending compressed data is a little more complicated however, because the work isn't done for you—but it may still have benefits for large data transfers.

If you want to further reduce the size of HTTP request/response payloads, another option is to switch from JSON to binary payloads. That way, you do not have to deal with compression, and processing the data may be faster, but the message size reduction is not as good.

Protocol Buffers

While it is usually not relevant, if your microservice deals with a lot of data, using an alternative format can be an attractive option to increase performance, and decrease the required network bandwidth without having to use extra processing power and time compressing and decompressing the data. Two widely used binary formats are **Protocol Buffers** (**protobuf**) (`https://developers.google.com/protocol-buffers`) and **MessagePack**.

Protocol Buffers requires you to describe data that's being exchanged into some schema that will be used to index the binary content. The schemas add some work because all data that is transferred will need to be described in a schema, and you will need to learn a new **Domain-Specific Language** (**DSL**). In a typed language, such as Rust, C++, or Go, defining these structures is something that already has to be done, so the overhead is far less.

However, the advantages are that the messages are well defined and can be easily validated before either end of the network conversation attempts to use the information. It is also possible to generate code for various languages—including Python—that let you construct the data in a way that is more suitable for the language being used. The following example is taken from the protobuf documentation:

```
syntax = "proto2";
package tutorial;

message Person {
  required string name = 1;
  required int32 id = 2;
```

```
    optional string email = 3;

    enum PhoneType {
      MOBILE = 0;
      HOME = 1;
      WORK = 2;
    }

    message PhoneNumber {
      required string number = 1;
      optional PhoneType type = 2 [default = HOME];
    }

    repeated PhoneNumber phones = 4;
  }

  message AddressBook {
    repeated Person people = 1;
  }
```

The schema is not very Pythonic, as it is intended to support multiple languages and environments. If you interact with statically typed languages or would like a feature to do basic syntax checking on data for you, then a definition like this may be helpful.

Using Protocol Buffers with a framework such as gRPC (`https://grpc.io/`) can abstract away the network interaction from your application, and instead provide a client with a function call in Python and little need to consider how it generates its return value.

MessagePack

Unlike Protocol Buffers, MessagePack (`http://msgpack.org/`) is schemaless, and can serialize your data by just calling a function. It's a simple alternative to JSON, and has implementations in most languages. The `msgpack` Python library (installed using the `pip install msgpack-python` command) offers the same level of integration as JSON:

```
>>> import msgpack
>>> data = {"this": "is", "some": "data"}
>>> msgpack.packb(data, use_bin_type=True)
b'\x82\xa4this\xa2is\xa4some\xa4data'
```

```
>>> msgpack.unpackb(msgpack.packb(data, use_bin_type=True))
{'this': 'is', 'some': 'data'}
```

Using MessagePack is simple compared to protobuf, but which one is faster and provides the best compression ratio depends a lot on your data. In some rare cases, plain JSON might be even quicker to serialize than a binary format.

In terms of compression, you can expect 10% to 20% compression with MessagePack, but if your JSON contains a lot of strings—which is often the case in microservices—GZIP will perform much better.

In the following example, a huge JSON payload of 48 KB that contains a lot of strings is converted using MessagePack and JSON and then GZIPped in both cases:

```
>>> sys.getsizeof(json.dumps(data))
35602
>>> sys.getsizeof(msgpack.packb(data))
30777
>>> sys.getsizeof(gzip.compress(bytes(json.dumps(data), 'utf8')))
3138
>>> sys.getsizeof(gzip.compress(msgpack.packb(data)))
3174
```

Using MessagePack reduces the size of the payload by approximately 14%, but GZIP is making it 11 times smaller with both JSON and MessagePack payloads!

It's clear that whatever format you are using, the best way to reduce the payload sizes is to use GZIP—and if your web server does not deal with decompression, it's straightforward in Python thanks to `gzip.uncompress()`.

Message serialization often only supports basic data types, as they must remain unaware of what environment is running in both the source and destination. This means that they cannot encode data that might be commonly used in Python, such as `datetime` objects to represent time. While other languages have date and time representation, it is not done in the same way, and so data like this and other Python objects need to be converted into a serializable form that other platforms can understand. For date and time, common options include an integer representing epoch time (the number of seconds since 1st January 1970) or a string in ISO8601 format, such as 2021-03-01T13:31:03+00:00.

In any case, in a world of microservices where JSON is the most accepted standard, taking care of dates is a minor annoyance to stick with a universally adopted standard.

Unless all your services are in Python with well-defined structures, and you need to speed up the serialization steps as much as possible, it is probably simpler to stick with JSON.

Putting it together

Before moving on, we will quickly recall what we have covered so far:

- Implementing HTTP cache headers is a great way to speed up repeated requests for data
- GZIP compression is an efficient way to lessen the size of requests and responses and is easy to set up
- Binary protocols are an attractive alternative to plain JSON, but it does depend on the situation

The next section will focus on asynchronous calls; everything your microservice can do that goes beyond the request/response pattern.

Asynchronous messages

In microservice architecture, asynchronous calls play a fundamental role when a process that is used to be performed in a single application now implicates several microservices. We touched briefly on this in the previous chapter with our change to the Jeeves application, which now communicates with its workers using an asynchronous message queue. To make the best use of these, we will investigate these tools in more depth.

Asynchronous calls can be as simple as a separate thread or process within a microservice app that is receiving some work to be done, and performs it without interfering with the HTTP request/response round trips that are happening at the same time.

But doing everything directly from the same Python process is not very robust. What happens if the process crashes and gets restarted? How do we scale background tasks if they are built like that?

It's much more reliable to send a message that gets picked by another program, and let the microservice focus on its primary goal, which is to serve responses to clients. If a web request does not need an immediate answer, an endpoint in our service can then become code that accepts an HTTP request, processes it, and passes it on, and its response to the client is now whether or not our service has successfully received the request rather than whether the request has been processed.

In the previous chapter, we looked at how Celery could be used to build a microservice that gets some work from a message broker like RabbitMQ. In that design, the Celery worker blocks—that is, it halts operation while it is waiting—until a new message is added to the RabbitMQ queue.

Message queue reliability

As with any distributed system, there are considerations with regard to reliability and consistency. Ideally, we would like to add a message to the queue and have it delivered—and acted upon—exactly once. In practice this is almost impossible to achieve in a distributed system, as components fail, experiencing high latency or packet loss, while all sorts of complex interactions occur.

We have two real choices, encoded in RabbitMQ's delivery strategies: "at-most-once" and "at-least-once."

A strategy to deliver a message at most once will not account for any unreliability in the message delivery system or failures in a worker. Once a worker has accepted the message, that is it: the message queue forgets about it. If the worker then suffers a failure and does not complete the chunk of work it has been given, that is something the wider system needs to cope with.

With a promise to deliver a message at least once, in the case of any failures the deliveries will be attempted again until a worker both accepts the message and acknowledges that it has acted upon it. This ensures that no data is lost, but it does mean that there are situations where the message can be delivered to more than one worker, and so some sort of **universally unique identifier** (**UUID**) is a good idea, so that while some work may be duplicated, it can be deduplicated when it is written to any database or storage. A wider discussion of distributed system reliability and consensus protocols like PAXOS would require a book of its own.

Basic queues

The pattern used by Celery workers is a push-pull tasks queue. One service pushes messages into a specific queue, and some workers pick them up from the other end and perform an action on them. Each task goes to a single worker. Consider the following diagram, shown in *Figure 6.1*.

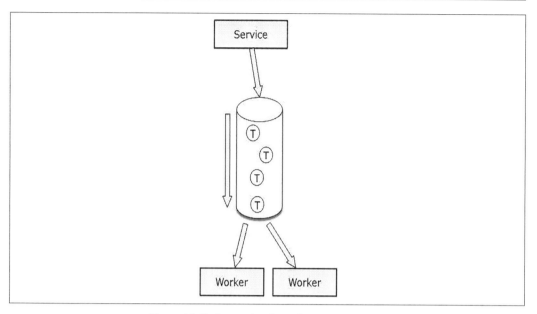

Figure 6.1: Tasks passing through a message queue

There is no bidirectional communication—the sender merely deposits a message in the queue and leaves. The next available worker gets the next message. This blind, unidirectional message passing is perfect when you want to perform some asynchronous parallel tasks, which makes it easy to scale.

In addition, once the sender has confirmed that the message was added to the broker, we can have message brokers—such as RabbitMQ—offer some message persistence. In other words, if all workers go offline, we don't lose the messages that are in the queue.

Topic exchanges and queues

Topics are a way of filtering and classifying messages that travel through the queue. When using topics, each message is sent with an extra label that helps to identify what sort of message it is, and our workers can subscribe to specific topics, or patterns that match several topics.

Let's imagine a scenario where we are releasing a mobile app to the Android Play Store and the Apple App Store. When our automation tasks finish building the Android app, we can send a message with a routing key of `publish.playstore`, so that RabbitMQ can route this message to the right topics. The reason that there is a difference between a routing key and a topic is that a topic can match a pattern. The worker that is capable of publishing files to the Play Store can subscribe to the topic `publish.playstore` and get its workload from those messages, but we could also have a queue for messages matching `publish.*` and a worker that sends notifications whenever something is about to be uploaded to the Play Store, the App Store, or any other place you might publish software.

In our microservices, this means we can have specialized workers that all register to the same messaging broker and get a subset of the messages that are added to it.

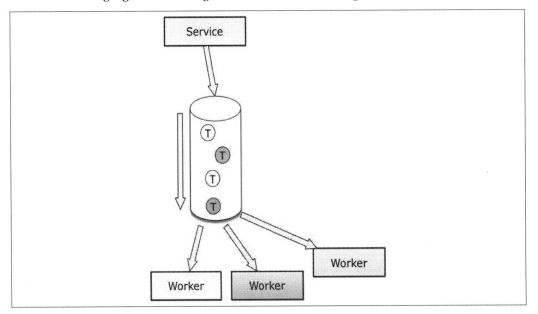

Figure 6.2: Tasks of different types passing through a message queue

This sort of behavior exists in most message queue services, in slightly different forms. Let's look at how to set this up in RabbitMQ.

To install a **RabbitMQ** broker, you can look at the download page at `http://www.rabbitmq.com/download.html`.

Running the container should be enough for any local experiments. RabbitMQ implements the **Advanced Message Queuing Protocol (AMQP)**. This protocol, described at `http://www.amqp.org/`, is a complete standard that has been developed for years by a group of companies working together.

AMQP is organized into three concepts: queues, exchanges, and bindings:

- A queue is a recipient that holds messages and waits for consumers to pick them
- An exchange is an entry point for publishers to add new messages to the system
- A binding defines how messages are routed from exchanges to queues

For our topic queue, we need to set one exchange, so RabbitMQ accepts new messages, and all the queues we want for workers to pick messages. Between those two ends, we want to route the messages to the different queues, depending on the topics, using a binding.

Let's look at how we would set up our app publishing example from earlier. We will assume we have two workers: one that publishes Android applications, and the other that sends notifications, such as updating a website or sending an email. Using the `rabbitmqadmin` command line that gets installed with RabbitMQ, we can create all the necessary parts. If the admin command does not come installed, you can find instructions on installing it at `https://www.rabbitmq.com/management-cli.html`:

```
$ rabbitmqadmin declare exchange name=incoming type=topic
exchange declared

$ rabbitmqadmin declare queue name=playstore
queue declared

$ rabbitmqadmin declare queue name=notifications
queue declared

$ rabbitmqadmin declare binding source="incoming" destination_
type="queue" destination="playstore" routing_key="publish.playstore"
binding declared

$ rabbitmqadmin declare binding source="incoming" destination_
type="queue" destination="notifications" routing_key="publish.*"
binding declared
```

In this setup, whenever a message is sent to RabbitMQ—and if the topic starts with `publish`—it will be sent to the notifications queue; and if it is `publish.playstore`, then it will end up in both the notifications and playstore queues. Any other topics will cause the message to be discarded.

To interact with RabbitMQ in the code, we can use **Pika**. This is a Python RPC client that implements all the RPC endpoints that a Rabbit service publishes: `https://pika.readthedocs.io`.

Everything we do with Pika can be done on the command line using `rabbitmqadmin`. You can directly get the status of all parts of the system, send and receive messages, and check what's in a queue. It is an excellent way to experiment with your messaging setup.

The following script shows how to publish two messages in RabbitMQ in the incoming exchange. One concerns a new app being published, and the other is about a newsletter:

```python
from pika import BlockingConnection, BasicProperties

# assuming there's a working local RabbitMQ server with a working
# guest/guest account
def message(topic, message):
    connection = BlockingConnection()
    try:
        channel = connection.channel()
        props = BasicProperties(content_type="text/plain", delivery_mode=1)
        channel.basic_publish("incoming", topic, message, props)
    finally:
        connection.close()

message("publish.playstore", "We are publishing an Android App!")

message("publish.newsletter", "We are publishing a newsletter!")
```

These RPC calls will each add one message to the incoming topic exchange. For the first message, the exchange will then add one message to the playstore queue, and for the second, two messages will be added—one to each queue. A worker script that waits for work that needs to be published to the Play Store would look like this:

```python
import pika

def on_message(channel, method_frame, header_frame, body):
    print(f"Now publishing to the play store: {body}!")
    channel.basic_ack(delivery_tag=method_frame.delivery_tag)

connection = pika.BlockingConnection()
channel = connection.channel()
```

```
channel.basic_consume("playstore", on_message)
try:
    channel.start_consuming()
except KeyboardInterrupt:
    channel.stop_consuming()

connection.close()
```

Notice that Pika sends back an ACK to RabbitMQ about the message, so it can be safely removed from the queue once the worker has succeeded. This is the at-least-once strategy approach to message delivery. The `notifications` receiver can be identical apart from the queue it subscribes to and what it does with the message body:

```
$ python ./playstore_receiver.py
Now publishing to the play store: b'We are publishing an Android App!'!
$ python ./publish_receiver.py
We have some news! b'We are publishing an Android App!'!
We have some news! b'We are publishing a newsletter!'!
```

AMQP offers many patterns that you can investigate to exchange messages. The tutorial page has many examples, and they are all implemented using Python and Pika: http://www.rabbitmq.com/getstarted.html.

To integrate these examples in our microservices, the publisher phase is straightforward. Your Quart application can create a connection to RabbitMQ using `pika.BlockingConnection` and send messages through it. Projects such as pika-pool (https://github.com/bninja/pika-pool) implement simple connection pools so you can manage RabbitMQ channels without having to connect/disconnect every time you are sending something through RPC.

The consumers, on the other hand, are trickier to integrate into microservices. Pika can be embedded into an event loop running in the same process as the Quart application, and trigger a function when a message is received. It will simply be another entry point into the same code, and could be run alongside a RESTful API if that's also required.

Publish/subscribe

The previous pattern has workers that handle the specific topics of messages, and the messages consumed by a worker are completely gone from the queue. We even added code to acknowledge that the message was consumed.

When you want a message to be published to several workers, however, the **Publish/ Subscribe (pubsub)** pattern needs to be used.

This pattern is the basis for building a general event system and is implemented exactly like the previous one, in which there is one exchange and several queues. The difference is that the exchange part has a fanout type.

In that setup, every queue that you bind to a fanout exchange will receive the same message. With pubsub in place, you can broadcast messages to all your microservices if necessary.

Putting it together

In this section, we have covered the following about asynchronous messaging:

- Non-blocking calls should be used every time a microservice can execute some work out of band. There's no good reason to block a request if what you are doing is not utilized in the response.

- Service-to-service communication is not always limited to task queues.

- Sending events through a message queue is a good way to prevent tightly coupled components.

- We can build a full event system around a broker—such as RabbitMQ—to make our microservices interact with each other via messages.

- RabbitMQ can be used to coordinate all the message passing, with messages sent using Pika.

Testing

As we learned in *Chapter 3, Coding, Testing, and Documentation: the Virtuous Cycle*, the biggest challenge when writing functional tests for a service that calls other services is to isolate all network calls. In this section, we'll see how we can mock asynchronous calls made using aiohttp.

Testing aiohttp and its outgoing web requests involves a different approach to traditional synchronous tests. The aioresponses project (https://github.com/ pnuckowski/aioresponses) allows you to easily create mocked responses to web requests made using an aiohttp ClientSession:

```
# test_aiohttp_fixture.py
import asyncio
import aiohttp
```

```
import pytest
from aioresponses import aioresponses


@pytest.fixture
def mock_aioresponse():
    with aioresponses() as m:
        yield m


@pytest.mark.asyncio
async def test_ctx(mock_aioresponse):
    async with aiohttp.ClientSession() as session:
        mock_aioresponse.get("http://test.example.com", payload={"foo":
"bar"})
        resp = await session.get("http://test.example.com")
        data = await resp.json()

    assert {"foo": "bar"} == data
```

In this example, we tell aioresponses that any GET request made to http://test.
example.com should return the data we specify. This way we can easily provide
mocked responses for several URLs, and even the same URL by invoking mocked.get
more than once to create multiple responses for the same endpoint.

If you are using Requests to perform all the calls—or you are using a library that
is based on Requests that does not customize it too much—this isolation work
is also easy to do thanks to the requests-mock project (https://requests-mock.
readthedocs.io), which implements mocked calls in a similar way, and likely
inspired aioresponses.

That said, mocking responses from other services is still a fair amount of work, and
can be difficult to maintain. It means that an eye needs to be kept on how the other
services are evolving over time, so your tests are not based on a mock that's no
longer a reflection of the real API.

Using mocks is encouraged to build good functional tests coverage, but make sure
you are doing integration tests as well, where the service is tested in a deployment
where it calls other services for real.

Using OpenAPI

The OpenAPI Specification (`https://www.openapis.org/`), previously known as Swagger, is a standard way of describing a set of HTTP endpoints, how they are used, and the structure of the data that is sent and received. By describing an API using a JSON or YAML file, it allows the intent to become machine-readable—this means that with an OpenAPI Specification, you can use a code generator to produce a client library in a language of your choosing, or to automatically validate data as it enters or leaves the system.

OpenAPI has the same goal that WSDL (`https://www.w3.org/TR/2001/NOTE-wsdl-20010315`) had back in the XML web services era, but it's much lighter and straight to the point.

The following example is a minimal OpenAPI description file that defines one single `/apis/users_ids` endpoint and supports the `GET` method to retrieve the list of user IDs:

```
---
openapi: "3.0.0"
info:
  title: Data Service
  description: returns info about users
  license:
    name: APLv2
    url: https://www.apache.org/licenses/LICENSE-2.0.html
  version: 0.1.0
basePath: /api
paths:
  /user_ids:
    get:
      operationId: getUserIds
      description: Returns a list of ids
      produces:
        - application/json
      responses:
        '200':
          description: List of Ids
          schema:
            type: array
            items:
              type: integer
```

The full OpenAPI Specification can be found on GitHub; it is very detailed and will let you describe metadata about the API, its endpoints, and the data types it uses: `https://github.com/OAI/OpenAPI-Specification`.

The data types described in the schema sections are following the JSON Schema specification (`http://json-schema.org/latest/json-schema-core.html`). Here, we are describing that the `/get_ids` endpoint returns an array of integers.

You can provide a lot of detail about your API in that specification—things such as what headers should be present in your requests, or what will be the content type of some responses and can be added to it.

Describing your HTTP endpoints with OpenAPI offers some excellent possibilities:

- There are a plethora of OpenAPI clients that can consume your description and do something useful with it, such as building functional tests against your service, or validating data that is sent to it.
- It provides a standard, language-agnostic documentation for your API
- The server can check that the requests and responses follow the spec

Some web frameworks even use the specification to create all the routing and I/O data checks for your microservices; for instance, Connexion (`https://github.com/zalando/connexion`) does this for Flask. Support for this within Quart is limited at the time of writing, but the situation is always improving. For this reason, we won't be using OpenAPI a great deal in the examples presented here.

There are two schools of thought when people are building HTTP APIs with OpenAPI:

- Specification-first, where you create a Swagger specification file and then create your app on top of it, using all the information provided in that specification. That's the principle behind Connexion.
- Specification-extracted, where it is your code that generates the Swagger specification file. Some toolkits out there will do this by reading your view docstrings, for instance.

Summary

In this chapter, we've looked at how a service can interact with other services synchronously, by using a Requests session, and asynchronously, by using Celery workers or more advanced messaging patterns based on RabbitMQ.

We've also looked at some ways to test a service in isolation by mocking other services, but without mocking the message brokers themselves.

Testing each service in isolation is useful, but when something goes wrong, it's hard to know what happened, particularly if the bug happens in a series of asynchronous calls.

In that case, tracking what's going on with a centralized logging system helps a lot. The next chapter will explain how we can tool our microservices to follow their activities.

7
Securing Your Services

So far in this book, all the interactions between services were done without any form of authentication or authorization; each HTTP request would happily return a result. This cannot happen in production for two simple reasons: we need to know who is calling the service (authentication), and we need to make sure that the caller is allowed to perform the call (authorization). For instance, we probably don't want an anonymous caller to delete entries in a database.

In a monolithic web application, simple authentication can happen with a login form, and once the user is identified a cookie is set with a session identifier so that the client and server can collaborate on all subsequent requests. In a microservice-based architecture, we cannot use this scheme everywhere because services are not users and won't use web forms for authentication. We need a way to accept or reject calls between services automatically.

The OAuth2 authorization protocol gives us the flexibility to add authentication and authorization in our microservices, which can be used to authenticate both users and services. In this chapter, we will discover the essential features of OAuth2 and how to implement an authentication microservice. This service will be used to secure service-to-service interactions.

A few things can be done at the code level to protect your services, such as controlling system calls, or making sure HTTP redirects are not ending up on hostile web pages. We will discuss how to add protection against badly formed data, some common pitfalls to avoid, and demonstrate how you can scan your code against potential security issues.

Lastly, securing services also means we want to filter out any suspicious or malicious network traffic before it reaches our application. We will look at setting up a basic web application firewall to defend our services.

The OAuth2 protocol

If you are reading this book, you are in all likelihood someone who has logged in to a web page with a username and password. It's a straightforward model to confirm who you are, but there are drawbacks.

Many different websites exist, and each needs to properly handle someone's identity and password. The potential for security leaks multiplies with the number of different places an identity is stored, and how many routes a password can take through the different systems involved. It also becomes easier for attackers to create fake sites, as people become used to entering their username and password in multiple different places that may all look slightly different. Instead, you have probably come across websites that let you "Login with Google," Microsoft, Facebook, or GitHub. This feature uses OAuth2, or tools built on top of it.

OAuth2 is a standard that is widely adopted for securing web applications and their interactions with users and other web applications. Only one service ever gets told your password or multi-factor authentication codes, and any site that needs to authenticate you directs you there. There are two types of authentication that we will cover here, the first being the Authentication Code Grant, which is initiated by a human using a browser or mobile app.

The process for a user-driven Authentication Code Grant looks complicated as it is depicted in *Figure 7.1*, but it serves an important purpose. Following the figure through, when a client requests a resource—whether it is a web page or some data, say—that they must log in to view, the application sends a 302 redirection to visit the authentication service. In that URL will be another address that the authentication service can use to send the client back to the application.

Once the client connects, the authentication service does the things you might expect—it asks for a username, password, and multi-factor authentication codes, and some may even display a picture or some text to demonstrate that you are visiting the right place. After logging in correctly, the authentication service redirects the client back to the application, this time with a token to present.

The application can validate the token with the authentication service, and can remember that result until the token expires, or for some other configurable length of time, occasionally rechecking it to check that the token hasn't been revoked. This way the application never has to deal with a username or password, and only has to learn enough to uniquely identify the client.

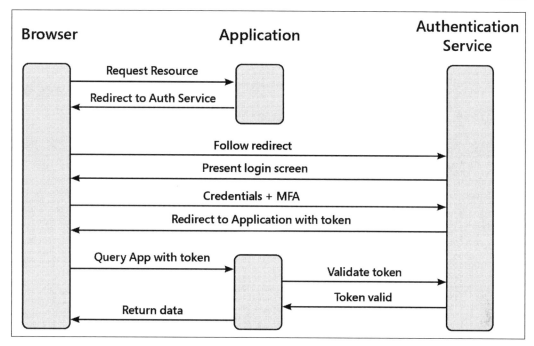

Figure 7.1: The OAuth2 authentication flow

When setting up OAuth2 for a program to use, so that one service can connect to another, there is a similar process called **Client Credentials Grant (CCG)** in which a service can connect to the authentication microservice and ask for a token that it can use. You can refer to the CCG scenario described in *section 4.4* of the OAuth2 Authorization Framework for more information: `https://tools.ietf.org/html/rfc6749#section-4.4`.

This works like the authorization code, but the service is not redirected to a web page as a user is. Instead, it's implicitly authorized with a secret key that can be traded for a token.

For a microservices-based architecture, using these two types of grants will let us centralize every aspect of authentication and authorization of the system. Building a microservice that implements part of the OAuth2 protocol to authenticate services and keep track of how they interact with each other is a good solution to reduce security issues — everything is centralized in a single place.

The CCG flow is by far the most interesting aspect to look at in this chapter, because it allows us to secure our microservice interactions independently from the users. It also simplifies permission management, since we can issue tokens with different scopes depending on the context. The applications are still responsible for enforcing what those scopes can and cannot do.

If you do not want to implement and maintain the authentication part of your application and you can trust a third party to manage this process, then Auth0 is an excellent commercial solution that provides all the APIs needed for a microservice-based application: `https://auth0.com/`.

X.509 certificate-based authentication

The `X.509` standard (`https://datatracker.ietf.org/doc/html/rfc5280`) is used to secure the web. Every website using TLS—the ones with `https://` URLs—has an `X.509` certificate on its web server, and uses it to verify the server's identity and set up the encryption the connection will use.

How does a client verify a server's identity when it is presented with such a certificate? Each properly issued certificate is cryptographically signed by a trusted authority. A **Certificate Authority (CA)** will often be the one issuing the certificate to you and will be the ultimate organization that browsers rely on to know who to trust. When the encrypted connection is being negotiated, a client will examine the certificate it's given and check who has signed it. If it is a trusted CA and the cryptographic checks are passed, then we can assume the certificate represents who it claims to. Sometimes the signer is an intermediary, so this step should be repeated until the client reaches a trusted CA.

It is possible to create a self-signed certificate, and this can be useful in test suites or for local development environments—although it is the digital equivalent of saying, "trust me, because I said so." A production service should not use self-signed certificates, and if the browser issues a warning, the human sitting in front of it will be right to be wary of the site they're accessing.

Obtaining a good certificate is significantly easier than it used to be, thanks to Let's Encrypt (`https://letsencrypt.org/`). Organizations that charge money for a certificate still offer value—there are features such as Extended Validation that aren't easily automated, and sometimes that extra display in the browser, often as a green padlock in the address bar, is worth it.

Let us generate a certificate using Let's Encrypt, and use some command-line tools to examine it. On the Let's Encrypt website there are instructions to install a utility called `certbot`. The instructions will vary slightly depending on the platform being used, so we won't include them here. Once `certbot` is installed, obtaining a certificate for a web server such as `nginx` is simple:

```
$ sudo certbot --nginx
No names were found in your configuration files. Please enter in your
domain
```

```
name(s) (comma and/or space separated)  (Enter 'c' to cancel): certbot-
test.mydomain.org
Requesting a certificate for certbot-test.mydomain.org
Performing the following challenges:
http-01 challenge for certbot-test.mydomain.org
Waiting for verification...
Cleaning up challenges
Deploying Certificate to VirtualHost /etc/nginx/sites-enabled/default
Redirecting all traffic on port 80 to ssl in /etc/nginx/sites-enabled/
default


- - - - - - - - - - - - - - - - - - - - - - - - - - - - - - - - - - - -

Congratulations! You have successfully enabled https://certbot-test.
mydomain.org
- - - - - - - - - - - - - - - - - - - - - - - - - - - - - - - - - - - -
```

Now we can examine our `nginx` configuration, and the site mentioned in the `certbot` output—`/etc/nginx/sites-enabled/default`. We can also see that the certificates have been set up for us, and we could have told `certbot` to just generate some certificates and let us install them if we wanted more fine-grained control over what happens with our configuration. In the following snippet of `nginx` configuration, we see the parts that `certbot` has added in order to secure the web service:

```
listen [::]:443 ssl ipv6only=on; # managed by Certbot
listen 443 ssl; # managed by Certbot
ssl_certificate /etc/letsencrypt/live/certbot-test.mydomain.org/
fullchain.pem; # managed by Certbot
ssl_certificate_key /etc/letsencrypt/live/certbot-test.mydomain.org/
privkey.pem; # managed by Certbot
include /etc/letsencrypt/options-ssl-nginx.conf; # managed by Certbot
ssl_dhparam /etc/letsencrypt/ssl-dhparams.pem; # managed by Certbot
```

We can use the OpenSSL toolkit to examine our certificate, both by looking at the file and by sending a query to the web server. Examining the certificate will provide a lot of information, although the important pieces for us include the sections on **Validity** and **Subject**. A certificate expiring without being renewed is a common error condition when running a service; certbot includes helpers to automatically refresh certificates that are about to expire, and so if we use the provided tools, this should not be a problem.

A certificate subject describes the entity that the certificate has been created for, and in this instance, that is a hostname. The certificate presented here has a subject **Common Name (CN)** of `certbot-test.mydomain.org`, but if that's not the hostname we are using then the clients connecting to our service will rightfully complain.

In order to examine a certificate's details, including the subject, we can use the openssl utility to display the certificate:

```
$ sudo openssl x509 -in /etc/letsencrypt/live/certbot-test.mydomain.
org/fullchain.pem  -text -noout
Certificate:
    Data:
    Version: 3 (0x2)
    Serial Number:
    04:92:e3:37:a4:83:77:4f:b9:d7:5c:62:24:74:7e:a4:5a:e0
    Signature Algorithm: sha256WithRSAEncryption
    Issuer: C = US, O = Let's Encrypt, CN = R3
    Validity
    Not Before: Mar 13 14:43:12 2021 GMT
    Not After : Jun 11 14:43:12 2021 GMT
    Subject: CN = certbot-test.mydomain.org
...
```

It is also possible to connect to a running web server using the openssl utility, which may be useful to confirm that the correct certificate is being used, to run monitoring scripts for certificates that will soon expire, or for other such diagnostics. Using the nginx instance we configured above, we can establish an encrypted session over which we can send HTTP commands:

```
$ openssl s_client -connect localhost:443
CONNECTED(00000003)
Can't use SSL_get_servername
depth=2 O = Digital Signature Trust Co., CN = DST Root CA X3
verify return:1
depth=1 C = US, O = Let's Encrypt, CN = R3
verify return:1
depth=0 CN = certbot-test.mydomain.org
verify return:1
---
Certificate chain
 0 s:CN = certbot-test.mydomain.org
   i:C = US, O = Let's Encrypt, CN = R3
 1 s:C = US, O = Let's Encrypt, CN = R3
   i:O = Digital Signature Trust Co., CN = DST Root CA X3
---
Server certificate
-----BEGIN CERTIFICATE-----
MII
```

```
# A really long certificate has been removed here
-----END CERTIFICATE-----
subject=CN = certbot-test.mydomain.org

issuer=C = US, O = Let's Encrypt, CN = R3

---
New, TLSv1.3, Cipher is TLS_AES_256_GCM_SHA384
Server public key is 2048 bit
Secure Renegotiation IS NOT supported
Compression: NONE
Expansion: NONE
No ALPN negotiated
Early data was not sent
Verify return code: 0 (ok)
---
```

We can easily read the public certificate in this exchange, and confirm it is the one we are expecting the server to use, from its configuration file. We can also discover which encryption suites have been negotiated between the client and server, and identify any that might be a cause of problems if older client libraries or web browsers are being used.

So far, we have only discussed the server using certificates to verify its identity and to establish a secure connection. It is also possible for the client to present a certificate to authenticate itself. The certificate would allow our application to verify that the client is who they claim to be, but we should be careful, as it does not automatically mean that the client is allowed to do something—that control still lies with our own application. Managing these certificates, setting up a CA to issue the appropriate certificates for clients, and how to properly distribute the files, are beyond the scope of this book. If it is the right choice for an application you are creating, a good place to start is the nginx documentation at http://nginx.org/en/docs/http/ngx_http_ssl_module.html#ssl_verify_client.

Let's take a look at authenticating clients that use our services, and how we can set up a microservice dedicated to validating client access.

Token-based authentication

As we said earlier, when one service wants to get access to another without any user intervention, we can use a CCG flow. The idea behind CCG is that a service can connect to an authentication service and ask for a token that it can then use to authenticate against other services.

Authentication services could issue multiple tokens in systems where different sets of permissions are needed, or identities vary.

Tokens can hold any information that is useful for the authentication and authorization process. Some of these are as follows:

- The username or ID, if it's pertinent to the context
- The scope, which indicates what the caller can do (read, write, and so on)
- A timestamp indicating when the token was issued
- An expiration timestamp, indicating how long the token is valid for

A token is usually built as a complete proof that you have permission to use a service. It is complete because it is possible to validate the token with the authentication service without knowing anything else, or having to query an external resource. Depending on the implementation, a token can also be used to access different microservices.

OAuth2 uses the JWT standard for its tokens. There is nothing in OAuth2 that requires the use of JWT—it just happens to be a good fit for what OAuth2 wants to do.

The JWT standard

The **JSON Web Token (JWT)** described in RFC 7519 is a standard that is commonly used to represent tokens: https://tools.ietf.org/html/rfc7519.

A JWT is a long string composed of three dot-separated parts:

- **A header**: This provides information on the token, such as which hashing algorithm is used
- **A payload**: This is the actual data
- **A signature**: This is a signed hash of the header and payload to verify that it is legitimate

JWTs are Base64-encoded so they can be safely used in query strings. Here's a JWT in its encoded form:

```
eyJhbGciOiJIUzI1NiIsInR5cCI6IkpXVCJ9
.
eyJzdWIiOiIxMjM0NTY3ODkwIiwibmFtZSI6IlNpbW9uIEZyYXNlciIsIm
lhdCI6MTYxNjQ0NzM1OH0
.
K4ONCpK9XKtc4s56YCC-13L0JgWohZr5J61jrbZnt1M
```

Each part in the token above is separated by a line break for display purposes—the original token is a single line. You can experiment with JWT encoding and decoding using a utility provided by Auth0 at `https://jwt.io/`.

If we use Python to decode it, the data is simply in Base64:

```
>>> import base64
>>> def decode(data):
... # adding extra = for padding if needed
... pad = len(data) % 4
... if pad > 0:
...     data += "=" * (4 - pad)
... return base64.urlsafe_b64decode(data)
...
>>> decode("eyJhbGciOiJIUzI1NiIsInR5cCI6IkpXVCJ9")
b'{"alg":"HS256","typ":"JWT"}'
>>> import base64
>>>
decode("eyJzdWIiOiIxMjM0NTY3ODkwIiwibmFtZSI6IlNpbW9uIEZyYXNlciIsImlhdC
I6MTYxNjQ0NzM1OH0")
b'{"sub":"1234567890","name":"Simon Fraser","iat":1616447358}'
>>> decode("K4ONCpK9XKtc4s56YCC-13L0JgWohZr5J61jrbZnt1M")
b"+\x83\x8d\n\x92\xbd\\\xab\\\xe2\xcez` \xbe\xd7r\xf4&\x05\xa8\x85\
x9a\xf9'\xadc\xad\xb6g\xb7S"
```

Every part of the JWT is a JSON mapping except the signature. The header usually contains just the `typ` and the `alg` keys: the `typ` key says that it is a JWT, and the `alg` key indicates which hashing algorithm is used. In the following header example, we have `HS256`, which stands for `HMAC-SHA256`:

```
{"typ": "JWT",  "alg": "HS256"}
```

The payload contains whatever you need, and each field is called a **JWT claim** in the RFC 7519 jargon. The RFC has a predefined list of claims that a token may contain, called **Registered Claim Names**. Here's a subset of them:

- `iss`: This is the issuer, which is the name of the entity that generated the token. It's typically the fully qualified hostname, so the client can use it to discover its public keys by requesting `/.well-known/jwks.json`.

- `exp`: This is the expiration time, which is a timestamp after which the token is invalid.

- `nbf`: This stands for *not before time*, which is a timestamp before which the token is invalid.

- aud: This indicates the audience, which is the recipient for whom the token was issued.

- iat: Stands for *issued at*, which is a timestamp for when the token was issued.

In the following payload example, we're providing the custom user_id value along with timestamps that make the token valid for the 24 hours after it was issued; once valid, that token can be used for 24 hours:

```
{
  "iss": "https://tokendealer.mydomain.org",
  "aud": "mydomain.org",
  "iat": 1616447358,
  "nbt": 1616447358,
  "exp": 1616533757,
  "user_id": 1234
}
```

These headers give us a lot of flexibility to control how long our tokens will stay valid. Depending on the nature of the microservice, the token **Time-To-Live (TTL)** can be anything from very short to infinite. For instance, a microservice that interacts with others within your system should probably rely on tokens that are valid for long enough to avoid having to regenerate tokens unnecessarily, multiple times. On the other hand, if your tokens are distributed in the wild, or if they relate to changing something highly important, it's a good idea to make them short-lived.

The last part of a JWT is the signature. It contains a signed hash of the header and the payload. There are several algorithms used to sign the hash; some are based on a secret key, while others are based on a public and private key pair.

PyJWT

In Python, the PyJWT library provides all the tools you need to generate and read back JWTs: https://pyjwt.readthedocs.io/.

Once you've pip-installed pyjwt (and cryptography), you can use the encode() and the decode() functions to create tokens. In the following example, we're creating a JWT using HMAC-SHA256 and reading it back. The signature is verified when the token is read, by providing the secret:

```
>>> import jwt
>>> def create_token(alg="HS256", secret="secret", data=None):
        return jwt.encode(data, secret, algorithm=alg)
...
```

```
>>>
>>> def read_token(token, secret="secret", algs=["HS256"]):
...   return jwt.decode(token, secret, algorithms=algs)
...
>>>  token = create_token(data={"some": "data", "inthe": "token"})
>>> print(token)
eyJ0eXAiOiJKV1QiLCJhbGciOiJIUzI1NiJ9.
eyJzb21lIjoiZGF0YSIsImludGhlIjoidG9rZW4ifQ.vMHiSS_vk-
Z3gMMxcM22Ssjk3vW3aSmJXQ8YCSCwFu4
>>> print(read_token(token))
{'some': 'data', 'inthe': 'token'}
```

When executing this code, the token is displayed in both its compressed and uncompressed forms. If you use one of the registered claims, PyJWT will control them. For instance, if the exp field is provided and the token is outdated, the library will raise an error.

Using a secret for signing and verifying the signature is great when you have a few services running, but it can soon become a problem due to it requiring you to share the secret among all services that need to verify the signature. So, when the secret needs to be changed, it can be a challenge to change it across your stack securely. Basing your authentication on a secret that you are sharing around is also a weakness. If a single service is compromised and the secret is stolen, your whole authentication system is compromised.

A better technique is to use an asymmetric key composed of a public key and a private key. The private key is used by the token issuer to sign the tokens, and the public key can be utilized by anyone to verify that the signature was signed by that issuer. Of course, if an attacker has access to the private key, or can convince clients that a forged public key is the legitimate one, you would still be in trouble.

But using a public/private key pair does still reduce the attack surface of your authentication process, often sufficiently to discourage most attackers; and, since the authentication microservice will be the only place that contains the private key, you can focus on adding extra security to it. For instance, such sensible services are often deployed in a firewalled environment where all access is strictly controlled. Let us now see how we can create asymmetric keys in practice.

Using a certificate with JWT

To simplify matters for this example, we will use the letsencrypt certificates we generated for nginx earlier on. If you are developing on a laptop or container that is not available from the internet, you may need to generate those certificates using a cloud instance or a certbot DNS plugin and copy them to the right place.

If `certbot` generated the certificates directly, they will be available in `/etc/letsencrypt/live/your-domain/`. To start with, we are interested in these two files:

- `cert.pem`, which contains the certificate
- `privkey.pem`, which has the RSA private key

In order to use these with PyJWT, we need to extract the public key from the certificate:

```
openssl x509 -pubkey -noout -in cert.pem  > pubkey.pem
```

RSA stands for **Rivest, Shamir, and Adleman**, the three authors. The RSA encryption algorithm generates crypto keys that can go up to 4,096 bytes, and are considered secure.

From there, we can use `pubkey.pem` and `privkey.pem` in our PyJWT script to sign and verify the signature of the token, using the `RSASSA-PKCS1-v1_5` signature algorithm and the `SHA-512` hash algorithm:

```python
import jwt

with open("pubkey.pem") as f:
  PUBKEY = f.read()

with open("privkey.pem") as f:
  PRIVKEY = f.read()

def create_token(**data):
  return jwt.encode(data, PRIVKEY, algorithm="RS512")

def read_token(token):
  return jwt.decode(token, PUBKEY, algorithms="RS512")

token = create_token(some="data", inthe="token")
print(token)

read = read_token(token)
print(read)
```

The result is similar to the previous run, except that we get a much bigger token:

```
eyJ0eXAiOiJKV1QiLCJhbGciOiJSUzUxMiJ9.eyJzb21lIjoiZGF0YSIsImludGh
lIjoidG9rZW4ifQ.gi5p3k4PAErw8KKrghRjsi8g1IXnflivXiwwaZdFEh84zvgw9RJRa
50uJe778A1CBelnmo2iapSWOQ9Mq5U6gpv4VxoVYv6QR2zFNO13GB_tce6xQ
OhjpAd-hRxouy3Ozj4oNmvwLpCT5dYPsCvIiuYrLt4ScK5S3q3a0Ny64VXy
3CcISNkyjs7fnxyMMkCMZq65Z7jOncf1RXpzNNIt546aJGsCcpCPGHR1cRj
uvV_uxPAMd-dfy2d5AfiCXOgvmwQhNdaxYIM0gPgz9_yHPzgaPjtgYoJMc9iK
ZdOLz2-8pLc1D3r_uP3P-4mfxP7mOhQHYBrY9nv5MTSwFC3JDA
{'some': 'data', 'inthe': 'token'}
```

Adding that much extra data to each request can have consequences for the amount of network traffic generated, so the secret-based JWT technique is an option to keep in mind if you need to reduce the network overhead.

The TokenDealer microservice

Our first step in building the authentication microservice will be to implement everything needed to perform a CCG flow. For that, the app receives requests from services that want a token and generates them on demand, assuming the request has a known secret in it. The generated tokens will have a lifespan of one day. This approach has the most flexibility, without the complexity of generating our own X.509 certificates, while allowing us to have one service responsible for generating the tokens.

This service will be the only service to possess the private key that is used to sign the tokens, and will expose the public key for other services that want to verify tokens. This service will also be the only place where all the client IDs and secret keys are kept.

We will greatly simplify the implementation by stating that once a service gets a token, it can access any other service in our ecosystem. When a service is accessed with a token, it can verify that token locally or call the TokenDealer to perform the verification. The choice between a network request and some CPU usage in the microservice will depend on what the application does and where its bottlenecks are. When balancing the security and performance requirements it might be necessary to validate the token, at most, once every few minutes, rather than every single time. This will cause a delay if the token needs to be invalidated, though, so we should consult the user stories and, if necessary, discuss the topic with the people who will be using the service to see which is most important.

To implement everything we've described, three endpoints will be created in this microservice:

- `GET /.well-known/jwks.json`: This is the public key published in the **JSON Web Key (JWK)** format, as described in RFC 7517, when other microservices want to verify tokens on their own. For more information, see the following: `https://tools.ietf.org/html/rfc7517`.

- `POST /oauth/token`: This endpoint accepts a request with credentials and returns a token. Adding the `/oauth` prefix is a widely adopted convention, since it is used in the OAuth RFC.

- `POST /verify_token`: This endpoint returns the token payload, given a token. If the token is not valid, it returns an HTTP 400 error code.

Using the microservice skeleton, we can create a very simple Quart application that implements these three views. The skeleton is available at `https://github.com/PacktPublishing/Python-Microservices-Development-2nd-Edition/`.

Let's look at these three OAuth views.

The OAuth implementation

For the CCG flow, the service that wants a token sends a `POST` request with a URL-encoded body that contains the following fields:

- `client_id`: This is a unique string identifying the requester.

- `client_secret`: This is a secret key that authenticates the requester. It should be a random string generated upfront and registered with the auth service.

- `grant_type`: This is the grant type, which here must be `client_credentials`.

We'll make a few assumptions to simplify the implementation. Firstly, we will keep the list of secrets in a Python data structure, for demonstration purposes. In a production service, they should be encrypted at rest and kept in a resilient data store. We will also assume that `client_id` is the name of the calling microservice, and for now we will generate secrets using `binascii.hexlify(os.urandom(16))`.

The first view will be the one that actually generates the tokens needed by the other services. In our example we are reading in the private key each time we create a token—this may be better stored in the application configuration for a real service, just to reduce the time spent waiting to read a file from the disk. We make sure the client has sent us a reasonable request, and that it wants some `client_credentials`. The error handling functions and utilities are available in the full source code samples for this chapter.

The token itself is a data structure with several fields: The issuer (iss) of the token, commonly the URL of the service; the intended audience (aud) for the token, that is, who the token is intended for; the time the token was issued (iat); as well as its expiry (exp) time. We then sign this data using the jwt.encode method and return it to the requesting client:

```
@app.route("/oauth/token", methods=["POST"])
async def create_token():
    with open(current_app.config["PRIVATE_KEY_PATH"]) as f:
        key = f.read().strip()
    try:
        data = await request.form
        if data.get("grant_type") != "client_credentials":
            return bad_request(f"Wrong grant_type {data.get('grant_
type')}")

        client_id = data.get("client_id")
        client_secret = data.get("client_secret")
        aud = data.get("audience", "")

        if not is_authorized_app(client_id, client_secret):
            return abort(401)

        now = int(time.time())

        token = {
            "iss": current_app.config["TOKENDEALER_URL"],
            "aud": aud,
            "iat": now,
            "exp": now + 3600 * 24,
        }
        token = jwt.encode(token, key, algorithm="RS512")
        return {"access_token": token}
    except Exception as e:
        return bad_request("Unable to create a token")
```

The next view to add is a function that returns the public keys used by our token generation, so that any client can verify the tokens without making further HTTP requests. This is often located at a well-known URL—the address literally contains the string .well-known/, which is a practice encouraged by the IETF to provide a way for a client to discover metadata about a service. Here we are responding with the JWKS.

In the data returned are the key type (kty), the algorithm (alg), the public key use (use)—here a signature—and two values used by the RSA algorithm that our cryptographic keys are generated with:

```
@app.route("/.well-known/jwks.json")
async def _jwks():
    """Returns the public key in the Json Web Key Set (JWKS) format"""
    with open(current_app.config["PUBLIC_KEY_PATH"]) as f:
        key = f.read().strip()
    data = {
        "alg": "RS512",
        "e": "AQAB",
        "n": key,
        "kty": "RSA",
        "use": "sig",
    }

    return jsonify({"keys": [data]})
```

The final view lets clients verify a token without doing the work themselves. Much more straightforward than the token generation, we simply extract the right fields from the input data and call the jwt.decode function to provide the values. Note that this function verifies the token is valid, but not that the token allows any particular access — that part is up to the service that has been presented with the token:

```
@app.route("/verify_token", methods=["POST"])
async def verify_token():
    with open(current_app.config["PUBLIC_KEY_PATH"]) as f:
        key = f.read()
    try:
        input_data = await request.form
        token = input_data["access_token"]
        audience = input_data.get("audience", "")
        return jwt.decode(token, key, algorithms=["RS512"],
audience=audience)
    except Exception as e:
        return bad_request("Unable to verify the token")
```

The whole source code of the TokenDealer microservice can be found on GitHub: https://github.com/PacktPublishing/Python-Microservices-Development-2nd-Edition.

The microservice could offer more features around token generation. For instance, the ability to manage scopes and make sure microservice A is not allowed to generate a token that can be used in microservice B, or managing a whitelist of services that are authorized to ask for some tokens. A client could also request a token that is intended for read-only use. Despite this, however, the pattern we have implemented is the basis for a simple token-based authentication system in a microservice environment that you can develop on your own, while also being good enough for our Jeeves app.

Looking back at our example microservice, TokenDealer now sits as a separate microservice in the ecosystem, creating and verifying keys that allow access to our data service, and authorizing access to the third-party tokens and API keys we need to query other sites:

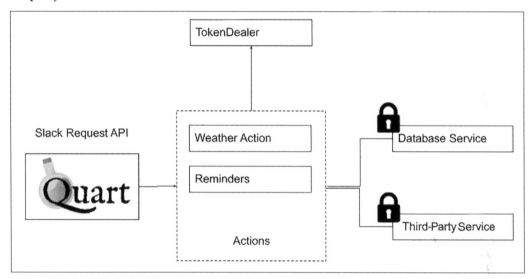

Figure 7.2: The microservice ecosystem with the CCG TokenDealer

Those services that require a JWT may validate it by calling the TokenDealer microservice. The Quart app in *Figure 7.2* needs to obtain tokens from TokenDealer on behalf of its users.

Now that we have a TokenDealer service that implements CCG, let us see how it can be used by our services in the next section.

Using TokenDealer

In Jeeves, the **Data Service** is a good example of a place where authentication is required. Adding information via the **Data Service** needs to be restricted to authorized services:

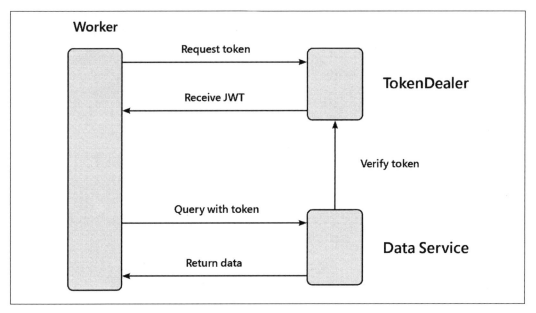

Figure 7.3: Requesting a CCG workflow

Adding authentication for that link is done in four steps:

1. **TokenDealer** manages a `client_id` and `client_secret` pair for the Strava worker and shares it with the Strava worker developers

2. The Strava worker uses `client_id` and `client_secret` to retrieve a token from **TokenDealer**

3. The worker adds the token to the header for each request to the **Data Service**

4. The **Data Service** verifies the token by calling the verification API of **TokenDealer** or by performing a local **JWT** verification

In a full implementation, the first step can be partially automated. Generating a client secret is usually done through a web administration panel in the authentication service. That secret is then provided to the client microservice developers. Each microservice that requires a token can now get one, whether it is the first time connecting, or because the tokens it has already obtained have expired. All they need to do to use it is add that token to the Authorization header when calling the Data Service.

The following is an example of such a call using the requests library — assuming our TokenDealer is already running on localhost:5000:

```python
# fetch_token.py
import requests

TOKENDEALER_SERVER = "http://localhost:5000"
SECRET = "f0fdeb1f1584fd5431c4250b2e859457"

def get_token():
    data = {
        "client_id": "worker1",
        "client_secret": secret,
        "audience": "jeeves.domain",
        "grant_type": "client_credentials",
    }
    headers = {"Content-Type": "application/x-www-form-urlencoded"}
    url = tokendealer_server + "/oauth/token"
    response = requests.post(url, data=data, headers=headers)
    return response.json()["access_token"]
```

The get_token() function retrieves a token that can then be used in the Authorization header when the code calls the Data Service, which we assume is listening on port 5001 for this example:

```python
# auth_caller.py
_TOKEN = None


def get_auth_header(new=False):
    global _TOKEN
    if _TOKEN is None or new:
        _TOKEN = get_token()
    return "Bearer " + _TOKEN


_dataservice = "http://localhost:5001"


def _call_service(endpoint, token):
    # not using session and other tools, to simplify the code
    url = _dataservice + "/" + endpoint
    headers = {"Authorization": token}
```

```
        return requests.get(url, headers=headers)


   def call_data_service(endpoint):
        token = get_auth_header()
        response = _call_service(endpoint, token)
        if response.status_code == 401:
            # the token might be revoked, let's try with a fresh one
            token = get_auth_header(new=True)
            response = _call_service(endpoint, token)
        return response
```

The call_data_service() function will try to get a new token if the call to the Data Service leads to a 401 response. This refresh-token-on-401 pattern can be used in all your microservices to automate token generation.

This covers service-to-service authentication. You can find the full implementation in the example GitHub repository to play with this JWT-based authentication scheme and use it as a basis for building your authentication process.

The next section looks at another important aspect of securing your web services, and that is securing the code itself.

Securing your code

Whatever we do, an application must receive data and act on it, somehow, or it will not be very useful. If a service receives data, then as soon as you expose your app to the world, it is open to numerous possible types of attack, and your code needs to be designed with this in mind.

Anything that is published to the web can be attacked, although we have the advantage that most microservices are not exposed to the public internet, which reduces the possible ways they could be exploited. The expected inputs and outputs of the system are narrower, and often better defined using specification tools, such as OpenAPI.

Attacks are not always due to hostile intent, either. If the caller has a bug or is just not calling your service correctly, the expected behavior should be to send back a 4xx response and explain to the client why the request was rejected.

The **Open Web Application Security Project (OWASP)** (https://www.owasp.org) is an excellent resource to learn about ways to protect your web apps from bad behaviors. Let's look at some of the most common forms of attack:

- **Injection**: In an application that receives data, an attacker sends SQL statements, shell commands, or some other instructions inside the request. If your application is not careful about how it uses that data, you can end up running code that is meant to damage your application. In Python, SQL injection attacks can be avoided by using SQLAlchemy, which constructs the SQL statements for you in a safe way. If you do use SQL directly, or provide arguments to shell scripts, LDAP servers, or some other structured query, you must make sure that every variable is quoted correctly.

- **Cross-Site Scripting** (**XSS**): This attack happens only on web pages that display some HTML. The attacker uses some of the query attributes to try to inject their piece of HTML on the page to trick the user into performing some set of actions, thinking they are on the legitimate website.

- **Cross-Site Request Forgery** (**XSRF/CSRF**): This attack is based on attacking a service by reusing the user's credentials from another website. The typical CSRF attack happens with POST requests. For instance, a malicious website displays a link to a user to trick that user into performing the POST request on your site using their existing credentials.

Things such as **Local File Inclusion (LFI)**, **Remote File Inclusion (RFI)**, or **Remote Code Execution (RCE)** are all attacks that trick the server into executing something via client input, or revealing server files. They can happen of course in applications written in most languages and toolkits, but we will examine some of Python's tools to protect against these attacks.

The idea behind secure code is simple, yet hard to do well in practice. The two fundamental principles are:

- Every request from the outside world should be carefully assessed before it does something in your application and data.

- Everything your application is doing on a system should have a well-defined and limited scope.

Let's look at how to implement these principles in practice.

Limiting your application scope

Even if you trust the authentication system, you should make sure that whoever connects has the minimum level of access required to perform their work. If there is a client that connects to your microservice and can authenticate themselves, that doesn't mean they should be allowed to perform any action. If they only need read-only access, then that's all they should be granted.

This isn't just protecting against malicious code, but also bugs and accidents. Any time you think, "the client should never call this endpoint," then there should be something in place that actively prevents the client using it.

That scope limitation can be done with JWTs by defining roles (such as read/write) and adding that information in the token under a permissions or scope key, for example. The target microservice will then be able to reject a call on a POST that is made with a token that is supposed to only read data.

This is what happens when you grant access to an application on your GitHub account, or on your Android phone. A detailed list of what the app wants to do is displayed, and you can grant or reject access.

This is in addition to network-level controls and firewalls. If you are controlling all parts of your microservices ecosystem, you can also use strict firewall rules at the system level to whitelist the IPs that are allowed to interact with each microservice, but that kind of setup greatly depends on where you are deploying your application. In the **Amazon Web Services (AWS)** cloud environment, you don't need to configure a Linux firewall; all you have to do is set up the access rules in the AWS Console. *Chapter 10, Deploying on AWS*, covers the basics of deploying your microservices on the Amazon cloud.

Besides network access, any other resource your application can access should be limited whenever possible. Running the application as a root user on Linux is not a good idea because if your application has full administrative privileges, then so does an attacker who successfully breaks in.

In essence, if a layer of security fails, there should be another behind it. If an application's web server is successfully attacked, any attacker should ideally be as limited as possible in what they can do, as they only have access to the well-defined interfaces between the services in the application—instead of full administrative control over the computer running the code. Root access to a system has become an indirect threat in modern deployments, since most applications are running in containers or a **Virtual Machine (VM)**, but a process can still do a lot of damage even if its abilities are limited by the VM it is running in. If an attacker gains access to one of your VMs, they have achieved the first step in getting control over the whole system. To mitigate the problem, there are two rules you should follow:

1. All software should run with the smallest set of permissions possible
2. Be very cautious when executing processes from your web service, and avoid it if you can

For the first rule, the default behavior for web servers such as nginx is to run its processes using the www-data user and group, so that standard user controls prevent the server accessing other files, and the account itself can be set up to not be allowed to run a shell or any other interactive commands. The same rules apply to your Quart processes. We will see in *Chapter 9*, *Packaging and Running Python*, the best practices to run a stack in the user space on a Linux system.

For the second rule, any Python call to os.system() should be avoided unless absolutely necessary, as it creates a new user shell on the computer, adding risks associated with badly formed commands being run, and increasing the risk of uncontrolled access to the system. The subprocess module is better, although it, too, must be used carefully to avoid unwanted side effects—avoid using the shell=True argument, which will result in the same trouble as os.system(), and avoid using input data as arguments and commands. This is also true for high-level network modules that send emails or connect to third-party servers via FTP, via the local system.

Untrusted incoming data

The majority of applications accept data as input: whose account to look up; which city to fetch a weather report for; which account to transfer money into, and so forth. The trouble is that data that comes from outside our system is not easily trusted.

Earlier, we discussed SQL injection attacks; let us now consider a very naive example, where we use a SQL query to look up a user. We have a function that treats the query as a string to be formatted, and fills it in using standard Python syntax:

```
import pymysql

connection = pymysql.connect(host='localhost', db='book')

def get_user(user_id):
    query = f"select * from user where id = {user_id}"
        with connection.cursor() as cursor:
        cursor.execute(query)
        result = cursor.fetchone()
        return result
```

This looks fine when the user_id is always a sensible value. However, what if someone presents a carefully crafted malicious value? If we allow people to enter data for get_user(), above, and instead of entering a number as a user_id, they enter:

```
'1'; insert into user(id, firstname, lastname, password) values (999,
'pwnd', 'yup', 'somehashedpassword')
```

Now our SQL statement is really two statements:

```
select * from user where id = '1'
insert into user(id, firstname, lastname, password) values (999,
'pwnd', 'yup', 'somehashedpassword')
```

get_user will perform the expected query, and a second query that will add a new user! It could also delete a table, or perform any other action available to SQL statements. Some damage limitation is there if the authenticated client has limited permissions, but a large amount of data could still be exposed. This scenario can be prevented by quoting any value used to build raw SQL queries. In PyMySQL, you just need to pass the values as parameters to the execute argument to avoid this problem:

```
def get_user(user_id):
    query = 'select * from user where id = %s'
        with connection.cursor() as cursor:
        cursor.execute(query, (user_id,))
        result = cursor.fetchone()
        return result
```

Every database library has this feature, so as long as you are correctly using these libraries when building raw SQL, you should be fine. Better still is to avoid using raw SQL completely, and instead use a database model through SQLAlchemy.

If you have a view that grabs JSON data from the incoming request and uses it to push data to a database, you should verify that the incoming request has the data you are expecting, and not blindly pass it over to your database backend. That's why it can be interesting to use Swagger to describe your data as schemas, and use them to validate incoming data. Microservices usually use JSON, but if you happen to use templates to provide formatted output, that's yet another place where you need to be careful with respect to what the template is doing with variables.

Server-Side Template Injection (SSTI) is a possible attack in which your templates blindly execute Python statements. In 2016, such an injection vulnerability was found on Uber's website on a Jinja2 template, because raw formatting was done before the template was executed. See more at https://hackerone.com/reports/125980.

The code was something similar to this small app:

```python
from quart import Quart, request, render_template_string

app = Quart(__name__)

SECRET = "oh no!"

_TEMPLATE = """
    Hello %s

    Welcome to my API!
    """

class Extra:
    def __init__(self, data):
    self.data = data


@app.route("/")
async def my_microservice():
    user_id = request.args.get("user_id", "Anonymous")
    tmpl = _TEMPLATE % user_id
    return await render_template_string(tmpl, extra=Extra("something"))

app.run()
```

By doing this preformatting on the template with a raw % formatting syntax, the view creates a huge security hole in the app, since it allows attackers to inject what they want into the Jinja script before it is executed. In the following example, the user_id variable security hole is exploited to read the value of the SECRET global variable from the module:

```
# Here we URL encode the following:
# http://localhost:5000/?user_id={{extra.__class__.__init__.__globals__
["SECRET"]}}
$ curl http://localhost:5000/?user_id=%7B%7Bextra.__class__.__init__.__
globals__%5B%22SECRET%22%5D%7D%7D

Hello oh no!

Welcome to my API!
```

That's why it is important to avoid string formatting with input data unless there is a template engine or some other layer that provides protection.

If you need to evaluate untrusted code in a template, you can use Jinja's sandbox; refer to `http://jinja.pocoo.org/docs/latest/sandbox/`. This sandbox will reject any access to methods and attributes from the object being evaluated. For instance, if you're passing a callable in your template, you will be sure that its attributes, such as ;__class__, cannot be used.

That said, Python sandboxes are tricky to get right due to the nature of the language. It's easy to misconfigure a sandbox, and the sandbox itself can be compromised with a new version of the language. The safest bet is to avoid evaluating untrusted code altogether and make sure you're not directly relying on incoming data for templates.

Redirecting and trusting queries

The same precaution applies when dealing with redirects. One common mistake is to create a login view that makes the assumption that the caller will be redirected to an internal page and use a plain URL for that redirect:

```python
@app.route('/login')
def login():
    from_url = request.args.get('from_url', '/')
    # do some authentication
    return redirect(from_url)
```

This view can redirect the caller to any website, which is a significant threat—particularly during the login process. Good practice involves avoiding free strings when calling `redirect()`, by using the `url_for()` function, which will create a link to your app domain. If you need to redirect to third parties, you cannot use the `url_for()` and `redirect()` functions, as they can potentially send your clients to unwanted places.

One solution is to create a restricted list of third-party domains that your application is allowed to redirect to and make sure any redirection done by your application or underlying third-party libraries is checked against that list.

This can be done with the `after_request()` hook that will be called after our views have generated a response, but before Quart has sent it back to the client. If the application tries to send back a 302, you can check that its location is safe, given a list of domains and ports:

```python
# quart_after_response.py
from quart import Quart, redirect
from quart.helpers import make_response
from urllib.parse import urlparse

app = Quart(__name__)

@app.route("/api")
async def my_microservice():
    return redirect("https://github.com:443/")

# domain:port
SAFE_DOMAINS = ["github.com:443", "google.com:443"]

@app.after_request
async def check_redirect(response):
    if response.status_code != 302:
        return response
    url = urlparse(response.location)
    netloc = url.netloc
    if netloc not in SAFE_DOMAINS:
        # not using abort() here or it'll break the hook
        return await make_response("Forbidden", 403)
    return response

if __name__ == "__main__":
    app.run(debug=True)
```

Sanitizing input data

In addition to the other practices for handling untrusted data, we can ensure the fields themselves match what we expect. Faced with the examples above, it is tempting to think that we should filter out any semicolons, or perhaps all the curly braces, but this leaves us in the position of having to think of all the ways in which the data could be malformed, and trying to outwit the inventiveness of both malicious programmers and also random bugs.

Instead, we should concentrate on what we know about what our data should look like—instead of what it should not. This is a much narrower question, and the answer can often be much easier to define. As an example, if we know that an endpoint accepts an ISBN to look up a book, then we know that we should only expect a series of numbers either 10 or 13 digits long, perhaps with dashes as separators. When it comes to people, however, data is much harder to clean up.

There are several fantastic lists of falsehoods that programmers believe about various topics at `https://github.com/kdeldycke/awesome-falsehood`. These lists are not meant to be exhaustive or authoritative, but they are helpful in reminding us that we may have false notions about how human information works. Human names, postal addresses, phone numbers: we should not make assumptions about what any of this data looks like, how many lines it has, or what order the elements are in. The best we can do is ensure that the human entering the information has the best chance to check that it is all correct, and then use the quoting and sandboxing techniques described earlier to avoid any incidents.

Even an email address is extremely complicated to validate. The permitted format has a lot of different parts to it, and not all of them are supported by every email system. An oft-quoted saying is that the best way to validate an email address is to try sending it an email, and this validation method is used by both legitimate websites—sending an email and informing you that they "have sent an email to confirm your account"—and by spammers who send nonsensical messages to millions of addresses and record which ones don't return an error.

To summarize, you should always treat incoming data as a potential threat, as a source of attacks to be injected into your system. Escape or remove any special characters, avoid using the data directly in database queries or templates without a layer of isolation between them, and ensure your data looks as you would expect it to.

There is also a way to continuously check your code for potential security issues using the Bandit linter, explored in the next section.

Using Bandit linter

Managed by the Python Code Quality Authority, Bandit (`https://github.com/PyCQA/bandit`) is another tool to scan your source code for potential security risks. It can be run in CI systems for the automatic testing of any changes before they get deployed. The tool uses the `ast` module to parse the code in the same way that `flake8` and `pylint` do. Bandit will also scan for some known security issues in your code. Once you have installed it with the `pip install bandit` command, you can run it against your Python module using the `bandit` command.

Adding Bandit to your continuous integration pipeline alongside other checks, as described in *Chapter 3, Coding, Testing, and Documentation: the Virtuous Cycle*, is a good way to catch potential security issues in your code.

Dependencies

Most projects will use other libraries, as programmers build on the work of others, and oftentimes there is not enough time to keep a close eye on how those other projects are doing. If there's a security vulnerability in one of our dependencies, we want to know about it quickly so that we can update our own software, without manually checking.

Dependabot (`https://dependabot.com/`) is a tool that will perform security sweeps of your project's dependencies. Dependabot is a built-in component of GitHub, and its reports should be visible in your project's **Security** tab. Turning on some extra features in the project's **Settings** page allows Dependabot to automatically create pull requests with any changes that need making to remain secure.

PyUp has a similar set of features but requires manually setting up—as does Dependabot if you're not using GitHub.

Web application firewall

Even with the safest handling of data, our application can still be vulnerable to attack. When you're exposing HTTP endpoints to the world, this is always a risk. You will be hoping for callers to behave as intended, with each HTTP conversation following a scenario that you have programmed in the service.

A client can send legitimate requests and just hammer your service with it, leading to a **Denial of Service (DoS)** due to all the resources then being used to handle requests from the attacker. When many hundreds or thousands of clients are used to do this, it's known as a **Distributed Denial of Service (DDoS)** attack. This problem sometimes occurs within distributed systems when clients have replay features that are automatically recalling the same API. If nothing is done on the client side to throttle calls, you might end up with a service overloaded by legitimate clients.

Adding protection on the server side to make such zealous clients back off is usually not hard to do, and goes a long way to protect your microservice stack. Some cloud providers also supply protection against DDoS attacks and a lot of the features mentioned here.

OWASP, mentioned earlier in this chapter, provides a set of rules for the `ModSecurity` toolkit's WAF that can be used to avoid many types of attacks: `https://github.com/coreruleset/coreruleset/`.

In this section, we will focus on creating a basic WAF that will explicitly reject a client that's making too many requests on our service. The intention of this section is not to create a full WAF, but rather to give you a good understanding of how WAFs are implemented and used. We could build our WAF in a Python microservice, but it would add a lot of overhead if all the traffic has to go through it. A much better solution is to rely directly on the web server.

OpenResty: Lua and nginx

OpenResty (http://openresty.org/en/) is an nginx distribution that embeds a Lua (http://www.lua.org/) interpreter that can be used to script the web server. We can then use scripts to apply rules and filters to the traffic.

Lua is an excellent, dynamically typed programming language that has a lightweight and fast interpreter. The language offers a complete set of features and has built-in async features. You can write coroutines directly in vanilla Lua.

If you install Lua (refer to http://www.lua.org/start.html), you can play with the language using the Lua **Read-Eval-Print Loop** (**REPL**), exactly as you would with Python:

```
$ lua
Lua 5.4.2  Copyright (C) 1994-2020 Lua.org, PUC-Rio
> io.write("Hello world\n")
Hello world
file (0x7f5a66f316a0)
> mytable = {}
> mytable["user"] = "simon"
> = mytable["user"]
simon
> = string.upper(mytable["user"])
SIMON
>
```

To discover the Lua language, this is your starting page: http://www.lua.org/docs. html.

Lua is often the language of choice to be embedded in compiled apps. Its memory footprint is ridiculously small, and it allows for fast dynamic scripting features — this is what is happening in OpenResty. Instead of building nginx modules you can extend the web server using Lua scripts and deploy them directly with OpenResty.

When you invoke some Lua code from your `nginx` configuration, the `LuaJIT` (`http://luajit.org/`) interpreter that's employed by OpenResty will run them, running at the same speed as the `nginx` code itself. Some performance benchmarks find that Lua can be faster than C or C++ in some cases; refer to: `http://luajit.org/performance.html`.

Lua functions are coroutines, and so will run asynchronously in `nginx`. This leads to a low overhead even when your server receives a lot of concurrent requests, which is exactly what is needed for a WAF.

OpenResty comes as a Docker image and a package for some Linux distributions. It can also be compiled from the source code if needed; refer to `http://openresty.org/en/installation.html`.

On macOS, you can use `Brew` and the `brew install openresty` command.

Once OpenResty is installed, you will get an `openresty` command, which can be used exactly like `nginx` to serve your applications. In the following example, the `nginx` configuration will proxy requests to a Quart application running on port `5000`:

```
# resty.conf
daemon off;
worker_processes  1;
error_log /dev/stdout info;
events {
worker_connections  1024;
}
http {
  access_log /dev/stdout;
  server {
    listen    8888;
    server_name  localhost;
    location / {
      proxy_pass http://localhost:5000;
      proxy_set_header Host $host;
      proxy_set_header X-Real-IP $remote_addr;
      proxy_set_header X-Forwarded-For $proxy_add_x_forwarded_for;
    }
  }
}
```

This configuration can be used with the openresty command line, and will run in the foreground (daemon off) on port 8888 to proxy pass all requests to the Quart app running on port 5000:

```
$ openresty -p $(pwd) -c resty.conf
2021/07/03 16:11:08 [notice] 44691#12779096: using the "kqueue" event
method
2021/07/03 16:11:08 [warn] 44691#12779096: 1024 worker_connections
exceed open file resource limit: 256
nginx: [warn] 1024 worker_connections exceed open file resource limit:
256
2021/07/03 16:11:08 [notice] 44691#12779096: openresty/1.19.3.2
2021/07/03 16:11:08 [notice] 44691#12779096: built by clang 12.0.0
(clang-1200.0.32.2)
2021/07/03 16:11:08 [notice] 44691#12779096: OS: Darwin 19.6.0
2021/07/03 16:11:08 [notice] 44691#12779096: hw.ncpu: 12
2021/07/03 16:11:08 [notice] 44691#12779096: net.inet.tcp.sendspace:
131072
2021/07/03 16:11:08 [notice] 44691#12779096: kern.ipc.somaxconn: 128
2021/07/03 16:11:08 [notice] 44691#12779096: getrlimit(RLIMIT_NOFILE):
256:9223372036854775807
2021/07/03 16:11:08 [notice] 44691#12779096: start worker processes
2021/07/03 16:11:08 [notice] 44691#12779096: start worker process 44692
```

Note that this configuration can also be used in a plain nginx server since we are not using any Lua yet. That's one of the great things about OpenResty: it's a drop-in replacement for nginx, and can run your existing configuration files.

The code and configuration demonstrated in this section can be found at https://github.com/PacktPublishing/Python-Microservices-Development-2nd-Edition/tree/main/CodeSamples.

Lua can be invoked at different moments when a request comes in; the two that are most attractive to this chapter are:

- access_by_lua_block: This is called on every incoming request before a response is built, and is where we can build access rules in our WAF
- content_by_lua_block: This uses Lua to generate a response

Let us now see how we can rate-limit incoming requests.

Rate and concurrency limiting

Rate limiting consists of counting how many requests a server accepts within a given period of time, and rejecting new ones when a limit is reached.

Concurrency limiting consists of counting how many concurrent requests are being served by the web server to the same remote user, and rejecting new ones when it reaches a defined threshold. Since many requests can reach the server simultaneously, a concurrency limiter needs to have a small allowance in its threshold.

These techniques avoid any trouble within our application when we know there is an upper limit to how many requests it can respond to concurrently, and that can be a factor in load balancing across multiple instances of our app. Both are implemented using the same technique. Let's look at how to build a concurrency limiter.

OpenResty ships with a rate-limiting library written in Lua called `lua-resty-limit-traffic`; you can use it in an `access_by_lua_block` section: `https://github.com/openresty/lua-resty-limit-traffic`.

The function uses Lua *Shared Dict*, which is a memory mapping that is shared by all `nginx` workers within the same process. Using an in-memory dictionary means that rate limiting will work at the process level.

Since we're typically deploying one `nginx` per service node, rate limiting will happen per web server. So, if you are deploying several nodes for the same microservice, our effective rate limit will be the number of connections a single node can handle multiplied by the number of nodes—this will be important to take into account when deciding on the overall rate limit and how many concurrent requests the microservices can process.

In the following example, we're adding a `lua_shared_dict` definition and a section called `access_by_lua_block` to activate the rate limiting. Note that this example is a simplified version of the example in the project's documentation:

```
# resty_limiting.conf
daemon off;
worker_processes  1;
error_log /dev/stdout info;
events {
    worker_connections  1024;
}
http {
    lua_shared_dict my_limit_req_store 100m;

    server {
```

```
        listen    8888;
        server_name   localhost;
        access_log /dev/stdout;
        location / {
            access_by_lua_block {
                local limit_req = require "resty.limit.req"
                local lim, err = limit_req.new("my_limit_req_store",
200, 100)

                local key = ngx.var.binary_remote_addr
                local delay, err = lim:incoming(key, true)
                if not delay then
                    if err == "rejected" then
                        return ngx.exit(503)
                    end
                    ngx.log(ngx.ERR, "failed to limit req: ", err)
                    return ngx.exit(500)
                end

                if delay >= 0.001 then
                    local excess = err
                    ngx.sleep(delay)
                end
            }
            proxy_pass http://localhost:5000;
            proxy_set_header Host $host;
            proxy_set_header X-Real-IP $remote_addr;
            proxy_set_header X-Forwarded-For $proxy_add_x_forwarded_for;
        }
    }
}
```

The access_by_lua_block section can be considered as a Lua function, and can use some of the variables and functions that OpenResty exposes. For instance, ngx.var is a table containing all the nginx variables, and ngx.exit() is a function that can be used to immediately return a response to the user—in our case, a 503 when we need to reject a call because of rate limiting.

The library uses the my_limit_req_store dictionary that is passed to the resty. limit.req function; every time a request reaches the server, it calls the incoming() function with the binary_remote_addr value, which is the client address.

The incoming() function will use the shared dictionary to maintain the number of active connections per remote address, and send back a rejected value when that number reaches the threshold; for example, when there are more than 300 concurrent requests.

If the connection is accepted, the `incoming()` function sends back a delay value. Lua will hold the request using that delay and the asynchronous `ngx.sleep()` function. The delay will be `0` when the remote client has not reached the threshold of `200`, and a small delay when between `200` and `300`, so the server has a chance to unstack all the pending requests.

This design is quite efficient to prevent a service from becoming overwhelmed by many requests. Setting up a ceiling like this is also a good way to avoid reaching a point at which you know your microservice will start to break. For instance, if some of your benchmarks concluded that your service could not serve more than 100 simultaneous requests before starting to crash, you can set the rate limit appropriately, so it is `nginx` that rejects requests instead of letting your Quart microservice try to process all those incoming connections only to reject them.

The key used to calculate the rate in this example is the remote address header of the request. If your `nginx` server is itself behind a proxy, make sure you are using a header that contains the real remote address. Otherwise, you will rate limit a single remote client, the proxy server. It's usually in the `X-Forwarded-For` header in that case.

If you want a WAF with more features, the `lua-resty-waf` (https://github.com/p0pr0ck5/lua-resty-waf) project works like `lua-resty-limit-traffic`, but offers a lot of other protections. It is also able to read `ModSecurity` rule files, so you can use the rule files from the OWASP project without having to use `ModSecurity` itself.

Other OpenResty features

OpenResty comes with many Lua scripts that can be useful to enhance `nginx`. Some developers are even using it to serve their data directly. The following components page contains some useful tools for having `nginx` interact with databases, cache servers, and so on: `http://openresty.org/en/components.html`.

There's also a website for the community to publish OpenResty components: `https://opm.openresty.org/`.

If you are using OpenResty in front of your Quart microservices, there will probably be other use cases where you can transfer some code that is in the Quart app to a few lines of Lua in OpenResty. The goal should not be to move the app's logic to OpenResty, but rather to leverage the web server to do anything that can be done before or after your Quart app is called. Let Python focus on the application logic and OpenResty work on a layer of protection.

For instance, if you are using a Redis or a Memcached server to cache some of your GET resources, you can directly call them from Lua to add or fetch a cached version for a given endpoint. The `srcache-nginx-module` (`https://github.com/openresty/srcache-nginx-module`) is an implementation of such behavior, and will reduce the number of GET calls made to your Quart apps if you can cache them.

To conclude this section about WAFs: OpenResty is a powerful `nginx` distribution that can be used to create a simple WAF to protect your microservices. It also offers abilities that go beyond firewalling. In fact, if you adopt OpenResty to run your microservices, it opens a whole new world of possibilities, thanks to Lua.

Summary

In this chapter, we have looked at how to centralize authentication and authorization in a microservices-based application environment using OAuth2 and JWTs. Tokens give us the ability to limit what a caller can do with one of the microservices, and for how long they can do it.

When used with public and private keys, it also limits the damage an attacker can inflict if one component of the whole application is compromised. It also ensures that each connection is cryptographically validated.

A secure code base is the first step to a secure application. You should follow good coding practices and make sure your code does not do anything bad when interacting with incoming user data and resources. While a tool like Bandit will not guarantee the safety and security of your code, it will catch the most obvious potential security issues, so there should be no hesitation about continuously running it on your code base.

Lastly, a WAF is also a good way to prevent some fraud and abuse on your endpoints and is very easy to do with a tool such as OpenResty, thanks to the power of the Lua programming language.

OpenResty is also an excellent way to empower and speed up your microservices by doing a few things at the web server level when they do not need to be done within the Quart application.

8

Making a Dashboard

Most of the work done so far has focused on building microservices and making them interact with each other. It is time to bring humans into the equation, adding a **User Interface** (**UI**) through which our end users can use the system with a browser and change settings that may be awkward or unwise to do through Slack.

Modern web applications greatly rely on client-side JavaScript (JS, also known as ECMAScript). Some JS frameworks go all the way in terms of providing a full **Model-View-Controller** (**MVC**) system, which runs in the browser and manipulates the **Document Object Model** (**DOM**), the structured representation of the web page that is rendered in a browser.

The web development paradigm has shifted from rendering everything on the side of the server, to rendering everything on the client side with data collected from the server on demand. The reason is that modern web applications change portions of a loaded web page dynamically instead of calling the server for a full rendering. It is faster, requires less network bandwidth, and offers a richer user experience. Delays of a few seconds can cause a user to navigate away from your page, unless they have a strong need to visit it, such as, more specifically, a need to shop or read. One of the biggest examples of this client-side shift is the Gmail app, which pioneered these techniques around 2004.

Tools like Facebook's **ReactJS** (https://facebook.github.io/react/) provide high-level APIs to avoid manipulating the DOM directly and offer a level of abstraction which makes client-side web development as comfortable as building Quart applications.

That said, there seems to be a new JS framework every other week, and it is often hard to decide which one to use. **AngularJS** (https://angularjs.org/) used to be the coolest toy, but now many developers have switched to implementing most of their application UIs with ReactJS. There are also newer languages, such as **Elm** (https://elm-lang.org), which offers a functional programming language that compiles to JavaScript, allowing the compile-time detection of many common programming errors while also having a runtime that will work with any browser. In the future, no doubt, another new player will be popular.

This volatility is not a bad sign at all. It simply means much innovation is happening in the JavaScript and browser ecosystem. Features like service workers allow developers to run JS code in the background natively: https://developer.mozilla.org/en/docs/Web/API/Service_Worker_API.

WebAssembly (https://webassembly.org/), an extremely fast and safe sandboxed environment, allows developers to produce resource-intensive tools, such as 3D rendered environments, all running in a web browser.

If you have a clean separation between your UI and the rest of the system, moving from one JS framework to another should not be too hard. This means that you should not change how your microservices publish data to make them specific to a JS framework.

For our purposes, we shall use ReactJS to build our little dashboard, and we will wrap it in a dedicated Quart application that bridges it to the rest of the system. We will also see how that app can interact with all our microservices. We have chosen this approach due to ReactJS's current popularity, though you will also get excellent results in any of the other popular environments.

This chapter is composed of the following three parts:

- Building a ReactJS dashboard — a short introduction to ReactJS with an example
- How to embed ReactJS in a Quart app and structure the application
- Authentication and authorization

By the end of this chapter, you should have a good understanding of how to build a web UI using Quart, with the knowledge of how to make it interact with microservices — whether you choose to use ReactJS or not.

Building a ReactJS dashboard

The ReactJS framework implements its abstraction of the DOM and provides fast and efficient machinery to support dynamic events. Creating a ReactJS UI involves creating classes with a few standard methods, which will get called when events happen, such as the DOM being ready, the React class having been loaded, or user input occurring.

In a similar way to a web server such as nginx, taking care of all the difficult and common parts of the network traffic and leaving you to deal with the logic in your endpoints, ReactJS lets you concentrate on the implementation in your methods instead of worrying about the state of the DOM and the browser. Implementing classes for React can be done in pure JavaScript, or using an extension called JSX. We will discuss JSX in the next section.

The JSX syntax

Representing XML markup in a programming language can be hard work. A seemingly simple approach might be to treat all the markup as strings and format the content as if it were a template, but this approach means that your code does not understand what all that markup means. The other extreme would be creating each markup element as an object and rendering it all to the text representation.

Instead, there is a better, hybrid model using a transpiler – a type of compiler that generates a different form of source code instead of a runnable program. The JSX syntax extension (https://facebook.github.io/jsx/) adds XML tags to JavaScript and can be transpiled into pure JavaScript, either in the browser or beforehand. JSX is promoted by the ReactJS community as the best way to write React apps.

In the following example, a `<script>` section contains a `greeting` variable whose value is an XML structure representing a `div`; this syntax is valid JSX. From there, the `ReactDOM.render()` function can render the `greeting` variable in the DOM at the `id` you specify:

```
<!DOCTYPE html>
<html>

<head lang="en">
    <meta charset="UTF-8">
</head>
```

```
    <body>
        <div id="content"></div>
        <script src="https://unpkg.com/react@17/umd/react.development.
js" crossorigin></script>
        <script src="https://unpkg.com/react-dom@17/umd/react-dom.
development.js" crossorigin></script>
        <script src="https://unpkg.com/babel-standalone@6/babel.min.js"
crossorigin></script>
        <script type="text/babel">
            var greeting = (
                <div>
                    Hello World
                </div>)
            ReactDOM.render(greeting, document.
getElementById('content'));
        </script>
    </body>
    </html>
```

The two ReactJS scripts are part of the React distribution, and here we are using the development versions, which will provide more helpful error messages while we are still writing our code. Smaller, encoded versions — known as minified — are preferred for production use, as they use less network bandwidth and cache storage space. The `babel.min.js` file is part of the Babel distribution and needs to be loaded before the browser encounters any JSX syntax.

Babel (`https://babeljs.io/`) is a transpiler that can convert JSX to JS on the fly, among other available conversions. To use it, you simply need to mark a script as being of type `text/babel`.

The JSX syntax is the only specific syntax difference to know about React, as everything else is done with common JavaScript. From there, building a ReactJS application involves creating classes to render markup and respond to events, and these will be used to render the web pages.

Let's now look at the heart of ReactJS – components.

React components

ReactJS is based on the idea that a web page can be constructed from basic components, which are invoked to render different parts of the display and respond to events such as typing, clicks, and new data appearing.

As an example, if you want to display a list of people, you can create a `Person` class that is in charge of rendering a single person's information, given its values, and a `People` class that iterates through a list of people and calls the `Person` class to render each item.

Each class is created with the `React.createClass()` function, which receives a mapping containing the future class methods. The `createClass()` function generates a new class, and sets a `props` attribute to hold some properties alongside the provided methods. In the following example, in a new JavaScript file, we define a `Person` class with a `render()` function, which returns a `<div>` tag, and a `People` class which assembles the `Person` instances:

```
class Person extends React.Component {
    render() {
        return (
            <div>{this.props.name} ({this.props.email})</div>
        );
    }
}

class People extends React.Component {
    render() {
        var peopleNodes = this.props.data.map(function (person) {
            return (
                <Person
                    key={person.email}
                    name={person.name}
                    email={person.email}
                />
            );
        });
        return (
            <div>
                {peopleNodes}
            </div>
        );
    }
}
```

The `Person` class returns a `div`—a section or division—containing details about the person by referring to the `props` attribute in the instance. Updating these properties will update the object, and so update the display.

The props array is populated when the Person instance is created; this is what happens in the render() method of the People class. The peopleNodes variable iterates through the People.props.data list, which contains a list of the people we want to show. Each Person class is also provided with a unique key so that it can be referred to later if needed.

All that is left to do is instantiate a People class and put a list of people to be displayed by React in its props.data list. In our Jeeves app, this list can be provided by the appropriate microservice — the data service for information that we store, or a different service if we are fetching data from a third party. We can load the data asynchronously using an **Asynchronous JavaScript and XML (AJAX)** pattern using the built-in fetch method, or another helper library.

That is what happens in the loadPeopleFromServer() method in the following code, which builds on the previous example – add it to the same jsx file. The code calls our data service on the endpoint that lists all users, using a GET request and expecting some JSON as a response. Then, it sets the properties of the React component with the result, which propagates down through the other classes:

```jsx
class PeopleBox extends React.Component {
    constructor(props) {
        super(props);
        this.state = { data: [] };
    }

    loadPeopleFromServer() {
        fetch('http://localhost:5000/api/users')
            .then(response => response.json())
            .then(data => {
                console.log(data);
                this.setState({
                    data: data,
                });
                console.log(this.state);
            })
            .catch(function (error) {
                console.log(error);
            });
    }
    componentDidMount() {
        this.loadPeopleFromServer();
    }
```

```
        render() {
            return (
                <div>
                    <h2>People</h2>
                    <People data={this.state.data} />
                </div>
            );
        }


    }

    const domContainer = document.querySelector('#people_list');
    ReactDOM.render(React.createElement(PeopleBox), domContainer);
```

When the state changes, an event is passed to the `React` class to update the DOM with the new data. The framework calls the `render()` method, which displays the `<div>` containing `People`. The `People` instance, in turn, passes data down to each `Person` instance in a cascade.

To trigger the `loadPeopleFromServer()` method, the class implements the `componentDidMount()` method, which gets called once the class instance is created and mounted in React, ready to be displayed. Last, but not least, the class's constructor provides an empty set of data so that in the time before anything has loaded, the display is not broken.

This whole process of decomposition and chaining may seem complicated at first but, once in place, it is powerful and straightforward to use: it allows you to focus on rendering each component and letting React deal with how to do it in the most efficient way in the browser.

Each component has a state, and when something changes, React first updates its own internal representation of the DOM — the virtual DOM. Once that virtual DOM is changed, React can apply the required changes efficiently on the actual DOM.

All the JSX code we've seen in this section can be saved in a JSX file – it's static content, so let's place it in a directory called `static` – and used in an HTML page as follows. There is also a small helper microservice to serve these files in the code samples at `https://github.com/PacktPublishing/Python-Microservices-Development-2nd-Edition/tree/main/CodeSamples`.

```
    <!DOCTYPE html>
    <html>

    <head lang="en">
```

```
        <meta charset="UTF-8">
    </head>

    <body>
        <div class="container">
            <h1>Jeeves Dashboard</h1>
            <br>
            <div id="people_list"></div>
        </div>

        <script src="https://unpkg.com/react@17/umd/react.development.
js" crossorigin></script>
        <script src="https://unpkg.com/react-dom@17/umd/react-dom.
development.js" crossorigin></script>
        <script src="https://unpkg.com/babel-standalone@6/babel.min.js"
crossorigin></script>
        <script src="/static/people.jsx" type="text/babel"></script>
        <script type="text/babel">

        </script>

    </body>

    </html>
```

The PeopleBox class is instantiated with the /api/users URL for this demonstration, and once the web page has loaded and been processed, the componentDidMount methods are triggered, React calls that URL, and it expects to get back a list of people, which it passes down the chain of components.

Notice that we have also set up where to render the components in the last two lines: first, we find the element in the HTML with the right identifier, and then tell React to render a class within it.

Using transpilation directly in the browser is unnecessary, as it can be done while building and releasing the application, as we will see in the next section.

This section described a very basic usage of the ReactJS library and did not dive into all its possibilities. If you want to get more info on React, you should try the tutorial at https://reactjs.org/tutorial/tutorial.html as your first step. This tutorial shows you how your React components can interact with the user through events, which is the next step once you know how to do some basic rendering.

Pre-processing JSX

So far, we have relied on the web browser to convert the JSX files for us. We could still do that, however, it will be the same work being done by each web browser that visits our site. Instead, we can process our own JSX files and provide pure JavaScript to people visiting our site. To do that we must install some tools.

Firstly, we need a JavaScript package manager. The most important one to use is npm (https://www.npmjs.com/). The npm package manager is installed via Node.js. On macOS, the brew install node command does the trick, or you can go to the **Node.js** home page (https://nodejs.org/en/) and download it to the system. Once Node.js and npm are installed, you should be able to call the npm command from the shell as follows:

```
$ npm -v
7.7.6
```

Converting our JSX files is straightforward. Move the .jsx file we have created from static/ to a new directory called js-src. Our directory layout should now look like this:

- mymicroservice/
    - templates/ – all of our html files
    - js-src/ – our jsx source code
    - static/ – the JavaScript results of the transpilation

We can then install the tools we need using:

```
$ npm install --save-dev @babel/core @babel/cli @babel/preset-env @babel/preset-react
```

Then, for our development, we can start a command that will continuously watch our js-src directory for any changes to the files, and automatically update them, in much the same way that the development version of Quart will reload Python files automatically. In a new terminal, type:

```
$ npx babel --watch js-src/ --out-dir static/  --presets @babel/preset-react
```

We can then see that it creates .js files for you and does so each time you save your changes to the JSX files in js-src/.

To deploy our application, we can either generate the JavaScript files and commit them into the repository or generate them as part of the CI process. In either case, the command to process the files once is remarkably similar—we just don't watch the directory, and we use the production presets:

```
$ npx babel js-src/ --out-dir static/ --presets @babel/preset-react
```

With all the changes, the final `index.html` file just needs a small change to use the `.js` file instead of the `.jsx` one:

```
<script src="/static/people.js"></script>
```

Now that we have the basic layout for building a React-based UI, let's see how we can embed it in our Quart world.

ReactJS and Quart

From the perspective of the server, the JavaScript code is a static file, and so serving React apps with Quart is no trouble at all. The HTML page can be rendered with Jinja2, and the transpiled JSX files can be provided as static content alongside it, much like you would do for plain JavaScript files. We can also get the React distribution and serve those files, or rely on a **Content Delivery Network (CDN)** to provide them.

In many cases a CDN is the better option, as retrieving the files will be faster, and the browser then has the option of recognizing that it has already downloaded these files and can use a cached copy to save time and bandwidth. Let's name our Quart application `dashboard`, and start off with a simple structure like this:

- setup.py
- dashboard/
  - __init__.py
  - app.py
  - templates/
  - index.html
  - static/
  - people.jsx

The basic Quart application that serves the unique HTML file will look like this:

```python
from quart import Quart, render_template

app = Quart(__name__)

@app.route('/')
def index():
    return render_template('index.html')

if __name__ == '__main__':
    app.run()
```

Thanks to Quart's convention on static assets, all the files contained inside the `static/` directory are served under the `/static` URL. The `index.html` template looks like the one described in the previous section and can grow into something Quart-specific later on. That is all we need to serve a ReactJS-based app through Quart.

Throughout this section, we have worked on the assumption that the JSON data that React picked was served by the same Quart app. Doing AJAX calls on the same domain is not an issue, but in case you need to call a microservice that belongs to another domain, there are a few changes required on both the server and the client side.

Cross-origin resource sharing

Allowing client-side JavaScript to perform cross-domain requests is a potential security risk. If the JS code that's executed in the client page for your domain tries to request a resource from another domain that you don't own, it could potentially run malicious JS code and harm your users. This is why all browsers use the W3C standard for cross-origin resources (`https://www.w3.org/TR/2020/SPSD-cors-20200602/`) when a request is made. They ensure that the requests can only be made to the domain that served the page to us.

Beyond security, it is also a good way to prevent someone from using your bandwidth for their web app. For instance, if you provide a few font files on your website, you might not want another website to use them on their page and use your bandwidth without any control. However, there are legitimate use cases for wanting to share your resources with other domains, and you can set up rules on your service to allow other domains to reach your resources.

That is what **Cross-Origin Resource Sharing (CORS)** is all about. When the browser sends a request to your service, an `Origin` header is added, and you can control whether it is in the list of authorized domains. If not, the CORS protocol requires that you send back a few headers listing the allowed domains. There is also a `preflight` mechanism where the browser questions the endpoint via an `OPTIONS` call to know whether the request it wants to make is authorized and what capabilities the server has available. On the client side, you do not have to worry about setting up these mechanisms. The browser makes the decisions for you, depending on your requests.

On the server side, however, you need to make sure your endpoints answer the `OPTIONS` calls, and you need to decide which domains can reach your resources. If your service is public, you can authorize all domains with a wildcard. However, for a microservice-based application where you control the client side, you should restrict the domains. The **Quart-CORS** (`https://gitlab.com/pgjones/quart-cors/`) project allows us to add support for this very simply:

```python
# quart_cors_example.py
from quart import Quart
from quart_cors import cors

app = Quart(__name__)
app = cors(app, allow_origin="https://quart.com")

@app.route("/api")
async def my_microservice():
    return {"Hello": "World!"}
```

When running this app and using `curl` to do a `GET` request, we can see the results in the `Access-Control-Allow-Origin: *` header:

```
$ curl -H "Origin: https://quart.com" -vvv http://127.0.0.1:5000/api
*    Trying 127.0.0.1...
* TCP_NODELAY set
* Connected to 127.0.0.1 (127.0.0.1) port 5200 (#0)
> GET /api HTTP/1.1
> Host: 127.0.0.1:5000
> User-Agent: curl/7.64.1
> Accept: */*
> Origin: https://quart.com
>
< HTTP/1.1 200
< content-type: application/json
< content-length: 18
```

```
< access-control-allow-origin: quart.com
< access-control-expose-headers:
< vary: Origin
< date: Sat, 10 Apr 2021 18:20:32 GMT
< server: hypercorn-h11
<
* Connection #0 to host 127.0.0.1 left intact
{"Hello":"World!"}* Closing connection 0
```

Quart-CORS allows finer-grained permissions, with decorators that allow protecting a single resource or blueprint instead of the whole app, or limiting methods to GET, POST, or others. It's also possible to set configuration using environment variables, which helps the app remain flexible and get the correct settings at runtime.

For an in-depth understanding of CORS, the MDN page is a great resource that can be found here: `https://developer.mozilla.org/en-US/docs/Web/HTTP/CORS`. In this section, we have looked at how to set up CORS headers in our services to allow cross-domain calls, which are useful in JS apps. What's still missing to make our JS app fully functional is authentication and authorization.

Authentication and authorization

The React dashboard needs to be able to authenticate its users and perform authorized calls on some microservices. It also needs to enable the user to grant access to any third-party sites we support, such as Strava or GitHub.

We assume that the dashboard only works when you are authenticated and that there are two kinds of users: first-time and returning. The following is the user story for first-time users:

> *As a first-time user, when I visit the dashboard, there's a "login" link. When I click on it, the dashboard redirects me to Slack to grant access to my resources. Slack then redirects me back to the dashboard, and I am connected. The dashboard then starts to fill with my data.*

As described, our Quart app performs an OAuth2 conversation with Slack to authenticate users—and we know that since we are setting up a Slack bot, people should already have an account there. Connecting to Slack also means we need to store the access token in the user profile so we can use it to fetch data later on.

Before going further, we need to make a design decision: do we want the dashboard merged with the dataservice, or do we want to have two separate apps?

A note about Micro Frontends

Now we are discussing authenticating our users with a web frontend, there is the question of where we should put the corresponding code. One recent trend in frontend architecture is the idea of Micro Frontends. Facing many of the same scaling and interoperability troubles as the backend has faced, some organizations are shifting towards small, self-contained user interface components that can be included in a larger site.

Let's imagine a shopping website. When you visit the front page, there will be several different parts, including:

- Shopping categories
- Site-wide news and events, such as upcoming sales
- Highlighted and promoted items for sale, including customized recommendations
- A list of items you have recently viewed
- A widget allowing you to sign in or register for an account, plus other administrative tools

If we develop a single web page to deal with all of these elements, it can become large and complex very quickly, especially if we need to repeat elements across different pages on the site. With many sites, these different features are kept separate by separating out the <div> tags that anchor them in the page, and keeping the code in separate JavaScript files — whether or not those files are separate by the time they are loaded into the web page, as they have likely been compiled and minified.

This approach introduces some of the same complications that a monolithic backend suffers from. A change to any of the backend or its user interface means updating a microservice and the user interface elements that query it, and those may well be in different source control repositories or managed by different teams. Perhaps support for both the old and new ways has to be introduced for a managed migration, or careful timing with different deployment mechanisms has to happen.

By using a Micro Frontend architecture, these UI features can all be the responsibility of different teams and services. If the "recommendations" feature suddenly requires a new backend or a different JavaScript framework, that is possible, as the main site only knows about it as a self-contained feature to be included. Any change can also be self-contained, as the Micro Frontend UI components for the recommendations engine would live in the same repository and be provided by the same service. As long as the technique to include the Micro Frontend component doesn't change, the main user interface doesn't need to be changed; changes can be controlled entirely through the microservice it depends on.

This also frees up the people working on each component, as they can release new features and bug fixes on their own schedule without large cross-team coordination to deploy updated features in multiple areas. The teams just have to ensure their UI is included in a consistent manner, accepts the same data, such as a customer identifier, and returns a UI element of the desired size.

Let's look at the Packt website as an example. When loading the main web page, we get to see a banner along the top containing the usual options we expect, a banner below for current promotions and events, and then a listing of recently added stock to be brought to the reader's attention:

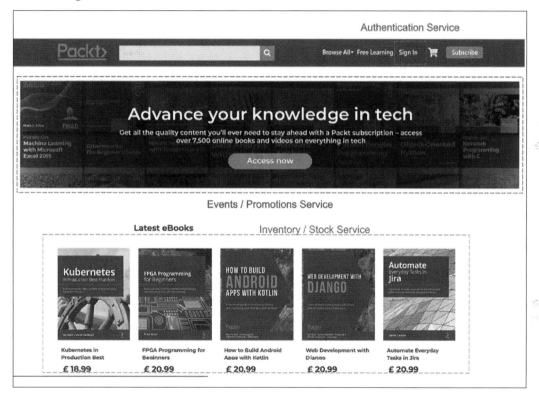

Figure 8.1: Packt home page and its constituent parts

If we were designing this page, we could construct at least three different micro-frontends: an authentication component that handles sessions and logging in, an events component that can display and react to upcoming conferences and promotions, and an inventory component that can display current stock. This approach isn't ideal for all situations; on many occasions, a user interface needs to interact closely with other elements, or perhaps the spread of knowledge within an organization doesn't allow it to produce many small user interface components this way.

It is also worth noting that this architecture does not require many different URLs. The same nginx load balancer could be configured to route different URLs to different backend services without the client being any the wiser—and this may give a useful approach to migrating to such an architecture, as it lowers the chance of you needing to update the endpoint URLs.

With all that said, the Micro Frontend model is still relatively new, and many best practices and even bits of terminology are still in flux. For that reason, we shall focus on a simpler variant of this approach and have the authentication service provide its own HTML for logging a user in and creating an account that can be included in an iframe within another page if desired.

Getting the Slack token

Slack provides a typical three-legged OAuth2 implementation, using a simple set of HTTP GET requests. Implementing the exchange is done by redirecting the user to Slack and exposing an endpoint the user's browser is redirected to once access has been granted.

If we request the special identify scope, then all we get from Slack is confirmation of the user's identity and the unique Slack ID string. We can store all this information in the Quart session, use it as our login mechanism, and pass the e-mail and token values to DataService for use with other components if we need to.

As we did in *Chapter 4, Designing Jeeves*, let us implement the function that generates the URL to send the user to, combined with the other information Slack needs, which is documented at https://api.slack.com/legacy/oauth:

```
@login.route("/login/slack")
async def slack_login():
    query = {
        "client_id": current_app.config["JEEVES_CLIENT_ID"],
        "scope": "identify",
        "redirect_uri": current_app.config["SLACK_REDIRECT_URI"],
    }
    url = f"https://slack.com/oauth/authorize?{urlencode(query)}"
    return redirect(url)
```

Here, we are running our Quart application behind nginx with a Let's Encrypt certificate, as we also set up in *Chapter 4, Designing Jeeves*. This is why we are using a callback URL from our configuration rather than attempting to work it out dynamically, as that URL is tied to nginx.

That function uses the `client_id` from the Jeeves application generated in Slack and returns a redirection URL we can present to the user. The dashboard view can be changed accordingly to pass that URL to the template.

```
@login.route("/")
async def index():
    return await render_template("index.html", user=session.
get("user"))
```

We also pass a `user` variable if there are any stored in the session. The template can then use the Strava URL to display a login/logout link as follows:

```
{% if not user %}
<a href="{{url_for('login.slack_login')}}">Login via Slack</a>
{% else %}
Hi {{user}}!
<a href="/logout">Logout</a>
{% endif %}
```

When the user clicks on the `login` link, they are redirected to Strava and back to our application on the endpoint, defined as `SLACK_REDIRECT_URI`. The implementation of that view could be like this:

```
@login.route("/slack/callback")
async def slack_callback():
    query = {
        "code": request.args.get("code"),
        "client_id": current_app.config["JEEVES_CLIENT_ID"],
        "client_secret": current_app.config["JEEVES_CLIENT_
SECRET"],
        "redirect_uri": current_app.config["SLACK_REDIRECT_URI"],
    }
    url = "https://slack.com/api/oauth.access"
    response = requests.get(url, params=query)
    response_data = response.json()
    session["user"] = response_data["user_id"]
    return redirect(url_for("login.index"))
```

Using the response we get from Slack's OAuth2 service, we put the temporary code received into a query to convert that into a real access token. Then we can store the token in the session or send it to the data service.

We are not detailing how Dashboard interacts with TokenDealer, since we have already shown this in *Chapter 7, Securing Your Services*. The process is similar—the Dashboard app gets a token from TokenDealer and uses it to access DataService.

The last part of authentication is in the ReactJS code, as we will see in the next section.

JavaScript authentication

When the Dashboard app performs the OAuth2 exchange with Slack, it stores user information in the session, which is a fine approach for the user authenticating on the dashboard. However, when the ReactJS UI calls the DataService microservice to display the user runs, we need to provide an authentication header. The following are two ways to handle this problem:

- Proxy all the calls to the microservices via the Dashboard web app using the existing session information.
- Generate a JWT token for the end user, which can be stored and used against another microservice.

The proxy solution seems simplest as it removes the need to generate one token per user for accessing DataService, although that does mean that if we want to trace a transaction back to an individual user, we have to connect the DataService event to the frontend's list of events.

Proxying allows us to hide the DataService from public view. Hiding everything behind the dashboard means we have more flexibility to change the internals while keeping the UI compatible. The problem then is that we are forcing all the traffic through the Dashboard service even when it is not needed. Our exposed API and the Dashboard appear, to the end user, to have different routes to the data, which may cause confusion. It also means that if there is an outage with the DataService, then the Dashboard is affected and may stop responding to any people trying to view the page. If the JavaScript contacts the DataService directly, then the Dashboard will continue operating, and notifications can be put up to let people know there is an ongoing problem.

This leads us strongly towards the second solution, generating a token for the end user for use in the React frontend. If we are already dealing tokens to the other microservices, the web user interface is just one of the clients. However, this also means that the client has a second authentication loop, as it must first authenticate using OAuth2, and then fetch a JWT token for internal services.

As we discussed in the last chapter, we can generate a JWT token once we have authenticated, and then use that to communicate with the other services under our control. The workflow is exactly the same—it simply gets called from JavaScript.

Summary

In this chapter, we looked at the fundamentals of building a ReactJS UI dashboard served by a Quart application. ReactJS is an excellent way to build a modern interactive UI in the browser, as it introduces a new syntax called JSX which speeds up JS execution. We also looked at how to use a toolchain, based on npm, and Babel, to manage JS dependencies and transpile JSX files into pure JavaScript.

The Dashboard application uses Slack's OAuth2 API to connect users and authenticate them with our own service. We made the design decision to separate the Dashboard application from DataService, so the token is sent to the DataService microservice for storage. That token can then be used by the periodic workers as well as the Jeeves actions to perform tasks on behalf of the user.

Lastly, the calls made to different services to build the dashboard are made independently of the dashboard, allowing us to focus on doing one thing well in each component. Our authorization service deals with all the token generation, and our dashboard can focus on being responsive to the viewer.

Figure 8.2 contains a diagram of the new architecture, which includes the Dashboard app:

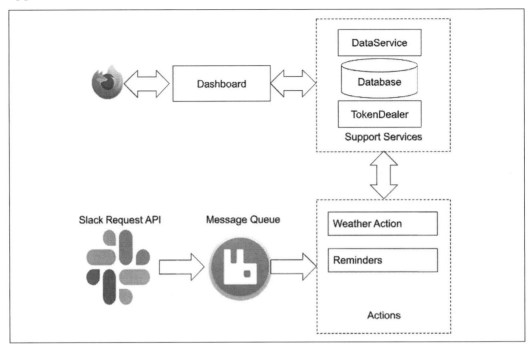

Figure 8.2: The full Jeeves microservice architecture

You can find the full code of the Dashboard in the PythonMicroservices organization on GitHub at https://github.com/PacktPublishing/Python-Microservices-Development-2nd-Edition/.

With several different Quart apps that compose it, developing an application like Jeeves can be a challenge when you are a developer. In the next chapter, we will look at packaging and running the application to make maintenance and upgrading much easier.

9
Packaging and Running Python

When the Python programming language was first released in the early 1990s, a Python application was run by pointing the Python scripts to the interpreter. Everything related to packaging, releasing, and distributing Python projects was done manually. There was no real standard back then, and each project had a long README on how to install it with all its dependencies.

Bigger projects used system packaging tools to release their work—whether it was Debian packages, RPM packages for Red Hat Linux distributions, or MSI packages under Windows. Eventually, the Python modules from those projects all ended up in the `site-packages` directory of the Python installation, sometimes after a compilation phase, if they had a C extension.

The Python packaging ecosystem has evolved a lot since then. In 1998, `Distutils` was added to the standard library to provide essential support to create installable distributions for Python projects. Since then, a lot of new tools have emerged from the community to improve how a Python project can be packaged, released, and distributed. This chapter is going to explain how to use the latest Python packaging tools for your microservices.

The other hot topic around packaging is how it fits in with your day-to-day work. When building microservices-based software, you need to deal with many moving parts. When you are working in a particular microservice, you can get away with using the TDD and mocking approach most of the time, which we discussed in *Chapter 3, Coding, Testing, and Documentation: the Virtuous Cycle*.

However, if you want to do some realistic testing, and examine all the parts of the system, you need the whole stack running either locally or on a test cloud instance. Moreover, developing in such a context can be tedious if you need to reinstall new versions of your microservices all the time. This leads to one question in particular: *how can you correctly install the whole stack in your environment and develop in it?*

It also means you have to run all the microservices if you want to play with the app. In the case of Jeeves, having to open multiple different shells to run all the microservices is not something a developer would want to do every time they need to run the app.

In this chapter, we are going to look at how we can leverage the packaging tools to run all microservices from the same environment, and then how to run them all from a single **Command-Line Interface** (**CLI**) by using a dedicated process manager. First, however, we will look at how to package your projects, and which tools should be utilized.

The packaging toolchain

Python has come a long way since the days of those early packaging methods. Numerous **Python Enhancement Proposals** (**PEPs**) were written to improve how to install, release, and distribute Python projects.

Distutils had some flaws that made it a little tedious to release software. The biggest pain points were its lack of dependency management and the way it handled compilation and binary releases. For everything related to compiling, what worked well in the nineties started to get old-fashioned ten years later. No one in the core team made the library evolve due to lack of interest, and also because Distutils was good enough to compile Python and most projects. People who needed advanced toolchains used other tools, like SCons (http://scons.org/).

In any case, improving the toolchain was not an easy task because of the existing legacy system based on Distutils. Starting a new packaging system from scratch was quite hard, since Distutils was part of the standard library, but introducing backward-compatible changes was also hard to do properly. The improvements were made in between. Projects like Setuptools and virtualenv were created outside the standard library, and some changes were made directly in Python.

As of the time of writing, you still find the scars from these changes, and it is still quite hard to know exactly how things should be done. For instance, the pyvenv command was added in early versions of Python 3 and then removed in Python 3.6, but Python still ships with its virtual environment module, although there are also tools such as virtualenv to help make life easier.

The best bet is to use the tools that are developed and maintained outside the standard library, because their release cycle is shorter than Python's. In other words, a change in the standard library takes months to be released, whereas a change in a third-party project can be made available much faster. All third-party projects that are considered as being part of the de facto standard packaging toolchain are now all grouped under the **PyPA** (https://www.pypa.io) umbrella project.

Besides developing the tools, PyPA also works on improving the packaging standards through proposing PEPs for Python and developing its early specifications—refer to https://www.pypa.io/en/latest/roadmap/. There are often new tools and experiments in packaging and dependency management that let us learn new things whether or not they become popular. For this chapter, we will stick with the core, well-known tools.

Before we start to look at the tools that should be used, we need to go through a few definitions to avoid any confusion.

A few definitions

When we talk about packaging Python projects, a few terms can be confusing, because their definitions have evolved over time, and also because they can mean slightly different things outside the Python world. We need to define a Python package, a Python project, a Python library, and a Python application. They are defined as follows:

- A **Python package** is a directory tree containing Python modules. You can import it, and it is part of the module namespace.

- A **Python project** can contain several packages, modules, and other resources and is what you release. Each microservice you build with Flask is a Python project.

- A **Python application** is a Python project that can be directly used through a user interface. The user interface can be a command-line script or a web server.

- Lastly, a **Python library** is a specific kind of Python project that provides features to be used in other Python projects and has no direct end-user interface.

The distinction between an application and a library can be quite vague, since some libraries sometimes offer some command-line tools to use some of their features, even if the first use case is to provide Python packages for other projects. Moreover, sometimes, a project that was a library becomes an application.

To simplify the process, the best option is to make no distinction between applications and libraries. The only technical difference is that applications ship with more data files and console scripts.

Now that we have defined the terminology around a Python package, project, application, and library, let's look at how projects are packaged.

Packaging

When you package your Python project, there are three standard files you need to have alongside your Python packages:

- `pyproject.toml`: A configuration file for the project's build system
- `setup.py` or `setup.cfg`: A special module that controls packaging and metadata about the project
- `requirements.txt`: A file listing dependencies

Let's look at each one of them in detail.

The setup.py file

The `setup.py` file is what governs everything when you want to interact with a Python project. When the `setup()` function is executed, it generates a static metadata file that follows the `PEP 314` format. The metadata file holds all the metadata for the project, but you need to regenerate it via a `setup()` call to get it to the Python environment you are using.

The reason why you cannot use a static version is that the author of a project might have platform-specific code in `setup.py`, which generates a different metadata file depending on the platform and Python versions. Relying on running a Python module to extract static information about a project has always been a problem. You need to make sure that the code in the module can run in the target Python interpreter. If you are going to make your microservices available to the community, you need to keep that in mind, as the installation happens in many different Python environments.

A common mistake when creating the `setup.py` file is to import your package into it when you have third-party dependencies. If a tool like `pip` tries to read the metadata by running `setup.py`, it might raise an import error before it has a chance to list all the dependencies to install. The only dependency you can afford to import directly in your `setup.py` file is `Setuptools`, because you can assume that anyone trying to install your project is likely to have it in their environment.

Another important consideration is the metadata you want to include to describe your project. Your project can work with just a name, a version, a URL, and an author, but this is obviously not enough information to describe your project. Metadata fields are set through `setup()` arguments. Some of them match directly with the name of the metadata, while some do not.

The following is a useful set of arguments you could use for your microservices projects:

- `name`: The name of the package; should be short and lowercase
- `version`: The version of the project, as defined in `PEP 440`
- `url`: A URL for the project; can be its repository or home page
- `description`: One sentence to describe the project
- `long_description`: A reStructuredText or Markdown document
- `author` and `author_email`: The name and email of the author — can be an organization
- `license`: The license used for the project (MIT, Apache2, GPL, and so on)
- `classifiers`: A list of classifiers picked from a fixed list, as defined in `PEP 301`
- `keywords`: Tags to describe your project — this is useful if you publish the project to the **Python Package Index (PyPI)**
- `packages`: A list of packages that your project includes — `Setuptools` can populate that option automatically with the `find_packages()` method
- `entry_points`: A list of `Setuptools` hooks, like console scripts (this is a `Setuptools` option)
- `include_package_data`: A flag that simplifies the inclusion of non-Python files
- `zip_safe`: A flag that prevents `Setuptools` from installing the project as a ZIP file, which is a historical standard (executable eggs)

If you are missing any critical options, then `Setuptools` will provide information about the ones it needs when you try to use it. The following is an example of a `setup.py` file that includes these options:

```
from setuptools import setup, find_packages

with open("README.rst") as f:
    LONG_DESC = f.read()

setup(
    name="MyProject",
```

```
        version="1.0.0",
        url="http://example.com",
        description="This is a cool microservice based on Quart.",
        long_description=LONG_DESC,
        long_description_content_type="text/x-rst",
        author="Simon",
        author_email="simon@example.com",
        license="MIT",
        classifiers=[
            "Development Status :: 3 - Alpha",
            "License :: OSI Approved :: MIT License",
            "Programming Language :: Python :: 3",
        ],
        keywords=["quart", "microservice"],
        packages=find_packages(),
        include_package_data=True,
        zip_safe=False,
        install_requires=["quart"],
    )
```

The `long_description` option is usually pulled from a `README.rst` file, so you do not have to deal with including a large piece of reStructuredText string in your function.

The `Twine` project (`https://pypi.org/project/twine/`)—which we will use later to upload packages to PyPI—has a check command to ensure the long description can be rendered properly. Adding this check to **Continuous Integration (CI)** as part of a standard test suite is a good idea, to ensure the documentation on PyPI is readable. The other benefit of separating the description is that it's automatically recognized, parsed, and displayed by most editors. For instance, GitHub uses it as your project landing page in your repository, while also offering an inline reStructuredText editor to change it directly from the browser. PyPI does the same to display the front page of the project.

The `license` field is freeform, as long as people can recognize the license being used. `https://choosealicense.com/` offers impartial advice about which open-source software license is most appropriate for you, if you plan to release the source code— and you should strongly consider it, as our progress through this book and the myriad of tools used have all been based on open-source projects, and adding more to the community helps everyone involved. In any case, you should add, alongside your `setup.py` file, a LICENCE file with the official text of that license. In open-source projects it is common practice now to also include a "Code Of Conduct," such as the `Contributor Covenant: https://www.contributor-covenant.org/`.

This is because working with people from around the world involves many different cultures and expectations, and being open about the nature of the community is another aspect that helps everyone.

The classifiers option is probably the most painful one to write. You need to use strings from `https://pypi.python.org/pypi?%3Aaction=list_classifiers` that classify your project. The three most common classifiers that developers use are the list of supported Python versions, the license (which duplicates and should match the license option), and the development status, which is a hint about the maturity of the project.

The `Trove` classifier is machine-parsable metadata that can be used by tools interacting with `PyPI`. For example, the `zc.buildout` tool looks for packages with the `Framework :: Buildout :: Recipe` classifier. A list of valid classifiers is available at `https://pypi.org/classifiers/`.

Keywords are a good way to make your project visible if you publish it to the Python Package Index. For instance, if you are creating a `Quart` microservice, you should use "quart" and "microservice" as keywords.

The `entry_points` section is an INI-like string that defines ways to interact with your Python module through callables—most commonly a console script. When you add functions in that section, a command-line script will be installed alongside the Python interpreter, and the function hooked to it via the entry point. This is a good way to create a CLI for your project. In the example, `mycli` should be directly reachable in the shell when the project is installed. Lastly, `install_requires` lists all the dependencies. It's a list of Python projects the project uses and can be used by projects like `pip` when the installation occurs. The tool will grab them if they are published in PyPI and install them. It is also possible to read the dependencies from the file we will be discussing next, `requirements.txt`, and to read the version from a separate text file—or JSON file—so that the version can be easily used in multiple places if it's needed in the release pipeline. Since the JSON module is part of the standard library, there is no extra dependency added by importing it.

Once this `setup.py` file is created, a good way to try it is by creating a local virtual environment.

Assuming you have `virtualenv` installed, and you run these commands in the directory containing the `setup.py` file, it will create a few directories, including a `bin` directory containing a local Python interpreter, and drop you into a local shell:

```
$ python3 -m venv ./my-project-venv
$ source ./my-project-venv/bin/activate
(my-project-venv) $
```

There are several helper tools to make managing your virtual environments easier, such as virtualenvwrapper (https://virtualenvwrapper.readthedocs.io/en/latest/), but we will keep to the core functionality with our examples.

From here, running the pip install -e command will install the project in editable mode. This command installs the project by reading its setup file, but unlike install, the installation occurs in-place. Installing in-place means that you will be able to work directly on the Python modules in the project, and they will be linked to the local Python installation via its site-packages directory.

Using a regular install call would have created copies of the files in the local site-packages directory, and changing the source code would have had no impact on the installed version.

The pip call also generates a MyProject.egg-info directory, which contains the metadata. pip generates version 1.1 of the metadata spec under the PKG-INFO name:

```
$ more MyProject.egg-info/PKG-INFO
Metadata-Version: 2.1
Name: MyProject
Version: 1.0.0
Summary: This is a cool microservice based on Quart.
Home-page: http://example.com
Author: Simon
Author-email: simon@example.com
License: MIT
Description: long description!

Keywords: quart,microservice
Platform: UNKNOWN
Classifier: Development Status :: 3 - Alpha
Classifier: License :: OSI Approved :: MIT License
Classifier: Programming Language :: Python :: 3
Description-Content-Type: text/x-rst
```

This metadata file is what describes your project, and is used to register it to PyPI via other commands, as we will see later in the chapter.

The pip call also pulls all the project dependencies by looking for them in PyPI on https://pypi.python.org/pypi and installs them in the local site-packages. Running this command is a good way to make sure everything works as expected.

The requirements.txt file

One standard that emerged from the pip community is to use a `requirements.txt`
file, which lists all the project dependencies, but also proposes an extended syntax
to install editable dependencies. Refer to `https://pip.pypa.io/en/stable/cli/pip_`
`install/#requirements-file-format`.

The following is an example of such a file:

```
arrow
python-dateutil
pytz
requests
six
stravalib
units
```

Using this file has been widely adopted by the community, because it makes it easier
to document your dependencies. You can create as many requirements files as you
want in a project, and have your users call the `pip install -r requirements.txt`
command to install the packages described in them.

For instance, you could have a `dev-requirements.txt` file, which contains extra
tools for development, and a `prod-requirements.txt`, which has production-specific
dependencies. The format allows inheritance to help you manage requirements files'
collections.

Using the `requirements` files duplicates some of the information contained in
the `setup.py` file's `install_requires` section. As noted earlier, we could read in
the `requirements.txt` file and include the data in `setup.py`. Some developers
deliberately keep these sources separate to distinguish between an application and a
library, allowing a library more flexibility in its dependencies in order to co-operate
with other installed libraries. This does mean keeping two sources of information up
to date, which is often a source of confusion.

As we said earlier in the chapter, we do not want to make our life complicated
by having two different ways to describe Python project dependencies, since the
distinction between an application and a library can be quite vague. To avoid
duplicating the information in both places, there are some tools in the community
that offer some syncing automation between `setup.py` and requirements files.

The `pip-tools` (https://github.com/jazzband/pip-tools) tool is one of these
utilities, and it generates a `requirements.txt` file (or any other filename) via a `pip-compile` CLI, as follows:

```
$ pip install pip-tools
...
$ pip-compile
#
# This file is autogenerated by pip-compile
# To update, run:
#
#     pip-compile
#
aiofiles==0.6.0
     # via quart
blinker==1.4
     # via quart
click==7.1.2
     # via quart
h11==0.12.0
     # via
     #    hypercorn
     #    wsproto
...
```

With no other arguments, `pip-compile` will examine `setup.py`. It's also possible to
pass it an unpinned version file, such as `requirements.in` as a list of packages to use
instead.

Notice that all the dependencies are pinned—the version we want is in the file. This
is always a good idea in a production environment, as we want our application to
be reproducible. If we do not specify a version to install, then we will get whatever
is the latest, and that may break our application. By specifying the version, we know
that all the tests we have run will still be valid no matter how far in the future we
deploy that version of our app.

It's also a good idea to add the hash of the dependency to the `requirements.txt`
file, as this avoids any issue with someone uploading a package without updating
the version number, or a malicious actor replacing an existing version of a package.
These hashes will be compared to the downloaded files on installation, and are only
used if they match:

```
$ pip-compile —generate-hashes
#
# This file is autogenerated by pip-compile
# To update, run:
#
#     pip-compile —generate-hashes
#
aiofiles==0.6.0 \
    —hash=sha256:bd3019af67f83b739f8e4053c6c0512a7f545b9a8d91aaeab55e6
e0f9d123c27 \
    —hash=sha256:e0281b157d3d5d59d803e3f4557dcc9a3dff28a4dd4829a9ff478
adae50ca092
    # via quart
blinker==1.4 \
    —hash=sha256:471aee25f3992bd325afa3772f1063dbdbbca947a041b8b89466d
c00d606f8b6
    # via quart
click==7.1.2 \
    —hash=sha256:d2b5255c7c6349bc1bd1e59e08cd12acbbd63ce649f2588755783
aa94dfb6b1a \
    —hash=sha256:dacca89f4bfadd5de3d7489b7c8a566eee0d3676333fbb5003026
3894c38c0dc
    # via quart
```

If you don't use pip-tools, pip has a built-in command called freeze, which you can use to generate a list of all the current versions that are installed in your Python virtual environment. Using pip freeze without a virtual environment is likely to result in a lot of packages that have been used for other projects, rather than just your own work:

```
$ pip freeze
aiofiles==0.6.0
blinker==1.4
click==7.1.2
h11==0.12.0
h2==4.0.0
hpack==4.0.0
…
...
```

The only problem when you pin your dependencies is when another project has the same dependencies, but is pinned with other versions. pip will complain and fail to meet both the requirements sets, and you will not be able to install everything. If you are producing a library, and you expect other people to use and add to their own list of dependencies, it is a good idea to specify a range of versions that you support, so that pip can try to sort out any dependency conflicts. For example:

```
quart>0.13.0,<0.15.0
```

It's also common practice to leave the dependencies unpinned in the `setup.py` file and pin the `requirements.txt` file. That way, pip can install the latest version for each package, and when you deploy, specifically in stage or production, you can refresh the versions by running the `pip install -r requirements.txt` command. pip will then upgrade/downgrade all the dependencies to match the versions, and if you need to, you can tweak them in the requirements file.

To summarize, defining dependencies should be done in each project's `setup.py` file, and requirements files can be provided with pinned dependencies if you have a reproducible process to generate them from the `setup.py` file to avoid duplication.

The next useful file your projects could have is the `MANIFEST.in` file.

The MANIFEST.in file

When creating a source or binary release, Setuptools will include all the package modules and data files, the `setup.py` file, and a few other files automatically in the package archive. Files like `pip requirements` will not be included. To add them to your distribution, you need to add a `MANIFEST.in` file, which contains the list of files to include.

The file follows a simple glob-like syntax, described at the following, where you refer to a file or a directory pattern and say whether you want to include or prune the matches: https://docs.python.org/3/distutils/commandref.html#creating-a-source-distribution-the-sdist-command.

Here's an example from Jeeves:

```
include requirements.txt
include README.rst
include LICENSE
recursive-include myservice *.ini
recursive-include docs *.rst *.png *.svg *.css *.html conf.py
prune docs/build/*
```

The `docs/directory` containing the Sphinx doc will be integrated in the source distribution, but any artifact generated locally in `docs/build/` when the doc is built will be pruned.

Once you have the `MANIFEST.in` file in place, all the files should be added in your distribution when your project is released.

A typical microservice project, as described in this book, will have the following list of files:

- `setup.py`: The setup file
- `README.rst`: The content of the `long_description` option
- `MANIFEST.in`: The MANIFEST template if it is needed
- A code of conduct, if the code is an open-source project
- `requirements.txt`: pip requirement files generated from `install_requires`
- `docs/`: The Sphinx documentation
- A directory containing the microservice code, which will typically be named after the microservice, or `src/`

From there, releasing your project consists of creating a source distribution, which is basically an archive of this structure. If you have some C extensions, you can also create a binary distribution.

Before we learn how to create those releases, let's look at how to pick version numbers for your microservices.

Versioning

Python packaging tools do not enforce a specific versioning pattern, although the version field should be one that can be converted using the packaging module into a meaningful version. Let's discuss what counts as a meaningful version number. To understand a versioning scheme, an installer needs to know how to sort and compare versions. The installer needs to be able to parse the string and know whether a version is older than another one.

Some software uses a scheme based on the date of release, like `20210101` if your software was released on January 1, 2021. For some use cases this works perfectly well. If you are practicing **Continuous Deployment** (**CD**), where every change that reaches the release branch is pushed to production, then there may be such a large number of changes that fixed version numbers are hard to work with. In that sort of situation, a date-based version, or a version from the version control hash, may work well.

Date- or commit-based versioning won't work very well if you do branched releases. For instance, if your software has a large change in behavior and you need to support the older version for a while as people transition, then having versions 1 and 2 makes things clear, but using dates in this situation will make some of your "version 1" releases appear as if they were more recent than some of the "version 2" releases, and confuse anyone trying to determine what they should install. Some software combines incremental versions and dates for that reason, but it became obvious that using dates was not the best way to handle branches.

There is also the problem of releasing beta, alpha, release candidates, and dev versions. Developers want to have the ability to mark releases as being pre-releases. For instance, when Python is about to ship a new version, it will ship release candidates using an rcX marker so that the community can try it before the final release is shipped, for example, 3.10.0rc1 or 3.10.0rc2.

For a microservice that you are not releasing to the community, using such markers is often unnecessary — but when you start to have people from outside your organization using your software, it may become useful.

Release candidates can be useful if you are about to ship a backward-incompatible version of a project. It's always a good idea to have your users try it out before it's published. For the usual release though, using candidate releases is probably overkill, as publishing a new release when a problem is found is cheap.

pip does a fairly good job of figuring out most patterns, ultimately falling back to some alphanumeric sorting, but the world would be a better place if all projects were using the same versioning scheme. PEP 386, then 440, was written to try to come up with a versioning scheme for the Python community. It's derived from the standard MAJOR.MINOR[.PATCH] scheme, which is widely adopted among developers, with some specific rules for pre and post versions.

The **Semantic Versioning (SemVer)** (http://semver.org/) scheme is another standard that emerged in the community, which is used in many places outside Python. If you use SemVer, you will be compatible with PEP 440 and the pip installer as long as you don't use pre-release markers. For instance, 3.6.0rc2 translates to 3.6.0-rc2 in SemVer.

Unlike PEP 440, SemVer asks that you always provide the three version numbers. For instance, 1.0 should be 1.0.0. The python-semver library will help a great deal with comparing different versions: https://github.com/python-semver/python-semver:

```
>>> import semver
>>> version1 = semver.parse_version_info('2.2.3-rc2')
```

```
>>> version2 = semver.parse_version_info('2.3.1')
>>> version1 < version2
    True
```

For your microservice project, or any Python project for that matter, you should start with the `0.1.0` version to make it clear that it is not yet stable and may change drastically during early development, and that backward compatibility is not guaranteed. From there, you can increment the `MINOR` number at will until you feel the software is mature enough.

Once maturity has been reached, a common pattern is to release `1.0.0`, and then start to follow these rules:

- `MAJOR` is incremented when you introduce a backward-incompatible change for the existing API.
- `MINOR` is incremented when you add new features that do not break the existing API.
- `PATCH` is incremented just for bug fixes.

Being strict about this scheme with the `0.x.x` series when the software is in its early phase does not make much sense, because you will make a lot of backward-incompatible changes, and your `MAJOR` version would reach a high number in no time.

The `1.0.0` release is often emotionally charged for developers. They want it to be the first stable release they will give to the world—that's why it's common to use the `0.x.x` versions and bump to `1.0.0` when the software is deemed stable.

For a library, what we call the API is all the public and documented functions and classes one may import and use. For a microservice, there's a distinction between the code API and the HTTP API. You may completely change the whole implementation in a microservice project and still implement the exact same HTTP API. You need to treat those two versions distinctly.

It's important to remember that version numbers are not decimals, or really any form of counting number, and so while it may look like the next version after `3.9` should be `4.0`, it does not have to be—`3.10` and onward are perfectly acceptable. The numbers are simply a way to order the values and tell which is lower or greater than another.

Now that we know how to deal with version numbers, let's do some releasing.

Releasing

To release your project, we must build a package that can be either uploaded to a package repository such as PyPI or installed directly wherever it is needed. Python has a build utility that makes this process straightforward.

In the following example, we install the build utility, and then run it in the example project we used earlier in this chapter. The output can be quite long, so only some of it is included below:

```
$ pip install --upgrade build
...
$ python -m build
...
running bdist_wheel
running build
installing to build/bdist.macosx-10.15-x86_64/wheel
running install
running install_egg_info
running egg_info
writing MyProject.egg-info/PKG-INFO
writing dependency_links to MyProject.egg-info/dependency_links.txt
writing requirements to MyProject.egg-info/requires.txt
writing top-level names to MyProject.egg-info/top_level.txt
reading manifest file 'MyProject.egg-info/SOURCES.txt'
writing manifest file 'MyProject.egg-info/SOURCES.txt'
Copying MyProject.egg-info to build/bdist.macosx-10.15-x86_64/wheel/
MyProject-1.0.0-py3.8.egg-info
running install_scripts
creating build/bdist.macosx-10.15-x86_64/wheel/MyProject-1.0.0.dist-
info/WHEEL
creating '/Users/simon/github/PythonMicroservices/CodeSamples/Chapter9/
pyproject-example/dist/tmpcqfu71ms/MyProject-1.0.0-py3-none-any.whl'
and adding 'build/bdist.macosx-10.15-x86_64/wheel' to it
adding 'MyProject-1.0.0.dist-info/METADATA'
adding 'MyProject-1.0.0.dist-info/WHEEL'
adding 'MyProject-1.0.0.dist-info/top_level.txt'
adding 'MyProject-1.0.0.dist-info/RECORD'
removing build/bdist.macosx-10.15-x86_64/wheel
```

The build command reads the information from setup.py and MANIFEST.in, collects all the files, and puts them in an archive. The result is created in the dist directory:

```
$ ls dist/
MyProject-1.0.0-py3-none-any.whl MyProject-1.0.0.tar.gz
```

Notice that the name of the archive is composed of the name of the project and its version. The archive is in the Wheel format, defined in PEP 427, which is currently the best format for distributing Python packages, although there have been different methods in the past, which you may encounter in existing projects. This archive can be used directly with pip to install the project as follows:

```
$ pip install dist/MyProject-1.0.0-py3-none-any.whl
Processing ./dist/MyProject-1.0.0-py3-none-any.whl
Collecting quart
  Using cached Quart-0.15.1-py3-none-any.whl (89 kB)
Collecting hypercorn>=0.11.2
  Using cached Hypercorn-0.11.2-py3-none-any.whl (54 kB)
Collecting itsdangerous
  Using cached itsdangerous-2.0.1-py3-none-any.whl (18 kB)
…
Installing collected packages: hyperframe, hpack, h11, wsproto,
priority, MarkupSafe, h2, werkzeug, jinja2, itsdangerous, hypercorn,
click, blinker, aiofiles, quart, MyProject
Successfully installed MarkupSafe-2.0.1 MyProject-1.0.0 aiofiles-0.7.0
blinker-1.4 click-8.0.1 h11-0.12.0 h2-4.0.0 hpack-4.0.0
hypercorn-0.11.2 hyperframe-6.0.1 itsdangerous-2.0.1 jinja2-3.0.1
priority-2.0.0 quart-0.15.1 werkzeug-2.0.1 wsproto-1.0.0
```

Once you have your archive ready, it's time to distribute it.

Distributing

If you are developing in an open-source project, it is good practice to publish your project to PyPI, so that it can be used by a wide range of people. This can be found at: https://pypi.python.org/pypi. If the project is private, or internal to a company, then you may have a package repository for your work that operates in a similar way to PyPI that is only visible to your own organization's infrastructure.

Like most modern language ecosystems, PYPI can be browsed by installers that are looking for releases to download. When you call the pip install <project> command, pip will browse PyPI to see whether that project exists, and whether there are some suitable releases for your platform.

The public name is the name you use in your `setup.py` file, and you need to register it at PyPI to be able to publish releases. The index uses the first-come, first-serve principle, so if the name you have picked is already taken, then you will have to choose another one.

When creating microservices for an application or organization, you can use a common prefix for all your projects' names. It is also possible to set up your own private version of PyPI for projects that should not be released to the wider world. If at all possible, though, it helps everyone to contribute to the open-source community.

At the package level, a prefix can also sometimes be useful to avoid conflicts. Python has a namespace package feature, which allows you to create a top-level package name (like `jeeves`), and then have packages in separate Python projects, which will end up being installed under the top-level `jeeves` package.

The effect is that every package gets a common `jeeves` namespace when you import them, which is quite an elegant way to group your code under the same banner. The feature is available through the `pkgutil` module from the standard library.

To do this, you just need to create the same top-level directory in every project, with the `__init__.py` file, containing and prefixing all absolute imports with the top-level name:

```
from pkgutil import extend_path
__path__ = extend_path(__path__, __name__)
```

For example, in Jeeves, if we decide to release everything under the same namespace, each project can have the same top-level package name. In the `tokendealer`, it could be as follows:

- jeeves
    - `__init__.py`: Contains the `extend_path` call
    - tokendealer/
        - ... the actual code...

And then in the `dataservice` directory, like this:

- jeeves
    - `__init__.py`: Contains the `extend_path` call
    - dataservice/
        - ... the actual code...

Both will ship a jeeves top-level namespace, and when pip installs them, the tokendealer and dataservice packages will both end up installed and available underneath the name jeeves:

```
>>> from jeeves import tokendealer, dataservice
```

This feature is not that useful in production, where each microservice is deployed in a separate installation, but it does not hurt, and it can be useful if you start to create a lot of libraries that are used across projects. For now, we will make the assumption that each project is independent, and each name is available at PyPI.

To publish the releases at PyPI, you first need to register a new user using the form at https://pypi.org/account/register/, which will look like that shown in *Figure 9.1*.

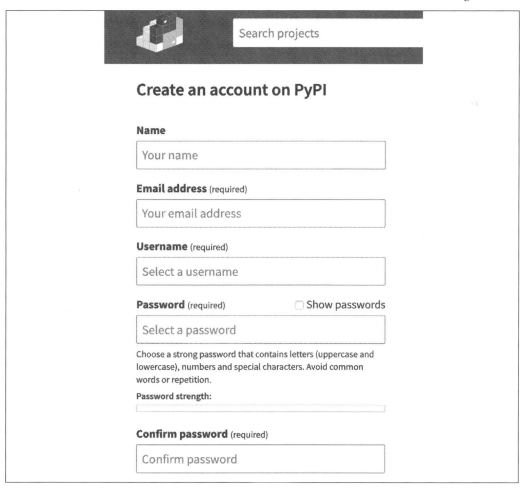

Figure 9.1: Creating an account on PyPI

It's also worth registering at the test version of PyPI, as this will let you experiment with uploads and try out all the commands without publishing anything to the real index. Use `https://test.pypi.org/account/register/` for an account on the test service.

Python `Distutils` has a `register` and `upload` command to register a new project at PyPI, but it is better to use `Twine` (`https://github.com/pypa/twine`), which comes with a better user interface. Once you've installed `Twine` (using the `pip install twine` command), the next step is to register your package using the following command:

```
$ twine register dist/jeeves-dataservice-0.1.0.tar.gz
```

Once done, you can go ahead and upload the releases. Let's upload to the test version of PyPI first, to make sure everything works. After the upload, we give pip some extra arguments so that it knows to use the test version of the PyPI version, and then to fall back to the real package index to sort out the other dependencies:

```
$ twine upload —repository testpypi dist/*
$ pip install —index-url https://test.pypi.org/simple/ —extra-index-url
https://pypi.org/simple jeeves-dataservice
```

Once we know everything is working, we can upload to the real package index:

```
$ twine upload dist/*
```

From there, your package should appear in the index, with an HTML home page at `https://pypi.python.org/pypi/<project>`. The `pip install <project>` command should work!

Now that we know how to package each microservice, let us see how to run them all in the same box for development purposes.

Running all microservices

So far, we have run our `Quart` applications using the built-in Quart wrapper, or using the `run()` function. This works well for development, as the app can detect changes to its source code and reload itself, saving time when making changes. However, there are limitations to this, not least of which is that this is running the server in a development mode, with extra diagnostics turned on that slow down the server's operation.

Instead, we should run our applications using Hypercorn (`https://pgjones.gitlab.io/hypercorn/`), an ASGI web server that allows Quart to run to its full potential, supporting HTTP/2, HTTP/3, as well as WebSocket. It's already installed alongside Quart and is very straightforward to use. For our dataservice application, we would run:

```
$ hypercorn dataservice:app
```

Hypercorn is the latest in a mine of WSGI and ASGI servers that aim to serve web applications, and if you are searching the Flask documentation when looking into extensions, you may come across mention of Gunicorn (`https://gunicorn.org/`), as it is a common equivalent to Hypercorn for synchronous applications, using a worker pool model to provide concurrency, an option we discussed in *Chapter 1, Understanding Microservices*. For Quart, though, we will stick with Hypercorn.

The last piece of the puzzle is to avoid having to run each console script in a separate Bash window. We want to manage those processes with a single script. Let's see in the next section how we can do this with a process manager.

Process management

Hypercorn specializes in running web apps. If you want to deploy a development environment with a few other processes, you have to manage several different Python microservices, a RabbitMQ instance, a database, and whatever else you use. In order to make life easier in your development environment, you will need to use another process manager.

A good option is a tool like Circus (`http://circus.readthedocs.io`), which can run any kind of process, even when they are not ASGI or WSGI applications. It also has the ability to bind sockets and make them available for the managed processes. In other words, Circus can run a Quart app with several processes, and can also manage some other processes if needed.

Circus is a Python application, so, to use it, you can simply run the command `pip install circus`. Once Circus is installed, it provides a few commands—through the `entry_points` method described earlier. The two principal commands are `circusd`, which is the process manager, and `circusctl`, which lets you control the process manager from the command line. Circus uses an INI-like configuration file, where you can list the commands to run in dedicated sections—and, for each one of them, the number of processes you want to use.

Circus can also bind sockets, and let the forked process use them via their file descriptors. When a socket is created on your system, it uses a **File Descriptor (FD)**, which is a system handle a program can use to reach a file or an I/O resource like sockets. A process that is forked from another one inherits all its file descriptors. That is, through this mechanism, all the processes launched by Circus can share the same sockets.

In the following example, two commands are being run. One will run five processes for the Quart application, located in the server.py module, using the virtualenv provided in the virtualenv path, and the second command will run one Redis server process:

```
[watcher:web]
cmd = hypercorn —bind fd://$(circus.sockets.web) server:app
use_sockets = True
numprocesses = 5
virtualenv = ./venvs/circus-virtualenv/
copy_env = True

[watcher:redis]
cmd = /usr/local/bin/redis-server
use_sockets = False
numprocesses = 1

[socket:web]
host = 0.0.0.0
port = 8000
```

The socket:web section describes what host and port to use to bind the TCP socket, and the watcher:web section uses it via the $(circus.sockets.web) variable. When Circus runs, it replaces that variable with the FD value for the socket. To run this script, you can use the circusd command line:

```
$ circusd myconfig.ini
```

For our microservices, using Circus means we can simply create a watcher and a socket section per service and start them all using the circusd command.

Circus also offers options to redirect the stdout and stderr streams to log files to facilitate debugging and numerous other features that can be found at https://circus.readthedocs.io/en/latest/for-ops/configuration/.

Summary

In this chapter, we have looked at how to package, release, and distribute each microservice. The current state of the art in Python packaging still requires some knowledge about the legacy tools, and this will be the case for some years until all the ongoing work in Python and PyPA becomes mainstream. But, provided you have a standard, reproducible, and documented way to package and install your microservices, you should be fine.

Having numerous projects to run a single application adds a lot of complexity when you are developing it, and it's important to be able to run all pieces from within the same box. Tools like pip's development mode and Circus are useful for this, as it allows you to simplify how you run the whole stack—but they still require that you install tools on your system, even if it is inside a `virtualenv`.

The other issue with running everything from your local computer is that you might not use an operating system that will be used to run your services in production, or you may have some libraries installed for other purposes, which might interfere.

The best way to prevent this problem is to run your stack in an isolated environment. This is what the next chapter will cover: how to run your services inside a container.

10
Deploying on AWS

In the previous chapters, we ran our different microservices directly in the host operating system, as it is sometimes the quickest way to get started, while also being a useful approach in general—especially for smaller installations or development where everything can be contained in a virtual environment. However, if the application requires a database or a compiled extension, then things start to be tightly coupled to the operating system and version. Other developers with slightly different systems will start to run into problems, and the more differences between a development environment and a production one, the more trouble you will have when releasing your software.

Virtual Machines (**VMs**) can be a good solution, as they provide an isolated environment in which to run your code. A VM is essentially a piece of software pretending to be a real computer, in which there is a real operating system running in the pretend computer. If you've ever used an Amazon EC2 instance or a Google Compute Engine instance, then you have used a virtual machine. It's possible to run them locally using tools such as VMware or VirtualBox.

However, VMs are heavyweights, precisely because they emulate a full computer. Using one from scratch involves installing an operating system or using a tool such as HashiCorp's Packer (https://www.packer.io/) to build a disk image—the sort of thing that comes prebuilt for you when selecting an AWS or GCP instance.

The big revolution came with **Docker**, an open-source virtualization tool first released in 2013. Docker allows the use of isolated environments called *containers* to run applications in a very portable way.

Cloud computing providers, such as Amazon Web Services (AWS), Google Cloud, and Microsoft Azure, allow people to rent space on their computers and make creating virtual machines and containers much easier. Provisioning these cloud resources, along with attached storage and databases, can be done with a few mouse clicks, or a few commands typed in a terminal. They can also be configured using configuration files to describe resources, using Infrastructure-as-Code tools, such as HashiCorp's **Terraform**.

In this chapter, we present Docker and explain how to run Quart-based microservices with it. We then cover deploying a container-based application using some common orchestration tools, such as Docker Compose, Docker Swarm, and, briefly, Kubernetes. Many of these topics could fill entire books by themselves, so this chapter will be an overview that relies on the installation instructions provided by the tools themselves to get started.

Most of the cloud computing providers will also have their own versions of these tools, modified to better integrate with the other services that they offer. If you are already using a particular company's services, it is worth investigating their tools. At the same time, it is also worth knowing the cloud-agnostic versions, as taking a more independent approach can make migrating from one provider to another much easier.

 Note that some of the instructions in this chapter may result in incurring a charge from AWS. While we will keep those costs to a minimum, it is important to understand what costs may be incurred by checking with AWS and also to unsubscribe from any unused resources after trying things out.

What is Docker?

The **Docker** (https://www.docker.com/) project is a *container* platform, which lets you run your applications in isolated environments. Using the Linux feature called cgroups (https://en.wikipedia.org/wiki/Cgroups), Docker creates isolated environments called containers that run on Linux without a VM. On macOS and Windows, installing Docker will create a lightweight VM for you to run containers in, although this is a seamless process. This means that macOS, Windows, and Linux users can all develop container-based applications without worrying about any interoperability trouble and deploy them to a Linux server where they will run natively.

Today, Docker is almost synonymous with containers, but there are other container runtimes, such as **CRI-O** (https://cri-o.io/), and historical projects such as **rkt** and **CoreOS** that, together with Docker, helped shape the standardized ecosystem that we have today.

Because containers do not rely on emulation when running on Linux, there is little performance difference between running code inside a container and outside. As there is an emulation layer on macOS and Windows, while it is possible to run containers in production on these platforms, there is little benefit to doing so. It is possible to package up everything needed to run an application inside a container image and distribute it for use anywhere that can run a container.

As a Docker user, you just need to choose which image you want to run, and Docker does all the heavy lifting by interacting with the Linux kernel. An image in this context is the sum of all the instructions required to create a set of running processes on top of a Linux kernel, to run one container. An image includes all the resources necessary to run a Linux distribution. For instance, you can run whatever version of Ubuntu you want in a Docker container even if the host OS is of a different distribution.

 As containers operate best on a Linux-based system, the rest of this chapter assumes that everything is installed under a Linux distribution, such as Ubuntu.

We used Docker in *Chapter 5, Splitting the Monolith,* when discussing metrics and monitoring, so you may already have Docker installed. With some older Linux distributions, you may have a very old version of Docker available. Installing a newer one directly from Docker itself is a good idea, to get the latest features and security patches. If you have a Docker installation, feel free to jump directly to the next section of this chapter, *Introduction to Docker.* If not, you can visit https://www. docker.com/get-docker to download it and find the installation instructions. The community edition is good enough for building, running, and installing containers. Installing Docker on Linux is straightforward—you can probably find a package for your Linux distribution.

For macOS, if you have Homebrew (https://brew.sh) installed, then you can simply use brew install docker. Otherwise, follow the instructions on Docker's website. Under Windows, Docker can either use the **Windows Subsystem for Linux (WSL2)**, or the built-in Hyper-V to run a virtual machine. We recommend WSL, as it is the most straightforward to get working.

If the installation was successful, you should be able to run the `docker` command in your shell. Try the `version` command to verify your installation, like this:

```
$ docker version
Client:
 Cloud integration: 1.0.14
 Version:           20.10.6
 API version:       1.41
 Go version:        go1.16.3
 Git commit:        370c289
 Built:             Fri Apr  9 22:46:57 2021
 OS/Arch:           darwin/amd64
 Context:           default
 Experimental:      true

Server: Docker Engine - Community
 Engine:
  Version:          20.10.6
  API version:      1.41 (minimum version 1.12)
  Go version:       go1.13.15
  Git commit:       8728dd2
  Built:            Fri Apr  9 22:44:56 2021
  OS/Arch:          linux/amd64
  Experimental:     false
 containerd:
  Version:          1.4.4
  GitCommit:        05f951a3781f4f2c1911b05e61c160e9c30eaa8e
 runc:
  Version:          1.0.0-rc93
  GitCommit:        12644e614e25b05da6fd08a38ffa0cfe1903fdec
 docker-init:
  Version:          0.19.0
  GitCommit:        de40ad0
```

A Docker installation is composed of a Docker Engine, which controls the running containers and a command-line interface. It also includes Docker Compose, which is a way of arranging multiple containers that will work together, as well as Kubernetes, an orchestration tool for deploying and managing container-based applications.

The engine provides an HTTP API, which can be reached locally through a UNIX socket (usually, `/var/run/docker.sock`) or through the network. This means it is possible to control a Docker Engine that is running on a different computer to the Docker client, or orchestration tooling.

Now that Docker is installed on your system, let's discover how it works.

Introduction to Docker

Let's experiment with Docker containers. Running a container that you can enter commands in is as simple as the following:

```
docker run --interactive --tty ubuntu:20.04 bash
```

With this command, we are telling Docker to run the Ubuntu image, which will be fetched from Docker Hub, a central registry of public images. We are providing a tag of `20.04` after the image name so that we download the container image that represents the Ubuntu 20.04 operating system. This won't contain everything that a regular Ubuntu installation has, but anything that's missing is installable.

We also tell Docker to run interactively—the `-i` argument—and to assign a `tty` with the `-t` argument, so that we can type commands inside the container. By default, Docker assumes that you want to start a container that runs in the background, serving requests. By using these two options and asking that the command `bash` is run inside the container, we can get a shell that we can use just like a Linux shell, outside the container.

Every existing Linux distribution out there provides a base image, not just Ubuntu. There are also pared-down base images for running Python, Ruby, or other environments, and base Linux images, such as Alpine, which aim to be even smaller. The size of the image is important because every time you want to update it or run it in a new place, it must be downloaded. Alpine is a little over 5MB in size, whereas the `ubuntu:20.04` image is nearly 73MB. You can compare sizes and manage the images your Docker Engine knows about with the following commands – the second command will remove any local copy of the `ubuntu:20.04` image, so if you run that, you will need to download that image again to use it:

```
$ docker images
REPOSITORY      TAG       IMAGE ID        CREATED       SIZE
python          3.9       a6a0779c5fb2    2 days ago    886MB
ubuntu          20.04     7e0aa2d69a15    3 weeks ago   72.7MB
alpine          latest    6dbb9cc54074    4 weeks ago   5.61MB
```

```
$ docker rmi ubuntu:20.04
Untagged: ubuntu:20.04
Untagged: ubuntu@sha256:cf31af331f38d1d7158470e095b132acd126a7180a54f26
3d386da88eb681d93
Deleted: sha256:7e0aa2d69a153215c790488ed1fcec162015e973e49962d438e1824
9d16fa9bd
Deleted: sha256:3dd8c8d4fd5b59d543c8f75a67cdfaab30aef5a6d99aea3fe74d8cc
69d4e7bf2
Deleted: sha256:8d8dceacec7085abcab1f93ac1128765bc6cf0caac334c821e01546
bd96eb741
Deleted: sha256:ccdbb80308cc5ef43b605ac28fac29c6a597f89f5a169bbedbb8dec
29c987439
```

You might think that the size means the Ubuntu image is always a better choice than the Python base image, but the Ubuntu image doesn't contain Python, and so to use it we must build an image that contains everything we need and install our own software on top of that. Rather than do all of this set up by hand, we can use a **Dockerfile** (https://docs.docker.com/engine/reference/builder/).

The standard name for these Docker configuration files is a Dockerfile, and the following is a basic example of one:

```
FROM ubuntu:20.04
RUN apt-get update && apt-get install -y python3
CMD ["bash"]
```

A Dockerfile is a text file with a set of instructions. Each line starts with the instruction in uppercase, followed by its arguments. In our example, there are these three instructions:

- FROM: Points to the base image to use
- RUN: Runs the commands in the container once the base image is installed
- CMD: The command to run when the container is executed by Docker

Now we should build our image and give it a useful name so that we can refer to it later on. Here we will run docker build and tag the new image with the name ubuntu-with-python, while using the current directory for a build environment – by default, this is also where docker build looks for a Dockerfile:

```
$ docker build -t ubuntu-with-python .
[+] Building 7.9s (6/6) FINISHED
 => [internal] load build definition from Dockerfile             0.0s
 => => transferring dockerfile: 125B                             0.0s
 => [internal] load .dockerignore                                0.0s
 => => transferring context: 2B                                  0.0s
 => [internal] load metadata for docker.io/library/ubuntu:20.04  0.0s
 => [1/2] FROM docker.io/library/ubuntu:20.04                    0.0s
 => [2/2] RUN apt-get update && apt-get install -y python3       7.3s
 => exporting to image                                           0.4s
 => => exporting layers                                          0.4s
 => => writing image sha256:02602f606721f36e95fbda83af09baaa9f8256e8303
0197e5df69fd444e5c604                                            0.0s
 => => naming to docker.io/library/ubuntu-with-python            0.0s

Use 'docker scan' to run Snyk tests against images to find
vulnerabilities and learn how to fix them
```

Now we can run our new image in the same way we ran the Ubuntu image earlier:

```
$ docker run -it ubuntu-with-python bash
root@42b83b0933f4:/# python3
Python 3.8.5 (default, Jan 27 2021, 15:41:15)
[GCC 9.3.0] on linux
Type "help", "copyright", "credits" or "license" for more information.
>>>
```

When Docker creates images, it creates a cache that has every instruction from the Dockerfile. If you run the build command a second time, without changing the file, it should be done within seconds. Permuting or changing instructions rebuilds the image, starting at the first change. For this reason, a good strategy when writing these files is to sort instructions so that the most stable ones (the ones you rarely change) are at the top.

Another good piece of advice is to clean up each instruction. For example, when we run apt-get update and apt-get install above, this downloads a lot of package index files, and the .deb packages that, once installed, we no longer need.

We can make our resulting image smaller by cleaning up after ourselves, which must be done in the same RUN command so that the data we are removing is not written out as part of the container's image:

```
$ cat Dockerfile
FROM ubuntu:20.04
RUN apt-get update && \
    apt-get install -y python3 && \
    apt-get clean && \
    rm -fr /var/lib/apt/lists
CMD ["bash"]
$ docker build -t cleaned-ubuntu-python .
$ docker images
REPOSITORY                TAG      IMAGE ID      CREATED         SIZE
cleaned-ubuntu-python     latest   6bbca8ae76fe  3 seconds ago   112MB
ubuntu-with-python        latest   dd51cfc39b5a  34 minutes ago  140MB
```

One great feature that Docker offers is the ability to share, publish, and reuse images with other developers. Docker Hub (https://hub.docker.com) is to Docker containers what PyPI is to Python packages.

In the previous example, the Ubuntu base image was pulled from the Hub by Docker, and there are numerous pre-existing images you can use. For instance, if you want to launch a Linux distribution that is tweaked for Python, you can look at the Python page on the official Docker Hub website and pick one (https://hub.docker.com/_/python/).

The python:version images are Debian-based, and are an excellent starting point for any Python project.

The Python images based on **Alpine Linux** are also quite popular, because they produce the smallest images to run Python. They are more than ten times smaller than other images, which means they are much faster to download and set up for people wanting to run your project in Docker (refer to http://gliderlabs.viewdocs.io/docker-alpine/).

To use Python 3.9 from the Alpine base image, you can create a Dockerfile like this:

```
FROM python:3.9-alpine
CMD ["python3.9"]
```

Building and running this Dockerfile places you in a Python 3.9 shell. The Alpine set is great if you run a Python application that does not require a lot of system-level dependencies nor any compilation. It is important to note, however, that Alpine has a specific set of compilation tools that are sometimes incompatible with some projects.

For a Quart-based microservice project, the slightly larger Debian-based Python images are probably a simpler choice, because of its standard compilation environment and stability. Moreover, once the base image is downloaded, it is cached and reused, so you do not need to download everything again.

 Note that it is important to use images from trusted people and organizations on Docker Hub, since anyone can upload an image. Beyond the risk of running malicious code, there's also the problem of using a Linux image that is not up to date with the latest security patches. Docker also supports digitally signing images to help verify that an image is the one you expect, with no modifications.

Running Quart in Docker

To run a Quart application in Docker, we can use the base Python image. From there, installing the app and its dependencies can be done via pip, which is already installed in the Python image.

Assuming your project has a `requirements.txt` file for its pinned dependencies, and a `setup.py` file that installs the project, creating an image for your project can be done by instructing Docker on how to use the `pip` command.

In the following example, we introduce the `COPY` command, which will recursively copy files and directories from outside the container into the image. We also add the `EXPOSE` directive to indicate to anyone running the container that this port should be exposed to the outside world. We still need to connect that exposed port when we run the container with the `-p` option. Any process inside the container can listen to any ports that it wants to, and communicate with itself using localhost, but anything outside the container won't be able to reach the inside unless that port has been exposed. It's also worth noting that localhost inside the container only refers to the container, not the computer that's hosting the running containers; so, if you need to communicate with other services, you will need to use its real IP address:

```
FROM python:3.9
COPY . /app/
RUN pip install -r /app/requirements.txt
RUN pip install /app/
CMD ["hypercorn", "--bind", "0.0.0.0:5000", "myservice:app"]
```

The 3.9 tag here will get the latest Python 3.9 image that was uploaded to Docker Hub. Now we can run our new container, exposing the port it needs:

```
$ docker run -p 5000:5000 quart_basic
[2021-05-15 15:34:56 +0000] [1] [INFO] Running on http://0.0.0.0:5000
(CTRL + C to quit)
# In another terminal:
$ curl localhost:5000
{}
```

Press *Ctrl + C* to stop the container, or from another terminal window, find the container and tell it to stop:

```
$ docker ps
CONTAINER ID    IMAGE             COMMAND               CREATED
STATUS                          PORTS
NAMES
040f7f01d90b    quart_basic       "hypercorn —bind 0.…"   2 seconds ago
Up Less than a second      0.0.0.0:5000->5000/tcp, :::5000->5000/tcp
stoic_bhabha
$ docker stop 040f7f01d90b
040f7f01d90b
```

The COPY command automatically creates the top-level app directory in the container and copies everything from "." in it. One important detail to remember with the COPY command is that any change to the local directory (".") invalidates the Docker cache, and builds from that step. To tweak this mechanism, you can create a .dockerignore file where you can list files and directories that should be ignored by Docker, such as the .git directory that stores all the history and metadata about your version control.

We are not using a virtual environment inside the container, as we are already in an isolated environment. We also run our Quart application using Hypercorn, a good practice for production use as we discussed in *Chapter 9, Packaging and Running Python*.

That is why the CMD instruction, which tells the container what command to run when it starts, uses **Hypercorn**. CMD can take a normal shell command as an argument, but this does get interpreted by the shell inside the container, meaning that it could go wrong if there are symbols the shell interprets differently, such as * and ?. It's much safer to provide a list, in a format you may be familiar with, if you have ever used the Python subprocess module (https://docs.python.org/3/library/subprocess.html) or used exec system calls.

The next thing we need to do is orchestrate different containers so that they can work together. Let's see in the next section how we can do that.

Docker-based deployments

Deploying a microservice at scale can be done by running several containers spread across either one or several instances. When we are developing our application locally, we are limited to what our one desktop or laptop computer can provide; but for a production service, it may run on dozens or hundreds of servers, with each one running a container that is providing different parts of the application. Each of the options for deploying your application in the cloud, or scaling it up to meet your needs, will involve running more instances, to run more containers.

The first to examine is Docker Compose, which is aimed at smaller-scale deployments, mostly contained in a single instance, but running multiple containers. This is ideal for a development environment, a staging environment, or a prototype. Other options we will look at are Docker Swarm and Kubernetes, which provide different levels of complexity for someone deploying an application, but also increasing levels of flexibility and power. Both options will also need someone to run cloud instances or bare-metal servers on which to run the containers.

Once your Docker image is created, every host that runs a Docker daemon can be used to run as many containers as you want within the limits of the physical resources. We will examine several different options, to gain a broad overview of the features and complexity involved.

> There is no need to over-complicate your initial application. It might be tempting to go with a large Kubernetes cluster, but if your application does not need to scale that way, it's a wasted effort. Use the metrics collected about your application and the knowledge of upcoming business changes to adjust to plan for what you need, not what you might want.

To experiment with the **Terraform**, **Docker Swarm**, and **Kubernetes** examples in this book and on `https://github.com/PacktPublishing/Python-Microservices-Development-2nd-Edition/tree/main/CodeSamples`, you will need to create an account on AWS by visiting `https://aws.amazon.com/`.

Once you have set up the account, visit the **Identity and Access Management (IAM)** page to create a service user that can create and change resources. You could use your root—or main—account to do all of the work, but it is better to create service accounts for this purpose, as it means that any leaked access keys or secrets can be easily revoked—and new ones created—without causing major trouble for accessing the account in general. We should follow the principle of least privilege, as we discussed in *Chapter 7, Securing Your Services*.

Once on the IAM page, click **Add User** and request **Programmatic Access** so that you can obtain API keys to use this account in a program.

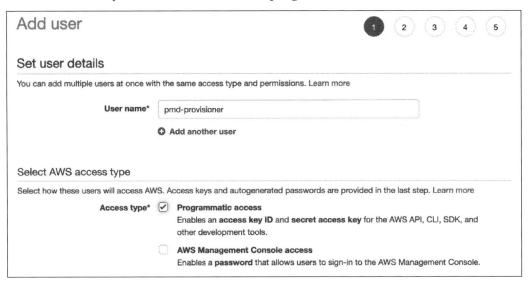

Figure 10.1: IAM Add user page in AWS

Create a group to control the user's permissions more easily. Grant this new group the permissions to modify EC2 instances, since it covers most of what we will be changing.

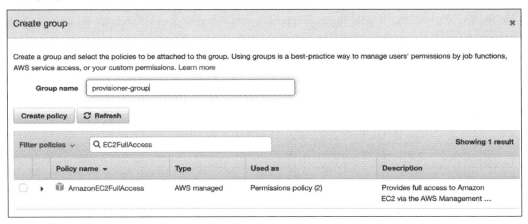

Figure 10.2: Naming the group and setting permissions

Once the group is created, you will get a chance to download the new **Access Key ID** and **Secret Access Key**. These will be used to grant access to any programs that we use to create instances and other cloud resources.

Most of these tools are Infrastructure-as-Code. That is to say, you will have a configuration file, or set of files, that describe what your running services will look like, and what resources they require. This configuration should also be kept in version control so that any changes can be managed. Whether it is in the same source control repository as your code will depend on how you need to deploy the software: If you are continuously deploying new versions, then it can be helpful to keep the configuration alongside the application, but in many cases, it is much clearer to keep it separate, especially if the CI pipelines will be difficult to coordinate between the deployments and the code's own test and packaging tasks.

Terraform

Before we head further into the different container orchestration tools, it's worth mentioning a different sort of tool that can organize the underlying cloud instances. **Terraform**, made by the company HashiCorp, is a widely adopted tool for defining resources as code. Using Terraform modules, you can define how you want your cloud instances to be set up, what the security groups will be, what storage is present, along with a whole suite of other variables. Describing an Amazon EC2 instance in Terraform will look a little like the following configuration snippet, with a full example at https://github.com/PacktPublishing/Python-Microservices-Development-2nd-Edition:

```
resource "aws_instance" "swarm_cluster" {
  count          = 3
  ami            = data.aws_ami.ubuntu_focal.id
  instance_type = "t3.micro" # Small for this demo.

  vpc_security_group_ids = [aws_security_group.swarm_security_group.id]
  key_name              = "your ssh key name here"

  root_block_device {
    volume_type = "gp2"
    volume_size = "40" # GiB
    encrypted   = true
  }
}
```

Here we are defining a resource called swarm_cluster, in which will create three new instances, using an Ubuntu Focal base image. We set the instance size to t3.micro because we are trying things out and want to minimize the cost.

This snippet of Terraform code does depend on other parts not quoted here, such as the security group resource, and discovering the latest identifier for an Ubuntu Focal image, but the full example is available at https://github.com/PacktPublishing/Python-Microservices-Development-2nd-Edition/tree/main/CodeSamples.

Using Terraform, we can create and destroy our cloud resources in a CI/CD pipeline in a similar way that we test and deploy our application code. The following has in-depth tutorials and worked examples, and there are many community-provided modules to perform common tasks: https://learn.hashicorp.com/terraform.

Terraform's `plan` command will show you what changes will be made to your cloud infrastructure when you run `terraform apply`:

```
$ terraform plan
...
  # module.docker-swarm.aws_instance.managers[2] will be created
  + resource "aws_instance" "managers" {
      + ami                          = "ami-0440ba4c79a163c0e"
      + arn                          = (known after apply)
      + associate_public_ip_address  = (known after apply)
      + availability_zone            = (known after apply)
...
$ terraform apply
[terraform plan output]
Do you want to perform these actions?
  Terraform will perform the actions described above.
  Only 'yes' will be accepted to approve.

  Enter a value: yes

aws_vpc.main: Creating...
module.docker-swarm.aws_iam_policy.swarm-access-role-policy:
Creating...
module.docker-swarm.aws_sns_topic.alarms: Creating...
module.docker-swarm.aws_iam_role.ec2: Creating...
module.docker-swarm.aws_s3_bucket.terraform[0]: Creating...
module.docker-swarm.aws_sns_topic.alarms: Creation complete after 0s
[id=arn:aws:sns:eu-central-1:944409847308:swarm-vpc-alarms]
module.docker-swarm.aws_iam_policy.swarm-access-role-policy: Creation
complete after 1s [id=arn:aws:iam::944409847308:policy/swarm-vpc-swarm-
ec2-policy]
...
```

Once you are done with any experiments, you can run `terraform destroy` to clear up any resources managed by Terraform—although this is a dangerous command for a production service!

Service discovery

While Docker tries to provide all the tools to deal with clusters of containers, managing them can become quite complex. When done properly, it requires sharing some configuration across hosts, and to make sure that bringing containers up and down is partially automated.

We very quickly come across scenarios that complicate a static configuration. If we need to move a microservice to a new AWS region, or a different cloud provider entirely, then how do we tell all the other microservices that use it? If we add a new feature that's controlled by a feature flag, how do we quickly turn it on and off? On a smaller scale, how does a load balancer know about all the containers that should receive traffic?

Service discovery is an orchestration method that aims to solve these problems. Tools such as **Consul** (https://www.consul.io/) and **etcd** (https://etcd.io/) allow values to be stored behind well-known keys and updated dynamically.

Instead of deploying your service with full knowledge of all the URLs it might connect to, you provide it with the address of a service discovery tool, and the list of keys it should look up for each element. When a microservice starts up, and at regular intervals, it can check where it should be sending traffic, or whether a feature should be turned on.

We will use `etcd` as an example, with a basic Quart service, while also utilizing the `etcd3` Python library. Assuming you have `etcd` running with the default options after following the instructions on their website, we can add some configuration-updating code to our service, and have an endpoint that returns the URL we would contact, if the application was more complete:

```
# etcd_basic.py
from quart import Quart, current_app
import etcd3


# Can read this map from a traditional config file
settings_map = {
    "dataservice_url": "/services/dataservice/url",
}
settings_reverse_map = {v: k for k, v in settings_map.items()}
```

```
etcd_client = etcd3.client()

def load_settings():
    config = dict()
    for setting, etcd_key in settings_map.items():
        config[setting] = etcd_client.get(etcd_key)[0].decode("utf-8")
    return config

def create_app(name=__name__):
    app = Quart(name)
    app.config.update(load_settings())
    return app

app = create_app()

def watch_callback(event):
    global app
    for update in event.events:
    # Determine which setting to update, and convert from bytes to str
        config_option = settings_reverse_map[update.key.
decode("utf-8")]
        app.config[config_option] = update.value.decode("utf-8")

# Start to watch for dataservice url changes
# You can also watch entire areas with add_watch_prefix_callback
watch_id = etcd_client.add_watch_callback("/services/dataservice/url",
watch_callback)

@app.route("/api")
def what_is_url():
    return {"url": app.config["dataservice_url"]}

app.run()
```

In this example, we load the keys in the settings_map when the application starts, including /services/dataservice/url, which we can then validate and use. Any time that value changes in etcd, the watch_callback function will be run in its own thread, and the app's configuration updated:

```
$ curl http://127.0.0.1:5000/api
{"url":"https://firsturl.example.com/api"}
$ etcdctl put "/services/dataservice/url" "https://secondurl.example.
com/api"
OK
$ curl http://127.0.0.1:5000/api
{"url":"https://secondurl.example.com/api"}
```

Updating the live configuration is a simple command!

If your application has configuration options that depend on each other, such as pairs of access tokens, it is best to encode them in a single option so that they are updated in a single operation. If something fails and only one of a co-dependent set of configuration settings is updated, your application will behave in unwanted and unexpected ways.

Docker Compose

The commands required to run several containers on the same host can be quite long once you need to add names and networks and bind several sockets. Docker Compose (https://docs.docker.com/compose/) simplifies the task by letting you define multiple containers' configuration in a single configuration file, as well as how those containers depend on each other. This utility is installed on macOS and Windows alongside Docker. For Linux distributions, there should be a system package available to install it, or you can obtain an installation script by following the instructions at https://docs.docker.com/compose/install/.

Once the script is installed on your system, create a yaml file containing the information about services and networks that you want to run. The default filename is docker-compose.yml, and so we will use that name for our examples to make the commands simpler.

> The compose configuration file has many options that let you define every aspect of the deployment of several containers. It's like a Makefile for a group of containers. This URL lists all options: https://docs.docker.com/compose/compose-file/.

In the following example, the .yaml file is placed one directory above two of our Jeeves microservices and defines three services: the dataservice and the tokendealer, which are built locally from their Dockerfile; the third is RabbitMQ, and we use an image published on Docker Hub to run that:

```
version: '3'
networks:
  jeeves:
services:
  dataservice:
    networks:
      - jeeves
    build:
        context: dataservice/
    ports:
      - "8080:8080"
  tokendealer:
    networks:
      - jeeves
    build:
        context: tokendealer/
    ports:
      - "8090:8090"
  rabbitmq:
    image: "rabbitmq:latest"
    networks:
      - jeeves
```

The Compose file also creates networks with its networks sections, allowing the containers to communicate with each other. They will get private DNS entries so they can be referred to with the image names, such as dataservice, tokendealer, and rabbitmq in the example above. To build and run those three containers, you can use the up command as follows:

```
$ docker compose up
[+] Building 9.2s (9/9) FINISHED
 ...
[+] Running 3/0
 ∷ Container pythonmicroservices_tokendealer_1   Created        0.1s
 ∷ Container pythonmicroservices_dataservice_1   Created        0.1s
```

```
:: Container pythonmicroservices_rabbitmq_1  Created            0.1s
Attaching to dataservice_1, rabbitmq_1, tokendealer_1
```

The first time that command is executed, the two local container images will be built. These will either be static, or you can assign volumes to them to mount in the source code and continue developing on them.

Using Docker Compose is great when you want to provide a full working stack for your microservices, which includes every piece of software needed to run it. For instance, if you are using a Postgres database, you can use the Postgres image (`https://hub.docker.com/_/postgres/`) and link it to your service in a Docker Compose file.

Containerizing everything, even the databases, is a great way to showcase your software, or simply a good option for development purposes. However, as we stated earlier, a Docker container should be seen as an ephemeral filesystem. So if you use a container for your database, make sure that the directory where the data is written is mounted on the host filesystem. In most cases, however, the database service is usually its dedicated server on a production deployment. Using a container does not make much sense and adds only a little bit of overhead.

Docker Swarm

Docker has a built-in cluster functionality called **swarm** mode (`https://docs.docker.com/engine/swarm/`). This mode has an impressive list of features, which lets you manage all your container clusters from a single utility. This makes it ideal for smaller deployments or ones that do not need to scale up and down as flexibly to meet changing demands.

Once you have deployed a cluster, you need to set up a load balancer so that all the instances of your cluster are sharing the workload. The load balancer is commonly software such as nginx, OpenResty, or HAProxy, and is the entry point to distribute the incoming requests on clusters.

To set up a swarm, all we really need are three EC2 instances, provided we can connect to them using port 22 for SSH access to configure them, and port 2377 for Docker's own communication. We should also allow any ports that our application needs, such as port 443 for HTTPS connections.

To create a swarm, we must create a manager node that will organize the rest. Using one of the nodes you have just created, connect to it using SSH, and convert it to a Docker Swarm manager:

```
$ sudo docker swarm init —advertise-addr <Public IP Address>
Swarm initialized: current node (16u7ljqhiaosbeecn4jjlm6vt) is now a
manager.
```

To add a worker to this swarm, run the following command:

```
docker swarm join —token <some long token> 52.212.189.167:2377
```

To add a manager to this swarm, run `docker swarm join-token manager` and follow the instructions.

Copy the `docker swarm` command provided, and paste it into an SSH session on the other instances you have created. You may need to run sudo to gain root access before the commands will work. On the manager node, we can now see all our workers:

```
$ sudo docker node ls
ID                              HOSTNAME           STATUS
AVAILABILITY    MANAGER STATUS  ENGINE VERSION
6u81yvbwbvb0fspe06yzlsi13       ip-172-31-17-183   Ready  Active
20.10.6
16u7ljqhiaosbeecn4jjlm6vt *     ip-172-31-26-31    Ready  Active
Leader            20.10.6
873cp1742grhkzoo5xd2aiqls       ip-172-31-28-17    Ready  Active
20.10.6
```

Now all we need to do is create our services:

```
$ sudo docker service create —replicas 1 —name dataservice jeeves/
dataservice
sikcno6s3582tdr91dj1fvsse
overall progress: 1 out of 1 tasks
1/1: running   [==================================================>]
verify: Service converged
$ sudo docker service ls
ID              NAME         MODE         REPLICAS    IMAGE
PORTS
sikcno6s3582    dataservice  replicated   1/1         jeeves/
dataservice:latest
```

From here, we can scale our service up and down as we need to. To create five copies of our dataservice, we would issue a scale command:

```
$ sudo docker service scale dataservice=5
```

As long as our manager node remains available, and some of the worker nodes are up, then our container service will remain active. We can terminate one of the cloud instances and watch things rebalance to the remaining instances with `docker service ps`. Adding more nodes is as easy as adjusting a variable in the Terraform configuration and re-running `terraform apply`, before then joining them to the swarm.

Looking after the suite of cloud instances is still work, but this environment provides a neat way of providing a resilient container deployment, especially early on in an application's life.

Kubernetes

Originally designed by Google, but now maintained by an independent foundation, **Kubernetes** (`https://kubernetes.io/`, also known as k8s) provides a platform-independent way of automating work with containerized systems, allowing you to describe the system in terms of different components, and issuing commands to a controller to adjust settings.

Like Docker Swarm, Kubernetes also runs on a cluster of servers. It's possible to run this cluster yourself, although some cloud providers do have a service that makes managing the fleet of instances much easier. A good example of this is the **eksctl** utility for AWS (`https://eksctl.io/`). While not created by Amazon, it is an officially supported client for creating clusters in Amazon's Elastic Kubernetes Service.

Rather than create all the AWS resources yourself, or create Terraform configuration to do so, `eksctl` performs all the work for you, with sensible defaults for experimenting with Kubernetes. To get started, it is best to use the AWS credentials we created for earlier examples and to install both `eksctl` and `kubectl`—the Kubernetes command line. The AWS credentials will be used by `eksctl` to create the cluster and other necessary resources, and once done, `kubectl` can be used to deploy services and software. Unlike Docker Swarm, kubectl's administrative commands are designed to be run from your own computer:

```
$ eksctl create cluster —name=jeeves-cluster-1 —nodes=4 —region=eu-
west-1
2021-05-27 20:13:44 [■]  eksctl version 0.51.0
2021-05-27 20:13:44 [■]  using region eu-west-1
```

```
2021-05-27 20:13:44 [■]  setting availability zones to [eu-west-1a eu-
west-1c eu-west-1b]
2021-05-27 20:13:44 [■]  subnets for eu-west-1a - public:192.168.0.0/19
private:192.168.96.0/19
2021-05-27 20:13:44 [■]  subnets for eu-west-1c -
public:192.168.32.0/19 private:192.168.128.0/19
2021-05-27 20:13:44 [■]  subnets for eu-west-1b -
public:192.168.64.0/19 private:192.168.160.0/19
2021-05-27 20:13:44 [■]  nodegroup "ng-4e138761" will use "ami-
0736921a175c8cebf" [AmazonLinux2/1.19]
2021-05-27 20:13:45 [■]  using Kubernetes version 1.19
...
```

It will take a few minutes to create the cluster, but once done, it will write the credentials kubectl needs to the correct file, so no further setup should be needed. We told eksctl to create four nodes, and that's exactly what it has done:

```
$ kubectl get nodes
NAME                                             STATUS   ROLES    AGE
VERSION
ip-192-168-2-113.eu-west-1.compute.internal      Ready    <none>   8m56s
v1.19.6-eks-49a6c0
ip-192-168-37-156.eu-west-1.compute.internal     Ready    <none>   9m1s
v1.19.6-eks-49a6c0
ip-192-168-89-123.eu-west-1.compute.internal     Ready    <none>   9m1s
v1.19.6-eks-49a6c0
ip-192-168-90-188.eu-west-1.compute.internal     Ready    <none>   8m59s
v1.19.6-eks-49a6c0
```

For the moment, we have nothing running on our k8s cluster, so we shall create some work for it to do. The fundamental unit of work for k8s is a pod, which describes a set of running containers on the cluster. We have not created any of our own yet, but there are some running in a different namespace to help k8s do its own work of managing the rest of the tasks we set it. Namespaces like this can be useful for grouping sets of tasks together, making it easier to understand what is important when looking at the cluster:

```
$ kubectl get pods
No resources found in default namespace…
$ kubectl get pods —namespace kube-system
NAME                READY   STATUS    RESTARTS   AGE
aws-node-6xnrt      1/1     Running   0          29m
aws-node-rhgmd      1/1     Running   0          28m
aws-node-v497d      1/1     Running   0          29m
```

```
aws-node-wcbh7              1/1    Running   0        29m
coredns-7f85bf9964-n8jmj    1/1    Running   0        36m
coredns-7f85bf9964-pk7sq    1/1    Running   0        36m
kube-proxy-4r7fw            1/1    Running   0        29m
kube-proxy-dw9sv            1/1    Running   0        29m
kube-proxy-p7qqv            1/1    Running   0        28m
kube-proxy-t7spn            1/1    Running   0        29m
```

A Pod is a low-level description of some work for the cluster, and to help make life easier, there are higher-level abstractions for different types of work, such as a Deployment for a stateless application, such as a web interface or proxy, a StatefulSet for when your workload needs storage attached rather than keeping its data in a different service, as well as Jobs and CronJobs for one-off tasks and scheduled repeating tasks, respectively.

Kubernetes accepts manifests of instructions that it should apply. A good starting point is to set up nginx, with a manifest such as this one:

```
# nginx.yml
apiVersion: apps/v1
kind: Deployment
metadata:
  name: nginx-deployment
  labels:
    app: nginx
spec:
  replicas: 3
  selector:
    matchLabels:
      app: nginx
  template:
    metadata:
      labels:
        app: nginx
    spec:
      containers:
        - name: nginx
          image: nginx:1.21.0
          ports:
          - containerPort: 80
```

We include some metadata about the type of resource we are requesting—a `Deployment`—and its name, and then dive into the specification for the service. Down at the bottom of the file, we can see that we've asked for a container based on the `nginx:1.21.0` image, and that it should have port `80` open. One layer up, we describe this container specification as a template that we use to create three different copies and run them on our cluster.

```
$ kubectl apply -f nginx.yml
deployment.apps/nginx-deployment created
$ kubectl get pods
NAME                                READY   STATUS    RESTARTS   AGE
nginx-deployment-6c4ccd94bc-8qftq   1/1     Running   0          21s
nginx-deployment-6c4ccd94bc-hqt8c   1/1     Running   0          21s
nginx-deployment-6c4ccd94bc-v7zpl   1/1     Running   0          21s
```

Using kubectl's `describe` subcommand, we get even more information about what was created for us:

```
$ kubectl describe deployment nginx-deployment
Name:                   nginx-deployment
Namespace:              default
CreationTimestamp:      Thu, 27 May 2021 21:06:47 +0100
Labels:                 app=nginx
Annotations:            deployment.kubernetes.io/revision: 1
Selector:               app=nginx
Replicas:               3 desired | 3 updated | 3 total | 3 available
| 0 unavailable
StrategyType:           RollingUpdate
MinReadySeconds:        0
RollingUpdateStrategy:  25% max unavailable, 25% max surge
Pod Template:
  Labels:  app=nginx
  Containers:
   nginx:
    Image:        nginx:1.21.0
    Port:         80/TCP
    Host Port:    0/TCP
    Environment:  <none>
    Mounts:       <none>
  Volumes:        <none>
Conditions:
  Type           Status  Reason
```

```
    Available       True   MinimumReplicasAvailable
    Progressing     True   NewReplicaSetAvailable
OldReplicaSets: <none>
NewReplicaSet:   nginx-deployment-6c4ccd94bc (3/3 replicas created)
Events:
  Type     Reason              Age    From                    Message
  Normal   ScalingReplicaSet   14m    deployment-controller   Scaled up
replica set nginx-deployment-6c4ccd94bc to 3
```

If we decide we need more nginx containers, we can update the manifest. Change the number of replicas in our `yaml` file from three to eight, and re-apply the manifest:

```
$  kubectl get pods -l app=nginx
NAME                                READY   STATUS             RESTARTS
AGE
nginx-deployment-6c4ccd94bc-7g74n   0/1     ContainerCreating  0
2s
nginx-deployment-6c4ccd94bc-8qftq   1/1     Running            0
17m
nginx-deployment-6c4ccd94bc-crw2t   1/1     Running            0
2s
nginx-deployment-6c4ccd94bc-fb7cf   0/1     ContainerCreating  0
2s
nginx-deployment-6c4ccd94bc-hqt8c   1/1     Running            0
17m
nginx-deployment-6c4ccd94bc-v7zpl   1/1     Running            0
17m
nginx-deployment-6c4ccd94bc-zpd4v   1/1     Running            0
2s
nginx-deployment-6c4ccd94bc-zwtcv   1/1     Running            0
2s
```

A similar change could be performed to upgrade the version of nginx, and Kubernetes has several strategies to perform updates of a service so that end users are unlikely to notice it happening. For example, it is possible to create an entirely new Pod of containers and redirect traffic to it, but it's also possible to do rolling updates inside a Pod, where a container is only destroyed when its replacement has successfully started. How can you tell the container was successfully started? Kubernetes allows you to describe what it should look for to check whether a container can do its work, and how long it should wait for a container to start, with its liveness and readiness checks.

If you have been following along with the examples, remember to delete the cloud resources when you are done, as they cost. To remove just the nginx-deeployment we created, use kubectl.

```
$ kubectl delete -f nginx.yml
deployment.apps "nginx-deployment" deleted
```

But to destroy the entire cluster, return to using eksctl:

```
$ eksctl delete cluster —name=jeeves-cluster-1 —region=eu-west-1
2021-05-27 21:33:22 [■]  eksctl version 0.51.0
2021-05-27 21:33:22 [■]  using region eu-west-1
2021-05-27 21:33:22 [■]  deleting EKS cluster "jeeves-cluster-1"
2021-05-27 21:33:23 [■]  deleted 0 Fargate profile(s)
2021-05-27 21:33:23 [✓]  kubeconfig has been updated
2021-05-27 21:33:23 [■]  cleaning up AWS load balancers created by
Kubernetes objects of Kind Service or Ingress
2021-05-27 21:33:25 [■]  2 sequential tasks: { delete nodegroup "ng-
4e138761", delete cluster control plane "jeeves-cluster-1" [async] }
2021-05-27 21:33:26 [■]  will delete stack "eksctl-jeeves-cluster-1-
nodegroup-ng-4e138761"
...
```

This is a very brief overview of an enormously powerful tool, as the topic could cover an entire book by itself. For those who need it, the time spent learning Kubernetes is well spent, but as ever, you must assess the needs of your own application, and whether something simpler will get the job done.

Summary

In this chapter, we looked at how microservices can be containerized with containers, and how you can create a deployment entirely based on Docker images. Containers are a well-established technology that is widely used to run internet services. The most important thing to keep in mind is that a containerized application is ephemeral: it is designed to be destroyed and recreated on demand, and any data that is not externalized using a mount point is lost.

For provisioning and clustering your services, there is no generic solution, as the tools you use will depend on your needs. From a simple Docker Compose setup to a full Kubernetes cluster, each option provides different complexity and benefits. The best choice often depends on where you are to deploy your services, how your teams work, and how large your application needs to be in the present—there is no sense in planning for an unknowable future.

The best way to tackle this problem is to take baby steps by first deploying everything manually, then automating where it makes sense. Automation is great, but can rapidly become difficult if you use a toolset you do not fully understand, or that is too complex for your needs.

As a guide, consider:

- Docker Compose when you need to deploy multiple containers in a small environment, and do not need to manage a large infrastructure.
- Docker Swarm when you need flexibility in how many containers are deployed, to respond to a changing situation, and are happy to manage a larger cloud infrastructure.
- Kubernetes when automation and flexibility are paramount, and you have people and time available to manage the infrastructure and handle the complexity.

You will not be locked into one orchestration tool once you choose it, as the containers you build can be used in any of them, but moving to a different orchestration tool can be hard work, depending on how complex your configuration is.

In that vein, to make their services easier to use and more appealing, cloud providers have built-in features to handle deployments. The three largest cloud providers are currently AWS, Google Cloud, and Microsoft Azure, although many other good options exist.

11
What's Next?

In this book, we have discussed the design and development of microservices written in Python using the Quart framework. We have built a monolithic application from which to work, and covered strategies to migrate from that architecture to one that makes the best use of microservices, along with the potential errors that could arise and how to avoid them. We have also learned about deploying our application to cloud providers using container-based services.

However, this is not the end of the story, and there are other topics that are beneficial to learn more about. There is always going to be more room for improvement in our automation and tooling to help services keep up to date, more questions to answer about performance and capacity management that our monitoring and logging can help with, and considerations about how to scale and change our deployment architecture to improve the service's reliability and availability. Finally, we need to remember that – unless writing code for a hobby – the software itself is not the end goal, and we must keep our promises to the people who need the software.

Automation

We briefly discussed **Terraform** as a way to automate the creation of cloud-based resources, and there is a lot more to learn about this tool as well as others that can automate some of the work involved in running a service.

To configure inside an instance, configuration management tools such as **Ansible**, **Chef**, and **Puppet** allow you to copy files, change file contents, install packages, and set up a computer how you like it in a repeatable, predictable manner.

Building operating system images for your own environment can be done with HashiCorp's **Packer**, which lets you use the configuration management tools above to create operating system images for use in AWS, GCP, VMware, or Docker, among many others.

Even if your infrastructure is small, using automation to create and maintain it is still valuable. In the event of a disaster, you are a few short commands away from recreating your entire suite of applications, instead of weeks of painstaking work.

When creating infrastructure as code, it's very easy to accidentally create a new monolith, responsible for creating and maintaining every component. If that is a deliberate, considered choice then it will work well, but it's also worth remembering the other principles of privilege separation and ease of maintenance that come with separating out the features into smaller projects. Here are some relevant links:

- Terraform: `https://www.terraform.io/`
- Ansible: `https://www.ansible.com/`
- Chef: `https://www.chef.io/`
- Puppet: `https://puppet.com/`

Scaling

When an application needs to do more work, the historical approach has been to run the application on a bigger computer. Give it more memory, more CPU cores, and even more disk space. This does not increase the application's reliability, as it still relies on a single computer, and it comes with added complications once your application is large enough that there simply aren't any computers large enough to run it on.

Giving a program a larger computer to run on is called scaling vertically. By contrast, scaling horizontally is the approach of using many smaller computers. We came across this idea when discussing deploying on container-based services and increasing the number of instances that our Docker swarm used. An application must have a replicated, scalable idea of its current state to operate in this way, for client sessions, shopping basket contents, and anything else that a visitor would expect to be persistent between different pages of a website.

Microservices allow you to scale an application much more easily, although it is important to remember that every component communicates with other microservices and that an increased load in one area will have consequences in others.

Careful monitoring will allow you to discover the bottlenecks in the overall system, and so prioritize which area needs the most urgent work in order to give the system more capacity.

Content Delivery Networks

Some of the content our applications deliver does not change very often, such as HTML pages, JavaScript, images, and video streams. **Content Delivery Networks (CDNs)** aim to provide static content that is distributed around the world. Acting either as a layer in front of your application or alongside it, they can provide cacheable content to clients much more quickly than a customized service. Some CDNs will also allow you to dynamically scale images and video based on the client and its network quality, or provide protection against distributed denial of service attacks, making them a valuable tool for any web-based service.

Multi-cloud deployments

When assessing the risks involved in running a service, it's easy to come to the realization that your organization is completely dependent on one cloud provider. A common desire to improve redundancy is to deploy services to multiple providers and spread the workload across Azure, GCP, Amazon, and others. This might seem like a great idea, but it also introduces a lot of complexity as different providers have different feature sets available, will need unique security arrangements, and be unable to share storage and secrets management.

While `Terraform` can help with this situation, it is often more achievable to aim for multiple regions within the same provider, and if several cloud providers are really required, to separate what's running in them based on how things interact. It's far easier to put a completely independent service somewhere else. There are parallels with the strategic approach and splitting a monolith into microservices, as a successful migration requires a clean interface between different components and well-structured isolation of concerns and requirements.

Lambda Functions

Lambda, or Cloud Functions, is a type of serverless deployment intended for small, short-lived tasks that can scale up and down very rapidly. While asynchronous frameworks have limited support in this area in 2021, they are widely used with synchronous code as the way they are run means that the responsiveness is controlled by the sheer number of them that can run simultaneously.

Expanding monitoring

In *Chapter 5, Splitting the Monolith*, we discussed monitoring and collecting metrics to record what an application is doing. Measurements can tell some of the story and give a picture involving a count, a size, or time passing. To get even more information, we can use logging services to record messages our application produces.

If you have set up a Linux server, you may be familiar with the logs that pass through `rsyslog` and end up in a file that exists in `/var/log`. In a cloud service, and especially in a container, logging locally is far less useful, as we would have to then investigate all the running containers and cloud instances to discover what was happening. Instead, we can use a centralized logging service.

This could be done using tools such as AWS CloudWatch or Google's Cloud Logging, but it's also possible to run services such as `Splunk` or `Logstash`. The latter is part of a popular open source trio of tools called the `ELK` stack, as it contains Elasticsearch, Logstash, and Kibana, to collect, search, and visualize logged data. Using these tools, all the logs from the systems and applications can end up in a single place and be easily examined.

Using structured logging techniques, it is also straightforward to annotate all the log entries to easily determine which microservice produced them, and so to better correlate events. A centralized logging service will allow you to connect the dots between errors in one component and reports from a separate area. At the same time, each microservice being more isolated means that any impact they have on other components should be through the designed interfaces, instead of being side effects due to resource constraints on the same server, or in the same process tree.

The ELK stack is a great starting point for collecting large numbers of logs and metrics, and you can discover more about it at `https://www.elastic.co/what-is/elk-stack`.

Making promises

When writing software, we are often not doing so in isolation, but instead to help our company or open source project achieve a goal. Relying on our intuition to tell us whether we're doing a good job is often misleading, as our instinct is affected by all the different biases humans have. Instead, we must measure – collect numbers, watch for patterns, and analyze data.

To demonstrate how well our software is doing, both to ourselves and to others, there are three levels we can think about. The first is the list of possible things we can measure, and these are known as **Service-Level Indicators** (**SLIs**). As developers, it is easy to come up with a list of technology-related SLIs, such as:

- The API response time in milliseconds
- A count of the different HTTP status codes
- The number of bytes transferred in each request

However, it is vitally important to include organization-level indicators as well, such as:

- How long an online shop's check-out process takes
- How many potential customers abandon a purchase during check-out
- The financial cost of running a service, especially one that automatically scales up and down

Both types of indicators, when used together, can make for very useful reports and dashboards for an organization, but you also don't want to be constantly checking on things – there is other work to be done! A **Service-Level Objective** (**SLO**) sets a threshold or alert value on top of an SLI, such as:

- Fewer than 1% of HTTP status codes must indicate a server error
- The rate of completed check-out operations must exceed 75%
- Users can successfully complete at least 99.9% of their requests without an error

What should we do if an SLO is not met? That's where **Service-Level Agreements** (**SLAs**) come in. SLAs are a contract – official or otherwise – between the providers of a service and the people using it and describe what should happen when an SLO is not met.

Here is an example covering all the levels:

- Service-level indicator: The number of HTTP 500 errors recorded
- Service-level objective: The HTTP 500 errors should not be more than 1% of the total requests
- Service-level agreement: A site reliability engineer is alerted and affected customers are informed

Creating SLOs helps developers and product team members understand what's important about an application and lets us demonstrate to everyone involved that the application is doing what it is meant to do.

Summary

As software developers we never stop improving our skills and knowledge, trying out new technologies and architectures, and building on the work of many others. Our profession's core skill is approaching a situation in a rational and methodical manner, breaking down each part of the problem into manageable chunks, and making sure that we – and others who have a stake in our work – can make sense of it all.

The microservices approach uses the same techniques in systems design, making each component easier to reason about and investigate. Like many approaches, it works very well when it is done with careful consideration, rather than a desire to follow a fashion.

Designing applications well takes a combination of knowledge, skill, and experience, and we hope that this book has contributed to the expertise that you bring to your work, whether it's paid, volunteering, or a hobby.

Subscribe to our online digital library for full access to over 7,000 books and videos, as well as industry leading tools to help you plan your personal development and advance your career. For more information, please visit our website.

Why subscribe?

- Spend less time learning and more time coding with practical eBooks and Videos from over 4,000 industry professionals
- Improve your learning with Skill Plans built especially for you
- Get a free eBook or video every month
- Fully searchable for easy access to vital information
- Copy and paste, print, and bookmark content

At www.packt.com, you can also read a collection of free technical articles, sign up for a range of free newsletters, and receive exclusive discounts and offers on Packt books and eBooks.

Other Books You May Enjoy

If you enjoyed this book, you may be interested in these other books by Packt:

Expert Python Programming

Michał Jaworski

Tarek Ziadé

ISBN: 9781801071109

- Explore modern ways of setting up repeatable and consistent Python development environments
- Effectively package Python code for community and production use
- Learn about modern syntax elements of Python programming, such as f-strings, dataclasses, enums, and lambda functions
- Demystify metaprogramming in Python with metaclasses
- Write concurrent code in Python
- Monitor and optimize the performance of Python application
- Extend and integrate Python with code written in different languages

Python Object-Oriented Programming

Steven F. Lott

Dusty Phillips

ISBN: 9781801077262

- Implement objects in Python by creating classes and defining methods
- Extend class functionality using inheritance
- Use exceptions to handle unusual situations cleanly
- Understand when to use object-oriented features, and more importantly, when not to use them
- Discover several widely used design patterns and how they are implemented in Python
- Uncover the simplicity of unit and integration testing and understand why they are so important
- Learn to statically type check your dynamic code
- Understand concurrency with asyncio and how it speeds up programs

Packt is searching for authors like you

If you're interested in becoming an author for Packt, please visit authors.packtpub.com and apply today. We have worked with thousands of developers and tech professionals, just like you, to help them share their insight with the global tech community. You can make a general application, apply for a specific hot topic that we are recruiting an author for, or submit your own idea.

Share your thoughts

Now you've finished *Python Microservices Development, Second Edition*, we'd love to hear your thoughts! Scan the QR code below to go straight to the Amazon review page for this book and share your feedback or leave a review on the site that you purchased it from.

https://packt.link/r/1801076308

Your review is important to us and the tech community and will help us make sure we're delivering excellent quality content.

Index

G

Get Docker
reference link 249
Gevent project
URL 19
GitHub Actions 87, 88
GitHub Pages 88
GitLab
URL 86
Global Interpreter Lock (GIL) 22
Graylog
URL 131
gRPC 9
reference link 153

H

HashiCorp Packer
reference link 247
Homebrew
reference link 249
Hypercorn 256
reference link 243

I

Identity and Access Management (IAM) 257
incoming requests
rate-limiting 199
InfluxDB
reference link 75
injection 187
integration tests 70, 71
Inter-Process Communication (IPC) 3
I/O operations 63

J

JavaScript
authenticating 220, 221
Jeeves
refactoring 137, 138
workflow 139
Jeeves bot 92
user stories 92, 93

Jinja
Jinja
reference link 46
Jinja's, features
reference link 48
Jinja's sandbox
reference link 192
JSON Web Key (JWK) format 180
JSON Web Token (JWT) 175, 176
header 174
payload 174
reference link 174
signature 174
JSX
pre-processing 211, 212
syntax 205, 206
JSX Specification
reference link 205
Just-In-Time (JIT) 23
JWT Claim in the RFC 7519 jargon 175

K

Kubernetes (k8s) 267-272
reference link 267

L

Lambda functions 277
**Linux-Apache-MySQL-Perl/PHP/Python
(LAMP) 4**
load tests 71-75
Local File Inclusion (LFI) 187
location
tracing 145
logging 128-131
loose coupling 10
Lua
installation link 196
LuaJIT
URL 197

M

Markdown
reference link 81
Memcached 11

OpenResty components
   URL 201
Open-Source Software (OSS) 6
Open Web Application Security Project
      (OWASP)
   URL 186
operational health monitoring 122
operations person (ops) 15

P

packaging toolchain 224, 225
Pika
   reference link 160
pika-pool
   reference link 161
Postgres
   reference link 265
process
   managing 243, 244
Prometheus
   reference link 75, 124
Prometheus, querying
   reference link 128
promises 278, 279
Protocol Buffers (protobuf)
   reference link 152
Publish/Subscribe (pubsub) pattern 162
Pull Request (PR) 86
Puppet
   URL 276
PyJWT library
   URL 176
PyPy interpreter
   URL 23
pytest
   using 76-79
Python
   installing 27, 28
   microservice, implementing with 15, 16
Python application 225
Python Enhancement Proposals (PEPs) 224
Python library 225
Python package 225
Python package index
   URL 44
Python Package Index (PyPI) 7, 227

reference link 239
Python packaging tools
   versioning 235-237
Python project 225
   distributing 239-242
   packaging 226
   releasing 238, 239
Python standard library
   reference link 82
Python, structlog
   reference link 130
Python subprocess module
   reference link 256

Q

quality assurance 122
Quart 7, 25
   features 40
   ReactJS apps, serving with 212, 213
   request 37, 38
   request, handling 28-32
   response 38-40
   routing 32, 33
Quart application
   running, in Docker 255, 256
quart-auth 116
Quart, features
   blueprints 50, 51
   configuration 48-50
   custom error handler 52-54
   error handling 52
   extensions 44, 46
   globals 41, 42
   middleware 44, 46
   session object 40, 41
   signals 42-44
   templates 46-48
Quart, routing
   converters 33-37
   url_for function 37
   variables 33-37

R

RabbitMQ 116
   URL 44, 113

TokenDealer microservice 179
  OAuth implementation 180-183
  TokenDealer, using 184, 185
tox
  using 76-79
Transport Layer Security (TLS) 112
Twine project
  reference link 228

U

Uniform Resource Locator (URL) 145
unit tests 63-67
universally unique identifier (UUID) 156
url_for function 37
use cases
  limiting, usage of mocks 63
User Interface (UI) 9, 75
user stories 92, 93

V

valid classifiers
  reference link 229
version control systems (VCS) 85, 86
virtualenv
  reference link 27
Virtual Machine (VM) 188, 247

W

web application firewall 195
web resources
  calling 142-144
Web Server Gateway Interface (WSGI) 16, 28
web services
  working with 16
WebTest, testing applications
  reference link 70
Windows Subsystem for Linux (WSL2) 249
WTForms 116

X

X.509 certificate-based authentication 170, 171, 173
  URL 170

Made in the USA
Coppell, TX
15 February 2022

73601810R00171